THE PERFECT BUSINESS PLAN MADE SIMPLE

William R. Lasher, PhD, JD, CPA

BOOKS

A Made Simple Book
Broadway Books
New York

Produced by The Philip Lief Group, Inc.

THE PERFECT BUSINESS PLAN MADE SIMPLE

For information, address: Broadway Books, a division of
Random House, Inc., 1745 Broadway, New York, NY 10019.

Produced by The Philip Lief Group, Inc.
Managing Editors: Judy Linden, Jill Korot, Albry Montalbano.
Design: Annie Jeon.

Broadway Books titles may be purchased for business or promotional use or for special sales.
For information, please write to: Special Markets Department, Random House, Inc.
1745 Broadway, New York, NY 10019.

MADE SIMPLE BOOKS and BROADWAY BOOKS are
trademarks of Broadway Books, a division of Random House, Inc.

Visit our website at www.broadwaybooks.com.
First Broadway Books trade paperback edition published 2005.

Disclaimer: Information in Chapter 11 is not meant as legal advice applicable to any specific situation
and is not a substitute for the advice of a competent attorney.

Library of Congress Cataloging-in-Publication Data
Lasher, William R.
    The Perfect Business Plan Made Simple / William R. Lasher—1st Broadway Books trade pbk. ed.
        p. cm.—(Made simple series)
    Includes index.
    ISBN 0-7679-1858-4
    1. New business enterprises—Planning. 2. New business enterprises—Finance.
    3. Proposal writing in business. I. Title. II. Made Simple (Broadway Books)
    HD62.5.L37 2005
    658.4'012—dc22   2004065047
10 9 8 7 6 5 4 3 2 1

CONTENTS

PART

I

THE BUSINESS PLAN AND ITS ENVIRONMENT

WHAT IS A BUSINESS PLAN? AN OVERVIEW

Business planning is the process of creating a picture or model of what a business unit will be. The model is a document made up of words and numbers, designed to give a reader an image of what the organization will look like at some time in the future.

The numbers represent projected financial statements. The words should describe the business in a realistic yet concise way, discuss broad strategic issues, detail the handling of short-term tactical questions, or amplify the financial projections. The image conveyed by a good plan is quite complete and includes information on products, markets, employees, technology, facilities, capital, revenue, profitability, and anything else that might be relevant in describing the organization and its affairs.

The plan describes the who, what, when, where, why, how, and how much that make the business concept come alive in the minds of its owners and managers. A good plan should be like an adventure story. It needs to excite an interested reader.

COMPONENTS AND STRUCTURE

Most business plans have a fairly standard structure that we can visualize as a table of contents with various chapter headings. Most plans tend to have more or less the same chapters, usually called sections.

Each section addresses a major business issue or function: marketing, finance, production, etc. It's useful to think of each section as a component of the business, and understand that a plan just like a business must have all of its components in working order to be effective. For example, virtually all plans have sections showing financial projections and dealing with marketing and management. What's in the sections depends on the type of business. A plan for retailing won't have a section on manufacturing, and a plan for manufacturing won't talk about merchandising. But they'll both have a section on operations under which the respective issues are covered.

What's most important is that a plan have all of the right pieces. This idea isn't as obvious as it may seem because some businesses have specialized requirements that other businesses don't need. For example, in Chapter 9 we'll be talking about the special features of service businesses while in Chapter 12 we'll deal with e-commerce. We'll see that certain issues need to be addressed for those types of business that simply don't exist for, say, a traditional retailer. In order to write the "perfect" business plan, it's necessary to know exactly what must be covered in detail and what can be glossed over or left out.

A GENERIC OUTLINE

What follows is a plan structure that works well for most enterprises.

Business Plan Outline

A. Contents

B. Executive Summary

C. Mission and Strategy Statement

D. Market
>   Background
>   The Customer Need
>   Who the Customers Are
>   Product/Service Description
>   Strategy/Approach
>   Competitive Analysis
>   Pricing/Profitability

E. Operations (of the Business)
>   Sources of Input and Costs
>   Processes
>   Equipment

F. Management/Staffing
>   Backgrounds and Qualifications of
>   Key Players
>   Staffing Plan

G. Financial Projections
>   Current Financials (If an Existing
>   Business)
>   Projected Financial Statements
>   Application of Funding Requested
>   Capital Structure

H. Contingency Planning
>   Appendices
>   Supporting Documents
>   Additional Detail as Required

In the chapters that follow, we'll talk about the meaning of each section and how to write them effectively.

SOME IMPORTANT IDEAS TO KEEP IN MIND

Inexperienced planners often become embroiled in the details of the various pieces of their business plans and end up with documents that don't hang together well when finished.

Understanding a few broad concepts will help you maintain perspective and put together an excellent document. The following paragraphs should be read thoughtfully and kept in mind as you pull your plan together.

Major Divisions

A business plan is a sales vehicle in which entrepreneurs sell themselves and their ideas. It can be divided into three parts:

1. Introduction

2. Descriptive sections

3. Financial projections

The introductory sections are the hook that has to catch the reader, usually an investor of some kind, and hold his or her attention long enough for you to get your more detailed ideas across. The introduction consists of the executive summary and the mission statement. They give the reader a quick overview of the business and why it's worth his or her time and investment. These sections should be relatively short but should establish why a business opportunity exists.

The descriptive sections explain how you'll make the business work. Each section addresses a different department or feature of the operation. The descriptive sections use both words and numbers, but tend to be mostly words. They have to *convince* the reader that the opportunity is real, establish the planner's *credibility* as a source of information in the area, and demonstrate that the planner/ entrepreneur is a *competent* business person.

The financial projections are packaged in a separate section and consist of a standard set of financial statements that are projections for the future, but include recent history if the company already exists. We'll talk a great deal about financials in Part Three. The important thing to understand for now is that financials must support the assumptions expressed in the descriptive sections of the plan and that the relationship between the two must be easy for the reader to understand.

This idea isn't as obvious as it sounds. Personal computers and spreadsheet software have enabled people to construct financial plans that are so complicated that no one but the planner can understand what's behind the numbers. That can be a big mistake because investors usually won't buy into businesses unless they understand how the financial figures flow from the operating assumptions.

Words, Numbers, and Technical Jargon—How Much of Each?

A business document's fundamental building blocks are words and numbers. How these are mixed and matched can make or break the document.

A plan that's all words, promises, and discussions gives the reader a sense of imprecision, the feeling that while the idea may be good, the author probably won't be too effective in implementing it. On the other hand, too many numbers or too much technical language can be confusing and irritating, especially if the material isn't adequately supported.

Don't minimize the importance of this balance. Imagine how your plan will be perceived by a reader whose background and skills may be very different from your own. Many plans fail because authors dwell on areas in which they themselves are the most comfortable. It's important to strike a readable balance among qualitative, quantitative, and technical material.

Size and Level of Detail

When people start thinking about writing business plans, one of the first questions they ask is about length. How long should it be, how many pages? As one might suspect, there isn't one answer to that question, but a few guidelines are appropriate.

Larger, more complicated businesses require longer, more detailed plans. A plan for a $200 million manufacturing start-up takes more justification than one for a restaurant in a shopping center.

Some businesses are more complex than others and take more explaining. For example, a manufacturing proposal generally requires more detail than a retail idea of the same size. The plan just needs to explain adequately what's going on in the business.

However, a bigger plan isn't necessarily a better plan because plans that are too long and complex will put people off.

So how much plan is enough? How do we package a full load of detailed thoughts, research, and analysis into something that looks and feels light, spirited, and easy to read?

The answer often lies in separately bound backup. Try to keep the basic plan document between twenty and sixty pages, but if that's not enough to explain the whole business, expand each section in an appendix that readers can request if they want to see more detail.

The Whole Plan—Four Parts

The business plan is a little like a résumé. Its purpose is to get you in the door and give you the chance to make your presentation. If we think in these terms, we can look at the entire business plan as consisting of at least four pieces:

1. The business plan document
2. Prepared backup carrying additional detail
3. The planner's presentation
4. What's in the planner's head

Everything you know about your business doesn't go into the plan document. It can't because you don't have that much space. But successful planners have thought-out answers for almost any question that might be asked about their businesses. Preparing those answers is as much a part of business planning as writing the plan document itself.

The Three Ms of Business Planning

The three Ms of business planning are the three most important areas in which a plan communicates with its readers. No plan will be successful if it doesn't tell its audience about:

The Market

The Management

The Money

Other sections may be more or less important depending upon the nature of the business, but *every* plan must be strong in these areas. Readers want to be convinced that there's a market for whatever you're selling and that you can reach it. They want to know who's running the business and what their qualifications are. And they want to be told how the business's financial performance will allow them to get their investments back.

Keep the three-M idea in mind while preparing your plan.

A Sample Business Plan

So far we've been talking about abstract concepts. At this point it's a good idea to get a sense of what a written plan actually looks like. Appendix E contains sample business plans. The first is for a relatively simple retail business. Look that one over now to get a general idea of the document's structure.

WHY DO WE NEED A BUSINESS PLAN?

THE VALUE OF BUSINESS PLANS AND PLANNING

Business plans are prepared by large and small companies so that they can chart where they're going in the future. Both the planning document and the processes by which it's created have separate values in that they each play an important role in effective management.

The business plan document serves two concrete purposes and provides an incidental benefit.

- It's indispensable for getting help from others, especially financial backers.

- It provides a guide for running operations once the enterprise is started and on its way.

The incidental benefit of planning is the actual process:

- The planning exercise pulls the management team together and forces the entrepreneur(s) or manager(s) to more fully appreciate the task ahead of them.

A few words about this last idea first.

Impact on Management

The planning process galvanizes the management team into a cohesive unit with common goals. It helps everyone understand what the objectives of the organization are, why they're important, and how management intends to achieve them. Creating a plan for a small business forces the entrepreneur to think through everything that has to be done to get the business going or to keep it afloat. If there's more than one owner, the planning process helps everyone understand what he or she has to do for the company and what each owner can expect out of it.

This is especially valuable for start-ups. Pre-start-up planning helps the entrepreneur establish his or her ideas and put them to a hard test of dollars and cents. The exercise often reveals an ill-conceived idea that isn't worth pursuing. Conversely, good ideas emerge buttressed with logic and calculations showing them to be viable.

Because it's far better to abandon a bad idea in the planning stage than after sinking thousands into it, would-be entrepreneurs should do careful plans for this purpose alone.

Financing Sources and Other Outsiders

If you want people to join you in an enterprise, they will expect you to show them a business plan. Plans explain the company's goals and methods to outsiders—especially in small businesses.

It's simply a fact of life that financial backers require high-quality business plans before considering requests. Therefore, people who want to start businesses must go through the business planning experience unless they already have all the money they need.

This reason for planning is so important and pervasive that many entrepreneurs think of business plans only as funding documents. But business owners shouldn't ignore the other benefits of planning, because they can be very significant.

A Road Map for Running the Business

Finally, business plans are marvelous retrospective devices. Owners and managers generally have an idea of where they want their businesses to go, but usually can't steer a straight course in getting there. Unfortunately, the realization that the firm isn't headed in the right direction often takes them by surprise and leaves them confused about what's wrong. In other words, being overdrawn at the bank is bad, but being overdrawn and not knowing why spells real trouble. Fortunately, prior business planning can just about always eliminate the confusion.

If a business is going off course, comparing its actual performance to the plan is the best way to understand the problems and come up with solutions. Being in business without a plan is like traveling without a road map. Things are okay as long as you're on familiar ground, but if you get a little lost, you're in big trouble. A plan projects where we're going and gives us the means of correcting our course along the way. It is truly a road map for running a business. For example, suppose profits in your first year are turning out below expectations. Without a plan you're unlikely to know if the problem is low sales volume, bad pricing, or higher than expected cost in one or more of a number of areas. A plan tells what you assumed at the outset for these elements and

lets you compare each to actual performance. Then you can immediately isolate the trouble spot and take corrective action.

THE BROAD BUSINESS PLANNING PROCESS

Business planning is a much bigger subject than most people think. In this chapter we'll review the full range of planning activity and explore how the entrepreneur's business plan fits in.

Four Kinds of Planning

People who look into the future of companies actually do so in four separate ways. Each is a distinct management process and can result in a different planning document. Large, sophisticated companies tend to do the four processes separately, while small firms tend to do one combined exercise and label the result "the business plan." It's important to understand all four parts to be sure your business plan picks up the right pieces.

Although there is some overlap in terminology, the four kinds of planning are commonly known as *strategic planning, operational planning, budgeting,* and *forecasting*. These differ according to three attributes: (1) the length of time over which we look at the business, often called the *planning horizon,* (2) the level of detail in which we plan, and (3) the kind of issues we consider.

NOTE: Terminology regarding the types of planning can sometimes be confusing. Some people talk about an *annual operating budget*, while others mention a *long-term forecast*. The words *outlook* and *view* are also used. The important distinction is the length of the planning horizon:
Multi year—Long term, strategic
One year—Intermediate term, operating
3 to 6 months—Short term, budgetary
Up to 3 months—Very short term, forecast

Strategic Planning

Strategic planning involves broad, conceptual thinking about the nature of the business, what it does, and who it serves. It's generally an exercise in which we try to predict in rough terms what the business will do and become over a period of several years (usually five).

Strategic planning begins by questioning the company's very existence. Why is the firm doing what it does? Would it be better off doing something else? What customer need does it serve? How? What opportunities exist in the marketplace? What threats? Strategic planning demands that a company develop a mission and a charter, that it define what it does and why, while it states its loftiest goals.

Once that is established, strategic planners look forward over several years and consider broad, sweeping issues. At the end of five years, will our business be in the same lines of endeavor? In the same geographic areas? How large will we have grown? Who will be our competition and how will we fight them? And so on.

Strategic planning deals with concepts and ideas expressed mostly with words rather than numbers. The numbers we do use tend to be simple and approximate. For example, a strategic plan might simply state the desire to be number one or two in the industry based on some defined measure. Or we might say that we want our sales to be about $50 million a year. Financial statements are projected in strategic planning, but they're approximate and ideal. The fifth year generally shows the best financial results anyone in the business could ever expect. The strategic plan is often called the long-range plan or the five-year plan.

The importance of strategic planning is a little hard to grasp in the context of small, family-run businesses, but it becomes immensely important as the company and its resources get larger and more complex. Some industries also seem to have more strategic issues than others.

Staying in business, earning a reasonable profit, and stocking what customers want may be the extent of strategy for a neighborhood grocery store. But even a modest-sized computer company must address issues of changing technology, developing a competence vis-à-vis the competition, marketing approach, customer requirements, level of service, and so on.

Most of today's entrepreneurial business planning considers strategy implicitly in the description of one's product and the market that exists for it. However, with modern strategic thinking, a planner can do a much better job of formulating why he or she is in business and where that business is going. Systematic strategic thinking says that a business must first analyze itself, its industry, and the competitive situation. Then, it must construct an approach that takes advantage of its strengths and minimizes the vulnerabilities caused by its weaknesses.

The key strategic question an entrepreneur must satisfactorily answer is: What distinctive competence does my business have that will set it apart from others?

Operational Planning

Operational planning involves translating business ideas into concrete, short-term projections, usually for about a year. The operational plan is sometimes referred to as the annual plan. Operational planning is more detailed than strategic planning, but it is still not highly detailed. We talk in terms of thousands of dollars rather than in dollars and cents.

In operational planning, we try to specify how much we will sell, to whom and at what prices. We also determine where we will get our labor, materials, and equipment, what they will cost, where we will produce, what we can expect to earn, and so on.

Major short-term goals are generally set in the operating plan. Revenue targets and profit objectives are established. Sales quotas and product development milestones are laid out. Compensation and bonus systems are generally specified in this exercise. The words *operational or operating* mean having to do with the actual running of the business.

An operational plan is typically about an even mix of words and numbers. What's going on is explained in words but backed up with fairly detailed financial projections.

Budgeting

Budgeting is the process of making accurate financial projections over a relatively short term, say, several months. Budgeting is commonly done quarterly.

Budgeting tries to determine exactly how much money will flow in and out of the organization and fixes responsibility on specific people for making it happen. The time frame is too short to make major changes in the business, but we do need to think about how we will guarantee our sales levels and control our expenses. We

try to predict exactly how many dollars will be spent in each department and on exactly what items: salary, material, travel, etc. Along with that, we try to predict precisely how much we will sell and at what cost.

There are fewer explanatory words in a budget because programs have already been established and the opportunity for conceptual change is limited.

Forecasting

Companies use forecasting when they want to know where they are financially, that is, how they'll close out the month or year with respect to profits and cash flows. Forecasting is simply a detailed estimate of where the business's *financial momentum* will carry it over a short period.

If the forecast yields an unsatisfactory result, we can sometimes take some very short-term actions to achieve our objectives. For example, if sales for the month look as though they'll be a little low, we can try to ship some product that normally wouldn't have gone out until the next month to make up the shortfall.

Forecasting is especially important with respect to cash requirements. If a company is to pay its bills and make its payroll, management needs a very accurate picture of the cash it expects to come in and go out over the next few weeks and months. If a temporary shortage is predicted, a relationship with a bank has to be set up to keep the firm running until collections catch up with disbursements.

RELATING THE SMALL BUSINESS PLAN TO THE BROAD PLANNING PROCESS

It helps to think of the entire planning process as a spectrum. On one end we have the broad, conceptual thinking of strategic planning, while on the other we have the numerical detail of forecasting:

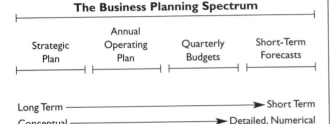

The Business Planning Spectrum

Strategic Plan · Annual Operating Plan · Quarterly Budgets · Short-Term Forecasts

Long Term ————→ Short Term
Conceptual ————→ Detailed, Numerical

As we move from left to right, the planning horizon (time covered) gets shorter, and the documents progress from qualitative to quantitative, that is, from being mostly words to mostly numbers.

Ideally, companies practice the whole spectrum. That's the way most large companies operate, producing different planning documents for each segment of the spectrum. When companies regularly prepare all the pieces, they gain the benefits of the process as well as the usefulness of the resulting documents. Hence, a company that periodically goes through a budgeting process does not do so just to come up with a profit figure, but also to make sure that everyone knows his or her responsibilities for the coming months.

Venture capitalists and small business entrepreneurs tend to think in terms of just one planning document, *the* business plan. It's the entrepreneur's document. Small companies tend to do only the plans that someone outside of the company demands of them, most notably the bank. They produce a plan when they are just getting started and update it later if they need something from the bank or another outside source of funding.

We certainly don't recommend such infrequent planning. Small companies should do a complete planning exercise at least once a year and establish budgets on a quarterly basis. But in the real world, time pressures get in the way, and people only do planning when they have to.

The small business business plan bears a definite relationship to the full planning spectrum we've been discussing. The people who read business plans for start-ups and relatively small companies have clear expectations of what should be included, so it's important that the writer understand those expectations in terms of the planning spectrum. If we lay the spectrum out again, we can indicate graphically how the small business plan relates to the overall picture.

The Business Planning Spectrum

Strategic Plan · Annual Operating Plan · Quarterly Budgets · Short-Term Forecasts

The Small Business "Business Plan"

The small business plan blends three of the exercises along the spectrum. It includes some of the elements of strategic planning and some of the elements we think of as budgeting. However, it generally includes everything under the heading of operational or annual planning.

The small business plan need not cover the broadest strategic issues. For example, an entrepreneur doesn't have to discuss why he or she chose this business over others, because that decision has already been made by the time the entrepreneur prepares a business plan. The plan does, however, have to establish that a market clearly exists and that it can be served by the proposed business. The small business plan must also make longer-term, strategic projections for what the business will be three to five and even ten years out.

The entrepreneur's plan must also do everything the big corporation's annual operating plan does: provide a thorough rationale for the concrete actions planned in the next (first) year and make some fairly detailed projections of quantities, headcounts, and dollars over that period.

Finally, the small business plan has to go beyond the operating-plan level and break the first year down into quarterly and monthly detail. This is a budget-like process. A small business plan must predict the detailed funding requirements that backers are being asked to provide. It need not, however, forecast how every dollar is to be spent.

The planning spectrum helps a planner focus on what his or her business plan has to accomplish. You're writing the plan to explain your strategy, operations, and budgets. Concentrate on the left-hand side of the spectrum. Your document has to have just the right amount of strategic thinking to capture and hold your readers' interest while you lock them in with the competence of the detail that follows.

That's crucial. The perfect business plan is convincing not only because it creates a conceptual excitement by discussing the business idea and why it will succeed but also because it demonstrates the author's business competence through a thorough, detailed discussion of what has to be done to make the idea happen.

THE PERFECT (SUCCESSFUL) BUSINESS PLAN AND THE TARGET AUDIENCE PRINCIPLE

When people are asked to define a business plan succinctly, their answer generally is something like: "A business plan is a portrayal of the future of a business unit. It's a forecast of how the business will fare over future months and years." No problem so far, but when people are pressed for more detail, definitions diverge, generally according to the respondent's background. An accountant says, "It's basically a budget." A marketeer maintains that, "It's primarily a market analysis describing customers, competitors, and our share strategy." Whereas an engineer tells us, "A business plan describes how we will overcome our product development obstacles and why our product is the best." Finally, the treasurer maintains, "It tells how much money you need and where it's coming from."

People will usually acknowledge that a complete business plan contains all of the elements of an actual business: financials, marketing analysis, product development detail, personnel evaluations, manufacturing methods, etc. In spite of that general agreement, when tasked with developing a plan, they produce entirely different documents.

FOCUSING ON THE PLAN AS A SALES TOOL

It is helpful if we focus for a moment on what we want a business plan to do for us rather than on what it is or who wrote it. A business plan should be a sales tool, a document used in selling an idea. The idea being sold is the business itself and how it is to be run whether we're talking about a proposed new venture, an existing concern, or a division of a larger company. In every case, the person responsible for the plan is selling to others his or her ideas on what the business is and how best to operate it. The others are people that the business planner wants something from, usually investment, cooperation, or, in the context of a large corporation, the continuation of his or her mandate to run the division.

The business plan is first a marketing tool for selling the business idea. (Although a plan is also an excellent control device for running a business, not many people go to the trouble of putting together a formal document unless they need to enlist the aid of another party.) A business plan is not something that has a value in and of itself; nor does it have to take some particular form or shape. It can be thought of as an advertisement: it needs to catch the reader's eye, hold it, and convey a message. And like an advertisement, it needs to be tailored to a specific audience. This is a central point: what a business plan should look like and what it should say depends on who the target audience is.

THE TARGET AUDIENCE PRINCIPLE

This idea is so important that it needs to be stated as a principle and kept in mind throughout all of our work in planning.

The Target Audience Principle of Business Planning

Business plans written for the right audience will win if they are otherwise well executed.

Business plans written for the wrong audience will lose no matter how well they are executed.

Putting the principle into practice involves following three simple rules:

1. The plan's emphasis must be in the area the audience sees as the most critical. This is usually defined by the criteria upon which the audience is measured.

AND...

2. The plan must offer to meet the measurable goals and objectives that are valued by the audience.

BUT...

3. Every business plan must have a section that at least addresses all business functions and critical issues.

The third point needs to be included because it's easy for the entrepreneur or executive planner to leave out things that have to do with business areas in which he or she is not experienced. This leaves a vulnerable area in the plan through which the entire proposal can be shot down.

This is very important to remember. Business plans are submitted to people who have a great deal more experience in the review and negotiating process than those who have done the planning. It's a little like negotiating with a car salesperson. The customer is inherently at a disadvantage because he or she goes through the process only once every few years while the salesperson does it every day. So, in order to succeed, the planner really has to do his or her homework. The planner must have thought through answers to all reasonable questions before submitting the plan. Otherwise, he or she can be trapped in a peripheral discussion and lose credibility before getting to the substantive issues for which he or she is best prepared.

TARGET AUDIENCES

At first glance, following rules 1 and 2 seems like a job for a mind reader. In fact, it isn't as difficult as it may appear. Business planning tends to fall into a limited number of categories, each with a particular type of audience. It is possible to set down broad guidelines for satisfying the audience in each case. The possibilities can be briefly summarized as follows:

1. A new venture looking for start-up equity capital

2. A business seeking a loan

3. A division or subsidiary of a larger corporation engaged in a periodic planning exercise

The first two groups are our main concern in this book, but knowledge of the third is important for perspective as well as for readers who are corporate planners.

Let's consider what makes each audience tick in a little more detail.

NEW VENTURES AND VENTURE CAPITALISTS

This is the most talked-about and the most exciting playing field for business plans. But in fact only a fraction of the planning done in business is aimed at either a venture capital firm or a wealthy investor.

The fundamental focus of venture investors is return on their investment. Backing new businesses is very risky. Investors know that many of the firms they fund will fail regardless of how carefully they're selected. To offset this, venture capital successes must really win big. Otherwise, backing new ventures won't pay off in the long run. As a result, to be considered for venture capital money a proposal must promise a return to the investor in the neighborhood of 50% compounded annually for a period of five or six years.

The VC Financial Model

Understanding how venture capitalists (VCs) get their money in successful deals is crucial to understanding their needs and how to satisfy them. The VC model works like this:

1. The VC puts money into a start-up in return for stock.

2. The firm operates and grows for about five years.

3. The company, now earning a profit, is either sold to a large corporation or taken public.

Going public is the procedure by which a corporation's stock is made available for sale to the general public. When a stock is publicly traded, its price and thereby a value for the firm are established. Then, if the venture has done well, the VCs can unload their stock on the open market at a big gain.

Either outright sale or going public allows the VC to recover his or her investment and profit.

It's important to understand that the starting point for the valuation of the firm in either case is generally about ten times earnings.

A Venture Capital Example

Given this model, devising a plan that meets the venture capitalist's financial needs requires certain calculations. Let's look at a numerical example. Assume the following:

1. The entrepreneur wants $2M from the investor.

2. For this he or she is willing to give the investor 40% ownership in the new venture.

3. Established businesses in similar fields earn a profit of approximately 8% of revenues.

The investor's interest must grow at 50% per year for five years, yielding a value of $15.2M:

$$\$2M \times 1.5 \times 1.5 \times 1.5 \times 1.5 \times 1.5 = \$15.2M$$

This amount represents 40% of the company's value, so the whole firm is worth $38M:

$$\$15.2M\ /\ .4 = \$38M$$

Since the firm is valued at about ten times earnings, this says that earnings in the fifth year must be around $3.8M, that is, one tenth of our targeted value. Finally, if earnings are to be 8% of revenues, fifth-year revenues must be around $47.5M:

$$\$3.8M\ /\ .08 = \$47.5M$$

Let's say $50M to use round numbers.

This gives us an idea of what it will take in terms of financial projections to get $2M out of a venture capitalist. We will have to have a plan that projects a revenue stream that will grow to $50M in five years. (To put this into perspective, a business of that size might employ as many as 500 people and have assets in the $40M range.) To achieve that kind of growth, we would probably need additional financing of debt or equity of as much as $20M during the five-year period.

So, a good rule of thumb is that your revenue forecast in the fifth year has to be about 25 times the investment you're looking for.

Other Guidelines on the Financial Projections

It's not advisable to submit a plan with financial projections that exceed these guidelines by very much. A more aggressive forecast will probably be viewed as unrealistically optimistic and will endanger the entrepreneur's credibility.

It's also not advisable to submit a plan with financial projections like these if the proposed business is to be in an industry characterized by slow or moderate growth. For example, if your proposal is for a grocery store, you can forget venture financing.

Other Requirements of VCs

The kind of projection described above will qualify a plan for further consideration, but it will by no means sell the idea.

The next requirement for a venture capital plan is establishing a credible market. The product or service must be presented in a way that satisfies a need perceived by the investor to exist. For example, the need for a product that will produce solar energy cheaply or one that will prevent heart disease will be recognized by almost anyone. The need for a new kind of frozen dessert is much harder to establish. A business plan must convince an investor that:

1. A market exists.

2. The product will satisfy the market need.

3. The marketing plan has a high probability of successfully connecting the two.

This last point requires special emphasis. Exactly how will the new business identify, contact, and sell to its customers? And, what experience have the entrepreneurs had in similar situations? More about that later.

Finally, the plan needs to convince the reader of the competence of each member of the management team. This is done with a summary of each person's background and education, including a listing of accomplishments in similar endeavors. The best experience possible is having participated in the successful launch of a venture before.

It should also be noted that many venture capitalists tend to develop expertise in specific industries like high tech and energy. It is probably useless to submit a plan that's outside their fields to specialized investors. They won't get excited about it regardless of how good it is.

In summary, a venture capitalist or investor will be impressed by a plan that reflects the following:

1. Financial projections that meet his or her return on investment requirements.

2. A credible market and a realistic plan to reach it in a field that's of interest to the investor.

3. A competent management team.

LENDERS—USUALLY BANKS

Business plans prepared to secure debt financing are usually submitted to loan officers or loan committees of banks. Both large and small companies prepare plans for this audience.

Although the bank is making a cash advance to the business in much the same way as the venture capitalist, its orientation is almost completely opposite that of the venture group.

The Difference Between Debt and Equity to the Investor

The difference between stocks and bonds is the same as the difference between equity and debt. For example, when a firm "sells" a bond it is actually borrowing money loaned by the bond buyer. In other words, a bond is a loan even though we say it is bought and sold rather than using the terms *borrow* and *lend* (more on this in Chapter 4). The following story illustrates the differences:

A business owner separately approaches two naïve investors for money. He proposes a stock sale (equity) to the first investor and a bond sale (debt) to the second. To his surprise, both ask him exactly the same two questions.

Question #1: "What happens to me if your company fails?"

Answer:
　Bond (debt) investor: "You lose all your money."

　Stock (equity) investor: "You lose all your money."

The answer is the same in both cases—disaster. Neither investor is very happy about that, but they proceed with the second question:

Question #2: "What happens to me if your company does spectacularly well?"

Answer:
　Bond (debt) investor: "You get your investment back plus interest."

Stock (equity) investor: "You get rich!"

Our business owner may be a little blunt in this example, but the point should be clear. The downside is the same for either investment method—total loss. But the upside is vastly different. The equity investor shares in the business's success, while the debt investor receives only a modest return.

What a Lender Wants to See in Financial Projections

This lack of upside potential differentiates the lender's focus from the stockholder's. Because a lender's return will be at best modest, he or she will look to ensure that any loss incurred will at worst be modest. That is, bankers will want to minimize their risk. In lending terms this means bankers generally demand collateral before extending loans to new businesses. *In terms of the business plan, it means the plan must focus on stability and the cash flows necessary to pay the interest and principle required by the loan.*

Bankers aren't likely to be impressed by the plan that hooked the venture capitalist. If you show bankers a plan with a 50% compounded growth rate, they probably won't believe it and is likely to label you an unrealistic optimist.

Even if the bankers do accept the numbers, they know that rapid growth can rarely be financed by internally generated funds—that is, by reinvested profits. When a plan forecasts very rapid growth, bankers, unlike venture capitalists, don't see a quickly rising stock price. They see a lack of cash available for paying interest and principle. Worse, they see the need for more cash to be injected into the business in the future.

Bankers will be impressed by a plan that shows modest growth, profitability, and a healthy balance sheet with relatively low levels of fixed assets, inventory, and receivables.

Other Financial Requirements

Bankers also need assurances and guarantees that depositors' money will be safe. We must keep in mind how the loan officers are graded. Their job is to make loans. A successful loan is, of course, one that gets repaid. But the loan officers don't get any prizes for making a successful loan—that's just what's expected. They do, however, get punished for making unsuccessful loans, ones which don't get repaid. Too many of those and they go back to the teller window. Hence, loan officers like high levels of assurance that loans are safe.

In the context of business loans, safety usually means either history or security, but it often takes both. History means bankers like to lend to businesses that have proven track records of solvency and whose owners are known to them and in the community.

Security means they like collateralized loans. These are loans backed by specific assets that will immediately belong to the bank in the event of default. Generally, the loan will be for only a fraction of the value of the collateral as a further guarantee that the bank will recover all of its money. Collateral usually consists of assets owned by the business or by the business owner.

The New Business and Borrowed Money

The bottom line is that you generally can't expect to start a business with borrowed money unless the loan is fully collateralized.

For many middle-class entrepreneurs that means putting up the equity in their homes. A partial exception to this rule is sometimes available through Small Business Administration (SBA) loans. Most of those loans are guaranteed by the federal government; thus, Uncle Sam is providing some of the bank's security.

It's unfortunate that in their advertising banks paint a somewhat misleading portrait of themselves. Phrases like "We like to say yes!" (to loan applicants) really mean "We like to say yes after you've met all of our conditions."

Nonfinancial Requirements

Once the cash flow requirements are understood, a plan for a bank depends upon the same key points as the venture plan: market and management. However, unlike the venture capitalist, bankers usually require that the market already be established. The best situation is an existing business with a satisfied and growing customer base. If the business is new, the bank will lend (collateralized) if the market is recognized and other businesses have been successful in it, for example, gas station, dry cleaner, plumber.

Management is also important to lenders. A common question to an entrepreneur is "What makes you think you can run this business profitably?" The best answer is that you have spent many years working in the field either in your own business or someone else's.

In summary, the emphasis points required in a plan aimed at borrowing money from a bank or another lending institution are:

1. Existence and stability of cash flows required to service the debt and/or collateral

2. A proven (existing) market with a credible plan for reaching it

3. The competence and experience of management

CORPORATE BUSINESS PLANNING

The bulk of the business planning done in the United States isn't done by entrepreneurs, it's done by corporate managers. This assertion is hard to prove but stands the test of logic. People tend to do business plans only when they have to. For small business owners, that's when they're going after some kind of financing or outside assistance.

Large corporations, on the other hand, have involved planning systems that keep their management employees engaged in a more or less continuous planning process. Each business unit is continually planning in good times and bad, although the frequency of revision is higher in bad times. This adds up to a great deal of planning activity.

The techniques involved in putting together a business plan are largely the same whether the business unit is an independent or a subdivision of a larger company, although the emphasis and focus need to be different.

The Focus of Corporate Executives—Stock Market Performance

When planning for a division or subsidiary, the target audience consists of senior operating officers of the corporation who tend to have predictable focuses. They will be looking at revenue growth and profitability as reflected on the income statement. It isn't difficult to understand why. Those are the criteria upon which Wall Street rewards stocks with high prices. Since stock price maximization is the most important goal of CEOs and board chairmen, it's not surprising that these criteria underlie the evaluation of business plans at the division level.

Although a great deal of sophisticated financial analysis goes on in the stock market, the overriding valuation formula is rather simple. It's based on the price–earnings ratio (P/E) and earnings per share (EPS). The price of a company's stock, P, is given by:

$$(1) \qquad P = EPS \times P/E$$

In this formula, EPS is bottom-line profit (earnings) divided by the number of shares of stock outstanding. EPS refers to accounting (income statement) profitability. Cash flows have little effect on the formula except in extreme cases. (See Chapter 14 for the difference between profit and cash flow and its importance.)

A company's price–earnings ratio (P/E) indicates how much the stock market will pay for each dollar of its earnings. Average P/Es are usually around 15 or 18, but more glamorous stocks command P/Es of 30 or more.

NOTE: Prior to the 1990s, average P/Es were in the neighborhood of 9 or 10. That decade saw a dramatic rise in stock prices and P/Es coupled with very low interest rates. There's a great deal of conjecture about whether both will last.

The P/Es of companies in the same industry tend to cluster in a range. Countless studies of stock market performance have shown that although P/Es depend on a number of things, their primary determinant is *expected* growth.

Hence in equation (1): more profit means a higher EPS, while more growth means a higher P/E, both of which mean a higher stock price, which is what executives like.

American business has been severely criticized for focusing on short-term stock performance, because it often leads to bad long-range decisions. Nevertheless, this is what makes top management tick, so planners must cater to that set of goals.

Supporting Revenue Growth

The corporation's emphasis on revenue growth means that a division's plan must include a thorough analysis of the marketing plan and sales projections. An increasing revenue stream must be justified by sales productivity estimates and a market share analysis. Burgeoning sales forecasts may be what the target audience wants to hear, but they have to be believable. Specifically, if revenue is growing, where is it coming from? Either the market must be growing or we are taking market share from someone else. If the latter, what are they doing in the meantime?

If a plan projects substantial revenue growth, profitability comes along almost automatically. Costs and expenses are simply forecast as increasing at a slower rate than revenues. This results in improving margins, which are generally put down to "economies of scale." These concepts are accepted without much question because they represent what the audience wants to hear.

Even when market conditions are such that revenue growth is unrealistic, profit improvement is still generally required. In such cases the plan needs to stress cost cutting and overhead reduction.

In summary, a successful business plan prepared for a corporate audience should stress:

(1) A strong revenue forecast supported by a believable marketing and sales plan.

(2) An improving profit projection regardless of how it is to be achieved.

OTHER IMPORTANT ISSUES

The **target audience principle** must be applied with some degree of caution. We aren't saying that these are the audience's only goals. We are saying that for the respective audiences these goals are virtually always at the top of the list. It is rare that some other goal conflicts with or overrides these. However, a wise planner should do a little research before presenting a plan to find out what other things might be high on the audience's current priority list.

Raising money to start a business is often the primary, if not the only, reason that entrepreneurs write business plans. As we've been saying, a good plan is an absolute requirement for getting funded by any professional money manager. However, it's important to understand that a good idea together with a good plan does not necessarily guarantee receiving money. In fact, getting money from venture capitalists and banks is a very difficult proposition for most new businesses.

Before going further, we need to be sure that we understand some basics about the forms funding can take and a few of the more important rules of the game.

We'll begin with the idea that money provided to businesses comes in the form of either *debt* or *equity*. We'll discuss each in some detail in the following pages.

DEBT

Debt simply means a loan. Some person or organization, such as a bank, lends your business money with the expectation of being repaid with interest. The two major forms of debt are straight loans, which can carry a variety of repayment terms, and bonds.

Bonds are simply a device that lets a number of people lend money to a company in one transaction. Suppose, for example, a firm wanted to borrow $1 million but couldn't find anyone willing to lend that much. Further suppose it could find a thousand people each willing to lend $1,000. Rather than make up a thousand different loan agreements, the firm "floats" a $1M bond issue. Each person who "buys" a bond for $1,000 is lending the company that amount. Notice we say that a lender "buys" a bond even though he or she is lending money. Few small companies can issue bonds, so we won't dwell on them here. The following concepts apply to all debt.

Term

Loans come in a variety of forms. The most important distinction among loans is *term*, the length of time over which they must be repaid. Loans are generally classified as follows:

Short-term	one year or less
Intermediate-term	one to five years
Long-term	longer than five years

Lenders generally expect the term of the loan to be matched to the use of the money. If you want a loan to buy equipment that will last 20 years, the banker will expect to make a long-term loan. On the other hand, if you need money to see you through a cash-short period when your receivables and inventory purchases get ahead of collections, the banker will want to lend short-term.

The expectation is that long- and intermediate-term money will be repaid out of profits, but short-term money will be repaid as soon as the short-term need is over, for example, as soon as your receivables are collected.

Most short-term loan agreements have a "clean-up" clause that stipulates that the borrower must be out of short-term debt for at least 60 days each year. This ensures that short-term money is really being used for short-term purposes.

It's important to understand that most lenders consider term an element of safety. A short-term loan is more secure than a long-term loan. That's because a bank makes a judgment about a borrower's financial condition when the loan is made. Because a short-term loan must be repaid within a year, there generally isn't time for the borrower's condition to deteriorate a great deal. On the other hand, anything can happen in the longer run.

Payments

Most loan agreements require payment of interest and principle over the term of the loan. Lenders will sometimes give a business a period in which principle repayments don't have to be made, but interest is always collected regularly.

This is an important feature of loans. The interest must be paid whether your business is making money or not! In fact, this require-ment to pay interest increases your risk of failure, because an unserviced loan can put you into bankruptcy.

Covenants

Most business loans have *covenants* attached. Covenants are clauses in the loan agreement that limit the way the entrepreneur can run his or her business while the loan remains

outstanding. Lenders put these in to ensure the safety of their investment.

A typical covenant might state that the com-pany can't pay dividends to stockholders during the life of the loan. The agreement might also preclude the entrepreneur's drawing or borrowing money from the business and limit the compensation paid to officers. Clearly, these rules are designed to ensure that the company's cash is used to service the loan before it is paid to owners. Covenants can also restrict the day-to-day operations of the firm.

If a covenant is broken, the loan is in *default* just as it would be if interest payments weren't made. When a loan goes into default, an *acceleration clause* makes the entire principle due and payable immediately. This means a lender can generally force a defaulted borrower into bankruptcy.

Collateral

Most lenders feel that small businesses are too risky to justify loans. Therefore, they require that some marketable asset back the loan obligation. In other words, if the company defaults, the asset becomes the property of the bank. The proceeds from the sale of the asset then pay off the loan. Such an asset is called *collateral*. Collateral can be an asset owned by the business or by the entrepreneur personally, such as his or her house.

Long-term loans that are used to buy equip-ment or real estate are usually collateralized by those assets themselves. Short-term loans that fund inventory and receivables are often collateralized by that inventory and those receivables.

Generally the collateral value of an asset is a fraction of its cost. For example, if a machine costs a million dollars, a bank might not lend more than about six hundred thousand on it. That's because if the bank has to repossess and sell the article, it has to do so on the used equipment market and absorb any expenses involved. So to come out whole, the bank can't be at risk for the entire million dollars.

This says that to buy an asset with a loan collateralized by that asset, you generally have to put in some of your own cash. This is a familiar concept. Residential mortgages and car loans are collateralized by the houses and cars they're used to purchase, and usually require a *down payment*.

We call the down payment our *equity* in the asset, meaning our own ownership as distinguished from the bank's interest.

A collateralized loan is also said to be *secured* by the asset. A loan without collateral is called an *unsecured* loan. Lenders will generally make unsecured loans only to businesses that have substantial track records of profitable operation.

Personal Guarantees

Theoretically, if a business that's a corporation owes money, creditors can only look to the assets of the business for recovery of their debts and not to the assets of the owners.

Understanding these rules of incorporation, banks, when lending to a small business, invariably require the entrepreneur's *personal guarantee* of the loan along with the business's agreement to repay the money. The entrepreneur's personal guarantee puts all of his or her personal assets at risk. We'll discuss this concept in Chapter 11.

Control

An advantage of debt financing is that a relatively small amount of control over the business is given up under normal circumstances. If covenants are negotiated carefully and aren't unreasonable, they won't get in the way of normal operations.

EQUITY

Equity means an ownership interest in the business. In a corporation, an equity investor gets stock. If the business is not a corporation, an equity investment means taking on a partner of some kind.

Partnerships

There are basically two kinds of partnerships. The most common is a *general partnership*. General partners usually participate in the running of the business, although not necessarily on an equal basis. They also usually contribute funds toward getting started, but again not necessarily equally. Taking on an additional general partner is rarely a viable way to raise money as it subjects the investors to the firm's liabilities and may require giving them some control over operations.

Limited partnerships are special legal devices designed to let people invest in businesses without being involved in management and without taking on personal liabilities beyond their initial investment. A limited partnership has two kinds of partners, at least one general partner who runs the business, and any number of limited partners who invest only money. The limited partners have no say in how the business is managed and are not liable for the debts of the business beyond their investments. Limited partnerships are popular in real estate enterprises.

General partnerships are easy to form, requiring only a comprehensive agreement between the partners. Limited partnerships are legally complex and should not be considered without the advice of a lawyer. We'll talk more about partnerships in Chapter 11.

Stockholders

If the business is a corporation, raising equity money means selling stock to outsiders. Investors are usually most interested in common stock, because it carries voting rights, which may imply a say in how the company is run. Voting means voting for seats on the board of directors, which appoints management, which in turn runs the company. A person or group owning a minority of stock in the company is unlikely to be able to elect any directors, so they may insist on being given a seat on the board as a prerequisite to buying stock.

There are other kinds of stock that don't carry voting rights. Although these are called equity, they really aren't, since they don't share in the control of the company.

We'll discuss the issues associated with stock ownership in Chapter 11.

Control

Unlike debt, an equity investment can involve giving up a substantial amount of control over the business. Investors often have little interest in day-to-day operations under relatively normal conditions, but can become very difficult in bad times if they feel that their investments are in jeopardy.

HYBRID INVESTMENTS

There are investment vehicles that combine some of the characteristics of debt and equity.

The advantage of debt to the investor is that it is generally safer than equity. This is because debt service is a legal obligation of the business, while payments to stockholders are not mandatory if times are tough. In addition, in the event of bankruptcy, debts are paid off before stockholders get anything. The advantage of equity is that a great gain may be made if the company does very well, mainly through price appreciation of the stock.

A *convertible bond* has the advantages of debt if things don't go too well and the advantages of stock in the event of great success. It is a debt instrument that can be converted into a specified number of shares of stock whenever the holder chooses. Clearly, the holder, who starts out as a lender, will only do this if the stock's price appreciates a great deal.

SOURCES OF FINANCING AND HOW TO DEAL WITH THEM

One basic financing fact must be understood at the outset by anyone interested in starting his or her own business. *Most of the money behind small business start-ups comes from the entrepreneurs themselves and from family and friends.* We're not saying that other financing sources cannot be found, but that a big chunk of the money generally comes from the entrepreneur's savings or from liquidating other assets. In other words, it's rarely realistic to assume you can start your own business without any of your own money.

The traditional arm's-length sources of funds for start-ups and relatively new businesses are banks for debt and venture capital for equity. By arm's length, we mean that there is no nonbusiness relationship between the entrepreneur and the source of the money. As we will discuss below, few start-ups have the characteristics that interest venture capitalists. Most successful funding comes out of banks. We will discuss dealing with banks and venture capitalists in turn, and then look at some other, less traditional sources of money.

BANKS

In Chapter 3 we discussed the things that were important to both banks and venture capitalists when advancing funds. Let's briefly review what banks like to see. The three big items were:

1. The existence and stability of the cash flows required to service the debt and/or collateral.

2. A proven (existing) market with a credible plan for reaching it.

3. The competence and experience of management.

You'll recall that the reason behind these preferences was that bankers invest other people's money and are essentially not big risk takers. The bank's reward system isn't consistent with risky investments. If the borrower does well, the bank just gets repaid with interest. It does not share in the company's success as does a stockholder. Understanding that, we can set down some general guidelines for securing a business loan from a bank whether your business is brand new or has been around for a while.

It's helpful to remember two things. One, the bank wants to make loans! That's the business they're in, and it's a competitive business. Check the rosters of your local Rotary, Kiwanis, and Lions clubs. You'll find bankers on all of them. Why? Because banks want to be involved in the business community and make loans to local businesses. Two, about 75% of loans to small businesses are made by small- and medium-sized banks. That says that your chances are better with a bank that's small enough to value your business. Keep in mind that the banking relationship is a two-way street. You need them, but they need business people like you, too.

Approach

When approaching a bank for a loan, you must make a complete, thorough presentation of your business. Don't try to do that by just walking in cold and pulling out your business plan. Go in the first time to meet the right person briefly and set up a second meeting. Be sure they block out enough time for you to get through your entire presentation. You may want to leave a copy of your plan with them so that they can look it over before your meeting.

Information

All banks have their own loan application forms. You will have to fill out their forms regardless of the fact that a great deal, if not all, of the information it requires is in your business plan. It's a good idea to pick up the forms early and have them completely filled out prior to your sit-down meeting with loan officers.

Commercial bankers work from a package of information about a business and the entrepreneur behind it. Applicants need to be sure that all the material is readily available to the loan officers. Loan information requirements can be roughly summarized as follows:

Typical Information Requirements for a Commercial Loan

Company/Business Information

1. A description of the nature and operation of the business. If it isn't new, a brief summary of its history.

2. The general plan for the future operation of the business, including a summary of how the proposed loan will help the company meet its goals.

3. The exact amount and purpose of the loan. People don't like to make "general-purpose" loans to businesses. The money should have a specific use.

4. Proposed repayment terms. Show how you plan to repay the loan and interest and where the cash will come from.

5. The capital structure of the business after the loan is made. In other words, if the bank makes the loan, what percentage of the company's total capital will be from debt and how much will be from equity? See Chapter 14 if you're unfamiliar with the concept of capital structure.

6. Details of any leasing agreements that the company has already entered into or contemplates, especially if they are not reflected on the financial statements.

7. The collateral being proposed for the loan. Banks are unlikely to make uncollateralized business loans to new businesses or to businesses and entrepreneurs they don't know well.

8. Insurance coverage carried on the business. List insurance policies for both the business itself and its owners.

9. Breakdown of assets owned by the business, including inventory, fixtures, equipment, real estate, etc. Include information on any intangibles considered of value, such as trademarks, patents, licenses, and goodwill.

10. Current and prior years' financial statements going back at least three years if the company or a predecessor has been around that long. Include balance sheets, income statements, and cash flow statements.

11. The company's federal tax returns for at least the past three years (for existing companies).

12. Projected financial statements for at least the next three years. Provide the first (next) year in monthly detail and subsequent years in quarterly detail. All three statements are required, but the order of importance is cash flow first and balance sheet second. Accounting profitability as reflected on the income statement isn't as important to a bank as is cash.

13. Summary of the assumptions that underpin the financial projections.

14. A worst-case scenario. In other words, a contingency plan. If things don't go as the business owner plans, how does the bank get its money?

Personal Information on the Business Owners

15. Professional qualifications, including complete work history and education. Essentially a résumé with references they can contact.

16. Credit history and references. They will also get credit bureau reports.

17. Personal financial statements stressing your net worth. Money in banks with verifiable account numbers, value of home, amount of mortgage, cars, and outstanding loans, etc.

18. Copies of your income tax returns for at least the last three years.

Several points should be made about loan information and the relationship with the loan officers. Most of the information needed by loan officers will already be included in a well-prepared business plan. The value of showing up with all the information, preassembled and well-organized, can't be overemphasized. You gain credibility and are perceived as competent and efficient when you've got it all together before you walk in the door.

Your Own Equity Investment

Banks don't really separate the business and the entrepreneur even if the company is incorporated. In small business, they lend primarily to the person. The entrepreneur's general character and experience are both important. From the bank's perspective, the best experience an entrepreneur can have is a track record of successful small business management in the industry proposed.

Banks prefer to lend to existing businesses with some operating history rather than to start-ups. They will lend to start-ups if the business and the person look good, the loan is collateralized, and the company shows substantial equity. This last point means that the entrepreneur has a sizable amount of his or her own money invested in the business.

The entrepreneur's own investment is important for two reasons. First, investors, including banks, feel that people simply try harder when their own money is at stake. They feel that people tend to manage and safeguard their own money more carefully than someone else's. Therefore, the business has an extra margin of safety and energy when a big chunk of the owner/operator's money is on the line. Second, if the business starts losing money, owner equity is lost first before debt money. Equity, therefore, cushions the bank's exposure to operating losses.

Attitude

Attitude is crucial when dealing with a bank. We advise that an entrepreneur strive to create the impression that he or she would like the loan but doesn't really need it. Someone who needs money too badly creates an impression of desperation, which signals a likely default in the eyes of a loan officer. Wanting the money for bigger and better things, on the other hand, signals prosperity and a successful business relationship.

Borrow Enough

Make sure to borrow enough money. Also, be careful of a banker who doesn't want to say no but won't lend you a sufficient amount. It's bad for a banking relationship, not to mention your business's health to take out a loan for some purpose and then go back and request more money for the same purpose. When applying for a loan, carefully document how you arrived at the amount you're requesting. If the loan officer suggests that you borrow significantly less, it might be a good idea to consider another source.

Perseverance

Don't be discouraged by a refusal. Try to learn something from the experience. Think about what you might have done to turn the loan committee off.

But keep in mind that you may not have done anything wrong. Refusals are sometimes for reasons that don't have much to do with the applicant. For example, the bank may already have too many loans in your line of business. There are also times when loan money is just tight, and there isn't much around for anyone. On the other hand, if you get six or eight refusals, it might make sense to rethink the whole idea and/or approach.

As Time Goes By

Once you get a loan and establish a relationship with a bank, keep your loan officer informed about how you're doing. When businesses aren't doing as well as hoped, people tend to be reluctant to share the bad news, especially with their backers. But remember that bankers don't like surprises, especially bad ones. Keep your loan officer informed in good times and bad, and your banking relationship will be one of your biggest assets.

SBA Loans

The Small Business Administration (SBA) is a government agency that exists to promote small business in the United States. SBA loans are misunderstood by many people. Although

there are rare exceptions, the SBA does not loan government money directly to businesses. What it does do is guarantee loans made to small businesses by banks. This government guarantee lowers the bank's risk, thereby allowing it to charge a slightly lower interest rate.

However, the key point is not the interest rate but the fact that some businesses are perceived as too risky to ever get bank financing without the SBA's guarantee. In order to get an SBA loan, you must have already been turned down by all available conventional channels. To learn more about SBA loans, contact the Small Business Development Center in your area. It is in the phone book. There's more about the SBA in Appendix D.

The Five Cs of Credit

Banks and other credit granting organizations are often said to make funding decisions based on the Five Cs of Credit. It's a good way to remember how banks think.

1. **Character** refers to the probability that people will attempt to pay off their debts. Do they intend to pay off the loan, and is that intention serious?

2. **Capacity** is a judgment made by the lender regarding the borrower's ability to pay.

3. **Capital** refers to the general financial condition of the borrower as reflected in its financial statements.

4. **Collateral** refers to the assets that are offered as security.

5. **Conditions** refers to general economic conditions and to circumstances peculiar to the borrower's industry or geographic area.

VENTURE CAPITAL

Entrepreneurs should realize that although a great deal is written about venture capitalists (VCs) and venture funding, few new business propositions will attract a VC's interest. Take the word *few* to heart; not one idea in hundreds rates a second look.

In the last chapter we went into some detail on how venture capitalists look at the world. The key for them is very rapid and sustained growth. Rapid and sustained means an annual rate of 40 to 50% compounded for five or six years. That kind of performance is generally associated with some new market. The invention of a new product with an instant demand is an example of a business where long-term supergrowth is possible. Good examples are cellular phones, personal computers, a variety of Internet-related dot.com businesses, and new medical drugs. If the market for the product grows immediately, firms in the business can grow with it.

Contrast personal computers with a more typical business, say, restaurants. In order to grow, a restaurant has to take business away from other restaurants, and that's unlikely to happen at extremely high rates.

Supergrowth opportunities tend to come about in high-technology industries. Those ventures come up with new ideas, which, every once in a while, find a ready and explosive market. There are examples of spectacular growth in lower-tech businesses, but they are far less common. A prominent example is Federal Express.

The Venture Capital Firm

The venture capitalist organization is usually a limited partnership sometimes called a fund. Limited partners put money into the fund and one or more general partners invest the money in businesses. The limited partners are usually investment companies, pension funds, and other institutions, but may include wealthy individuals. The general partner is someone who typically doesn't put in a great deal of money but manages the fund. That means he or she selects the ventures in which the fund invests. For that, the general partner gets a percentage of the earnings of the fund.

Entrepreneurs commonly approach venture capitalists by simply sending them business plans under cover letters. Unfortunately, venture people receive a great many unsolicited proposals, and conventional wisdom is that such blind approaches rarely result in securing VC money. Therefore, it helps immensely to have some kind of contact that can introduce an entrepreneur and his or her ideas to the venture capital community.

Venture firms often have definite preferences for the type of business in which they invest. Some also look for bigger rather than smaller deals and vice versa.

OTHER SOURCES OF MONEY

Occasionally entrepreneurs find private sources of either debt or equity funding. These so-called "angels" are typically wealthy individuals looking for an unusual investment opportunity. Success generally depends on some personal contact or nonbusiness relationship with the investor. Ask your accountant and banker if they know of anyone who might be interested. Personal financial planners sometimes have such leads among their clients. However, this kind of financing is hard to find.

An often overlooked source of limited amounts of short-term money can be vendors. If anxious to do business, a vendor may extend credit on his or her sales to your business. It never hurts to ask.

HOW FINANCIAL PEOPLE WILL READ YOUR PLAN

People who evaluate business plans for funding may have to sift through a hundred plans a week. The process is similar to that gone through by those who receive résumés in response to employment advertisements. Since evaluators don't have enough time to read every document carefully, they eliminate most of the candidates on the basis of a five-minute reading. The interesting ones are put aside and read more carefully later. If we assume that everyone gets a five-minute reading the first time around, the question is, how do we make sure we get on the read-more-carefully-later pile?

The first thing people look at is the executive summary, which, if well written, tells the financial people all that they initially need to know about the qualitative aspects of the business. That means that on the first pass they probably never look at the detailed sections describing the business and the approach to the market.

The next thing an analyst looks at is the financial projections, especially the cash forecast. That shows how the funding is to be used, and, in the case of a loan, it shows where the money to pay it back is coming from. In the case of venture capital, the analyst will make a quick estimate of the projected size and market value of the proposed company. He or she will also look at the balance sheet to see if more cash infusions are likely to be required in the first few years. Both will check the balance sheet and income statement to see if the assumptions made about the account balances that lead to the cash projections are reasonable.

In other words, once the analyst knows what kind of business the plan is describing, he or she focuses on the financial projections and tries to determine if the requirements laid out in Chapter 3 are met.

Finally, your reader will take a look at the background of the entrepreneur and the management team and make a quick judgment about their quality and character as business people.

In short, people try to very quickly grasp three things:

1. What the business is.

2. The MONEY.

3. Who's behind it.

It's a very good idea to put the best pieces of news you've got about each of these things in the executive summary. If that's done right, your plan is put on the read-again-later pile without being read past page one on the first pass.

PART 2

HOW TO *WRITE* THE PERFECT BUSINESS PLAN

Chapters 5–13 deal with how to structure the written parts of the plan. In Chapter 5 we deal with the executive summary and the ideas of mission and strategy. Earlier we referred to these as introductory sections in which the plan has to catch its reader's attention and interest. The remainder of Part 2 deals with the descriptive sections in which the plan sells the details of the business and the competence of the planner to the reader.

The level of depth and detail required in the descriptive sections varies a great deal with the nature and size of the business being planned. The treatment in Part 2 is rather complete and is designed to help an entrepreneur write a relatively complicated plan. All plans don't need to be as detailed. Those contemplating less complex businesses shouldn't feel they have to do everything that is described in the following chapters. You should pick and choose among the ideas presented in Part 2 and construct a document that makes sense for your business.

THE EXECUTIVE SUMMARY AND STATEMENTS OF MISSION AND STRATEGY

The business plan begins with the executive summary and statements of mission and strategy. These two sections condense many of the plan's involved ideas into a few paragraphs so that they can be read and absorbed quickly. Each section will be looked at by readers who aren't sure if they'll continue with the entire plan document as well as by those who are beginning to study it in earnest. The two sections introduce and summarize the entire plan at the same time. They should give readers an idea of where the plan is going while capturing their interest and attention.

In this chapter we'll look at the nature and purpose of the executive summary and then examine the concepts of mission and strategy in some detail. Mission and strategy statements are very important in some plans. To appreciate their impact, it's necessary to understand a few ideas from the field of strategic management. We'll present those ideas briefly but in enough detail to make you a better planner.

THE EXECUTIVE SUMMARY

It is common to include executive summaries in long, complex business documents. Summaries are popular because busy executives don't have time to read all of the detailed reports they receive, but they need to be aware of what's going on in their fields and within their organizations. To keep themselves informed, they insist that report writers con-

dense their work into single pages that contain the information they need to know.

Notice that the burden of communication falls on the report writers. They must decide what their readers need to know and put it in the summaries. The danger from the executive's perspective is that those doing the writing put in only what they *want* the reader to know and leave out less favorable information.

It's important to see that a summary can have two different purposes. The classic executive summary is produced to enable a reader to *avoid* reading the whole report. But for a business planner, a truly effective executive summary catches the readers' interest and entices them into reading the entire document.

The Purpose of the Business Plan's Executive Summary

In a business plan, an effective summary is like a plot synopsis. It should be designed to attract attention and pique interest. It should tell enough to convince the reader that the business idea has what he or she wants, but it should leave enough unsaid to require a deeper look.

The Reader's Perspective

Unfortunately, people who read plans and their summaries may have a different perspective. Those who review plans for funding generally look at large numbers of them and eliminate all but a few. When faced with that kind of task, people usually search for reasons to eliminate rather than reasons to retain.

The Writer's Perspective

An entrepreneur writing an executive summary has to keep these different perspectives in mind. That means emphasizing the positives and avoiding the negatives whenever reasonably possible. Don't give your reader a reason to eliminate your plan by pointing out a big negative in the summary.

For example, if you've found a great niche market that no one else serves, put that in, but leave out the fact that you haven't had any previous experience in that field. It's also important to consider the needs of your audience as outlined in Chapter 3.

How to Write the Executive Summary

The executive summary is simply a one-page condensation of what's in the rest of the plan. It can only touch on the highlights, and should generally follow the three Ms of business planning that we talked about in Chapter 1: Market, Money, and Management.

The summary should begin with a brief statement of the nature of the business (retail, manufacturing, service, etc.) and a description of the product and market. Then, it should mention who the people behind the business are and emphasize any special or unique qualifications they might have. Finally, it should summarize what the readers are being asked for, usually money, how it will be used, and what kind of a return the investor can expect (or when the money will be repaid in the case of a loan).

Try to keep the summary under one page in length.

It's important to emphasize the positive in the summary while tantalizing the reader. For example, a statement like, "A current investment of $500,000 will yield a $3 million value in five years," conveys just enough information about money. If the readers want more detail, they have to look into the plan more deeply, but they've been exposed to the idea that this may be a very high yield venture.

When to Write the Executive Summary

When people first sit down to write a business plan, their heads are filled with lots of unorganized information about their proposed enterprises. Nevertheless, there's a temptation to write the summary before the rest of the plan.

Writing the summary first is unwise because you can wind up trying to write a business plan to fit your summary rather than thinking through each piece of the venture independently. That defeats one of the most valuable benefits of business planning: gaining a better understanding of what you're trying to do and testing the concept for realism and viability.

Write the executive summary *last*, after you've finished everything else, including the financial projections. Look at the sample plans in Appendix E for examples of the executive summary.

STATEMENTS OF MISSION AND STRATEGY

The concepts of mission and strategy are part of a body of thought known as strategic management. The field deals with fundamental ideas, such as the structure of industries and the nature of competition. It attempts to uncover the underlying factors that explain why some companies succeed while others fail. Countless books and articles have been written on the subject, and all business schools teach at least one course in Strategy. The strategic planning we talked about in Chapter 2 is a big part of the overall idea of strategic management.

Mission and strategy statements rarely occupy more than a page or two of the business plan, but the thinking behind them is both critical and fundamental. This is especially true of plans that propose relatively sophisticated businesses. A strong strategic analysis can be the difference between success and failure for a business plan. Because of the importance of the ideas involved, we'll present an overview of the concepts and then look at how they function in a typical business plan.

THE MISSION

The mission statement has two essential parts. It tells exactly what the enterprise will do, and it provides a broad statement of the firm's long-term goals.

Defining the Business

The first piece of thinking behind a mission statement involves defining the business. People often think defining one's business is trivial or obvious. It usually isn't.

A good business definition always addresses three questions:

1. What customer need will be satisfied?

2. Who will the customers be?

3. What technology and functions will be used in satisfying the customer's need?

Customer Need

Products and services themselves are rarely of interest to customers. What makes an available product or service a business opportunity is the customer need that it satisfies.

Suppose we're in the software industry and want to write a business plan for a venture that will develop and market a personnel management system for small businesses. It's important to establish that small businesses need a software package to maintain and access their personnel records. If we don't do that at the outset of our business plan, our readers will never be convinced that the business will work.

In the mission statement it's usually enough to state that the need exists without much proof if it makes logical sense. The proof comes later when we discuss the market in detail. In many mission statements, the need is implied rather than explicitly stated. The statement gets the reader thinking in the right terms: there's an opportunity for a business to fill that need.

Customer Identification

The next step is to delineate the customer groups to which we expect to sell. This can be a crucial exercise. By focusing on exact customer groups with particular characteristics, planners often discover new opportunities or decide that their ideas weren't as good as they thought in the first place.

Our software system is a good example. If we intend to sell a personnel management system to smaller companies, we have to decide how big those firms will be, where they're located, how they're managing personnel records now, and how much money they have.

Suppose we target firms with 50 to 200 employees and call a few to see how receptive they'd be to what we're proposing. We might find that these potential customers would love a system like the one we're planning to offer. On the other hand, we might find that most of them use accounting systems that have personnel modules attached that are tied into their payroll systems so that they'd have to dump their whole financial package in order to use our product! That information might make us rethink the entire idea, because it would make it very difficult for customers to use our service even if they liked it.

Establishing who the customer is gives credibility to the plan at its outset. It implies that the planner has thought through problems like the one just described and hasn't found any that are insurmountable. The reader takes you more seriously as soon as he or she realizes that you've identified a concrete customer profile and have established that those people or organizations are likely to buy what you're selling.

Technology and Function

The tools and methods we'll use to satisfy the customer need also should be briefly established in the mission.

Don't be put off by the word technology. It's often used in the context of complex, high-tech businesses, but here it just refers to the tools and methods of our trade. For example, the technology of a restaurant is a kitchen, which may have a gas or an electric stove and which may prepare prefrozen dishes in a microwave oven or may cook everything from scratch.

Stating the Long-Term Goals

Most mission statements include a few sentences that are conceptual and visionary. These look to the long-term future and say something about what the entrepreneurs hope the business will become in terms that matter to them. Such statements usually portray the firm's future position in its market or say something about how it will be perceived by its customers. The ideas are often stated in qualitative terms relating to size, prominence, quality, excellence, or customer perceptions. Phrases like "we strive to become the leading producer of ...," "ranked first in customer satisfaction ...," or "number one developer of ..." are common.

The idea is straightforward. If the business is successful, state what place it will occupy in the community and market.

Making Money

We never state making money as a mission of the business. It's understood that profit is a fundamental reason for being in business. However, it is a byproduct of the mission, which addresses what the business can do for its customers and the community.

Mission Statement Examples

Let's consider a few examples of mission statements and analyze each one. We'll begin with the Decorator's Art Gallery in Anytown presented as a sample business plan in Appendix E. (The statement in the example itself is a combination of mission and strategy, and therefore reads somewhat differently.)

The Decorator's Art Gallery

The Decorator's Art Gallery will retail traditional wall hangings and accessories designed for middle-class homes at moderate prices. Discounts will be offered to professional decorators who place orders of $1,500 or more for a single client. The Gallery will offer limited consultation on decorating themes and color arrangements. Products will include original paintings, prints, and sculptures ranging in price from $50 to $500.

The Gallery will operate in an indoor regional shopping mall with a market radius of approximately 40 miles containing 75,000 households with incomes over $50,000.

Product will be procured from several large distributors. In addition, the Gallery will develop relationships with a number of as-yet unknown local artists, carrying their work for a reasonable commission.

The Decorator's Art Gallery will strive to become widely known as a leading source of wall hangings and accessories for households and the decorating trade in the Anytown area.

Notice that Decorator's mission statement answers all three questions, although some of the answers are implicit. The customer need is for moderately priced decorating items. The target customer population is the 75,000 households in the area with incomes over $50,000. And the technology or delivery technique is retailing in an enclosed mall. This statement also gives some information on sources of product. The visionary portion of the statement reflects the enterprise's long-term goal, to become a decorating institution in the area.

Next, let's look at Marcel's, an upscale French restaurant. Assume Marcel is already in business in Hometown and has prepared a business plan to secure a bank loan for expansion.

Marcel's Cuisine Française

Marcel's Cuisine Française offers an elegant dining experience to the more affluent residents of the Hometown area. Exquisite French cuisine is augmented by an old-world atmosphere, impeccable service, and an extensive wine cellar to create a memorable experience for the discriminating customer.

A limited menu and two seatings per evening ensure that gourmet meals are prepared to the most exacting standards by European-trained chefs.

Marcel's is becoming recognized as the finest restaurant in the Hometown area.

Marcel's mission statement reads a lot like an advertisement, but it does the job. It defines the need, clearly an entertainment experience rather than just food. It tells us who the customers are: the more affluent residents of Hometown. And it tells us how all this is to be accomplished, through painstaking and highly skilled labor. Finally, it gives us Marcel's vision of how he wants the business to be perceived in the long run.

Next, let's look at our personnel consulting business and its software package. Let's call them ABC Personnel Services.

ABC Personnel Services

ABC Personnel Services provides a wide range of personnel-related services to medium-sized companies having between 200 and 1,500 employees. ABC enables customer companies to provide their employees with a full range of human resources services without employing an extensive personnel staff of their own. Our proprietary PC-based software automates most standard record keeping and retrieval functions, and is available in conjunction with our broad range service or as a stand-alone package.

ABC intends to become nationally known as a source of state-of-the-art human resources information and technology for medium-sized companies. We will employ a staff with expertise in each human resources subarea and will maintain special expertise in PC-based support systems.

Notice that ABC's statement defines the customer's need implicitly. Customers need to manage their personnel records and services, but many don't want to hire a full-time personnel staff with the necessary skills. ABC will provide the expert services as needed, basically on a part-time basis. The technology and function of ABC's approach is a combination of personal consulting and a prewritten computer program. Finally, ABC has big aspirations. It wants to do this on a national basis. Implicit in that idea is multiple offices and a large staff.

STRATEGY

Strategy is a broad term that encompasses a firm's overall approach to doing business. A firm's strategy has roots in all the things it does that make a difference in its survival and success. The term comes out of the field of strategic planning, which we discussed briefly in Chapter 2. Volumes have been written on strategy; the idea has enormous implications. We don't intend to go into great detail here, but a few features of strategic thinking are important to the kind of business planning that we're talking about here.

Keep in mind that first and foremost the small business plan is a tool to sell an idea to others. In that context a concise statement of strategy in the beginning of a business plan is vital to building and maintaining credibility with the reader.

In a nutshell, the strategy statement tells the reader why your business will succeed in an environment where countless others have failed. We don't want to keep the reader guessing about the strategy which, along with the mission statement, is like the first paragraph in a newspaper article. Its purpose is to catch the reader's attention and give him or her a reason to work through the detail that follows. We have to tell the reader why this plan will work, and we have to do it quickly. Strategy gives us the framework in which to do that job.

Strategy Basics

You can't expect to say to the world, "I'm in business, buy from me, too," and have it work. People have to be given a reason to choose your product over what they were doing before. Somehow your business has to differentiate itself from the others that are already out there. You have to be better, faster, cheaper, offer more variety, better training, better service—something, to distinguish yourself from the others. And, you have to provide that distinguishing feature well.

This seemingly simple statement underlies the idea of strategy. However, the idea is more complex than just that. In order to fully appreciate what's involved, we have to master a few basic ideas from the field of strategic thinking.

Strength, Distinctive Competence, and Competitive Advantage

A *strength* is something that your business does especially well. It can also be some characteristic that gives you a unique capability over your competitors. A particularly good sales force or a talent for research and development are examples of strengths. Having access to a patent or some piece of proprietary knowledge, owning a scarce resource, having access to an effective distribution system, or owning a widely known brand name are characteristics rather than abilities that represent strengths.

It's important to recognize that not all strengths are important in all circumstances. For example, exceptional marketing talent probably wouldn't be very important if you came up with a cure for cancer. Such a product would sell itself once it got through the FDA.

Strategy, or one's approach to the market, must be grounded on strengths. Put another way, a company's strategy must be suited to what it is capable of doing well.

A *distinctive competence* is something a firm does particularly well relative to its competitors. It is a strength that matters and that has been developed effectively in the marketplace. There are many examples of distinctive competences: efficient service, the ability of a sales force to identify and satisfy customer requirements, manufacturing excellence, near-perfect quality control, particularly creative research, and so on.

It's important to realize that a strength in something that isn't particularly critical to the business doesn't develop into a distinctive competence.

A *competitive advantage* is an edge over other firms in the market. It is something that is used to make your company more attractive and more effective than the competition. Continually coming up with new products that are attractive to customers is a competitive advantage, as is producing extremely reliable products for users whose applications are sensitive to down time.

Clearly, there's a logical chain here. A strength in an area that matters leads to a distinctive competence, which, if used effectively in the marketplace, can lead to a competitive advantage:

$$\text{STRENGTH} \longrightarrow \begin{array}{c}\text{DISTINCTIVE}\\\text{COMPETENCE}\end{array} \longrightarrow \begin{array}{c}\text{COMPETITIVE}\\\text{ADVANTAGE}\end{array}$$

Key Success Factors (KSFs)

In every business there are a few things that are more important for success than most others. For example, in the restaurant business you must have good food. If you're delivering packages, you have to be reasonably prompt and reliable. If you run a discount store, you have to be cheap.

It's important that a business planner think through the entire process of the enterprise, and identify the two to five key success factors that matter in his or her business. Don't put down too many things—there are rarely more than a few—but don't leave anything important out, either.

The idea of key success factors doesn't mean we can get along without other things, it just means they aren't strategy critical. For example, most businesses need an accounting function, but it usually isn't strategy critical. It's relatively easy to get an accounting staff that's adequate, and if they're a little worse than average, it won't sink the business. On the other hand, suppose we sell a consumer product, say, cosmetics, and our sales force is a little better or a little worse than average. That's likely to make the difference between success and failure. Although we can't do without either, sales is a KSF and accounting isn't.

Don't make the mistake of thinking that the sales function is always a KSF and accounting is unimportant. In many businesses, sales is just an order-taking process, and success depends primarily on something else: quality, reliability, advertising, service, etc. Accounting can be a KSF if we're trying to produce a complex product at the lowest possible cost in a highly price-competitive market.

Effective Strategy

Strategies that work are based on putting the ideas in the last section together. Some entrepreneurs do that instinctively, others have to work at it. Using the framework of concepts and definitions that we've outlined here makes it easier to think through the logic involved in structuring a concise statement that will convince a reader that you can do it.

An effective strategy must be built on one or more strengths of the organization. In other words, it doesn't do much good to pursue a business opportunity in which your organization doesn't have especially good skills.

The strengths we build on must be things that matter in the competitive environment. Using our strategic terminology, we can say that such strengths must lead to distinctive competences.

Finally, distinctive competences must be managed well enough to develop at least one sustainable competitive advantage. That implies the competences have to be in areas critical to at least one of the key success factors of the business.

Generic Strategies

Many business strategists believe that a successful strategy must be a variant on one of three "generic strategies":

Low-cost producer

Differentiation

Focus or Niche

Low-Cost Producer

The low-cost producer strategy, as the name implies, is based on producing a product or service of reasonable quality for the lowest possible cost. A firm pursuing such a strategy may or may not offer the product to customers at the lowest price available on the market. If the price is held high to match that of other producers, one expects to capture a substantial profit margin on each unit. On the other hand, if the product is offered at a minimal price so unit margins are low, volume is expected to be high enough to generate acceptable overall profits.

The low-cost producer strategy works best where customers are very price sensitive, and it doesn't cost them much to switch to another supplier.

It's important to notice that the low-cost strategy doesn't make sense in many small business situations. For example, suppose you own a store that sells television sets. You won't get far trying to underprice Kmart. You'll never succeed because Kmart's buying volume gives them a wholesale cost advantage you can never match. Nevertheless, stores successfully sell appliances against discounters all the time. They must compete based on something other than price, perhaps service or convenience.

Differentiation

The differentiation strategy involves adding features to the package so that customers perceive added value. The differentiating feature may be attached to the product, like a bigger engine on a car, or it may be some ancillary feature like being located close to the customer, offering better service, training, or a warranty.

Differentiating features create customer loyalty, because some customers like specific features and are reluctant to give them up to switch to other suppliers. Differentiating items can be add-ons or variations in fundamental product attributes, such as the taste of a brand of beer. Features can be real or perceived. Advertising creates a great deal of perceived differentiation that's grounded in very little actual difference in product.

The key to a successful differentiation strategy is to differentiate on issues that are important to the buyer and to make sure that the cost of differentiating doesn't exceed the increment that customers are willing to pay for the altered product.

Focus or Niche

A focus strategy involves finding a small segment in a market that is not well served by other suppliers and tailoring an offering to suit that customer group specifically. In other words, the business *focuses* on the requirements of a particular market segment. The term *niche strategy* refers to the same idea. The word niche refers to a small segment of the market.

Focus strategies often involve creating products that fit the specific needs of particular user groups. For example, extra-wide shoes might be made for people with extra-wide feet. However, it's also possible to define a segment without modifying the product. For example, suppose a rural town doesn't have a clothing store, and it's a two-hour drive to the nearest city that does. Putting a clothing store in that town could be a successful focus strategy. The residents aren't well served by anyone else because there's no one else there.

The focus strategy can sometimes be thought of as an extreme case of differentiation. We differentiate the product so far that no one else wants it. The difference between focus and differentiation is that a differentiated product still maintains a broad appeal, while a focused product's appeal is quite narrow. Only the customers in the niche want it.

A risk associated with the focus strategy is that it doesn't pay to be too successful. If a focuser makes too much money, it will attract either larger firms or more small competitors into the niche, and that can spell the end of the opportunity. Take the wide shoes example. If someone is extremely successful with wide shoes, his or her success may attract a large shoe manufacturer's attention. The big guy might then start putting out a wide line. If that happens, the chances are the original focuser is doomed, because it can't match the big firm's resources in head-to-head competition.

Writing a Strategy Statement

The concise statement of strategy comes near the beginning of the business plan. The statement has to summarize what makes your business work and why customers will choose you over others.

The statement has to be based on serving a market need with an ability or talent your firm has that's superior to others. You have to convince your reader that you'll take a strength and build it into a distinctive competence, which will turn into a competitive advantage because it's grounded in something that's critically important to the business.

It isn't necessary or advisable to use these strategic terms in the actual plan. They simply help us focus our thinking. It is necessary to give your readers a brief statement to believe in. Something that makes them say, "Ahh, that makes sense. Now let's see how they plan to do that in detail."

Let's look at a few examples.

The Decorator's Art Gallery

The Decorator's Art Gallery will base its appeal on providing traditional decorating items and expertise in a wider variety than is available at any other single location in the area. The upscale format will lend a sense of the quality of fine art to the store's offerings as will the perceived expertise of the staff.

Comparable items are available in department stores and framing studios in small quantities and limited variety, so customers are faced with a hit-or-miss decorating task. There is also little or no expert advice available in such establishments, so customers are entirely on their own. The Gallery will provide a breadth of product sufficient to guarantee that customers or professional decorators will be able to find everything they need in one or two visits. People unsure of their requirements will be assisted in their selections by an expert staff.

Notice that the strength here is product expertise and the ability to carry variety. A sense of the competition is given by describing the customers' other alternatives in department stores and framing studios. People will come to the Gallery because they can get everything done at once and feel good about it. Readers of the plan see the point immediately. If they have questions or concerns about exactly how it will all work, they're led toward the detailed sections in the body of the document.

ABC Personnel Services

Most companies would like to provide a full range of personnel services to their managers and employees. Doing that involves employing expertise in a variety of fields: recruiting, compensation, counseling, employee relations, pension administration, and so on. Mid-size firms have the full range of need, but generally don't have the financial resources to employ expertise in each subarea. Consultants tend to specialize in one area or another, so dealing with them is fragmented and expensive.

ABC offers customers the ability to hire a complete, "big company" personnel department on a part-time basis at a reasonable price. Thus customers can have whatever expertise they need without adding to their payroll. The service comes with a sophisticated computer system appropriate for mid-sized companies. No other firms currently offer this broad type of service. ABC will market its services by calling on CEOs of companies in the target size range.

In this case, the strategy statement involves providing the reader with a fairly thorough understanding of the need ABC plans to fill. ABC's strength is clearly the breadth of its expertise in personnel services.

A big part of the competitive advantage is alleged to be the fact that no one else is doing exactly the same thing at the moment. Notice that this doesn't make the strategy one of focus or niche. The market is broad; there just doesn't happen to be anyone there yet. The strategy is differentiation. ABC differentiates itself from other consultants by providing a full range of services while others specialize.

In this example, ABC is hoping to capture what strategists call a "first-mover advantage" by being first to market a new idea. In situations like that, once the first mover has a customer, it's difficult for a competitor to take away the account. The customer's internal procedures become enmeshed in ABC's way of doing things and changing vendors is costly and difficult.

The last sentence brings up an important point. An experienced businessperson will recognize that the real key to this business will be getting customers to sample ABC's services. It's going to be a tough sell, because the client will have to get rid of most of the personnel department he or she already has if he or she decides to use ABC. Therefore, the strategy statement briefly outlines how we'll sell the service, implying that a great deal more explanation follows in the detailed marketing section.

Summary—Strategy

In short, think about what's important to the business's success and what your organization will be especially good at. Also think about what others are doing now and will be doing after you get started. Pull these thoughts together into a short statement of why your company will succeed.

MISSION AND STRATEGY IN THE BUSINESS PLAN

In a nutshell, mission is what you want your business to be, at first and in the long run, and strategy is what makes you think that's possible. The importance of making explicit statements about these ideas varies tremendously from business to business.

In simple enterprises, the ideas can be self-evident, and a separate business plan section may not be necessary. For example, if you want to open a car wash or a luncheonette,

the mission and strategy are inherent in the business's location and your argument that a market exists around that location.

On the other hand, if you've invented a new product or intend to provide some sophisticated consulting service, your mission and strategy aren't obvious and should be stated rather carefully. You have to establish exactly what you're going to do, for whom, and how you'll do it. In such ventures, a short but explicit statement of mission and strategy is an important part of a well-written business plan.

In order to focus readers and capture their attention, the mission and strategy statements should come at the beginning of the business plan. The statements tell the readers where the plan is going.

The Value of Thinking It Through

Thinking through the ideas of mission and strategy can be more important for the plan writer than for the audience. This is especially true for new or unusual business ideas.

The structured thinking involved in putting together these statements provides a test for the business idea and the entrepreneur's understanding of what he or she is getting into. Formulating a mission makes us come to grips with exactly where we want to go, while articulating strategy forces us to focus on what has to happen in order to get there.

THE ENTREPRENEUR AND THE MANAGEMENT TEAM

THE IMPORTANCE OF THE PEOPLE

Business plan readers are very interested in the personal characteristics of entrepreneurs who write plans and of individuals who will play key roles in running the proposed businesses. We'll begin by developing an understanding of why.

Small Business Failures

The overwhelming majority of small businesses fail! Statistics vary as to just how many fail and exactly how long they stay in business, but it's probably safe to say that more than 50% go under within the first two years and that fewer than 10% are left after five years.

Countless attempts have been made to determine why so many entrepreneurial ventures end in disaster. Dun & Bradstreet has compiled a number of categories into which failures are grouped. Here are a few:

Poor choice of business type

Owner not suited to small business

Emotional selection of location

Lack of knowledge of advertising/attracting customers

Failure to get proper professional advice

Insufficient planning and investigation

Poor choice of legal form

Insufficient capital

Too many noncritical assets

Poor pricing practices

Owner living beyond income from business

No knowledge of finances and record keeping

Poor credit granting practices

Poor inventory management

Inadequate borrowing practices

Notice that the majority of these things don't involve a lack of knowledge of the business's product or service. Rather they're issues related to *running* the business. For example, most people who open restaurants know how to cook. If they weren't into food and cooking, they probably wouldn't be interested in the restaurant business in the first place. Nevertheless, the restaurant industry has one of the highest failure rates around. Why? Because too many chef-entrepreneurs don't have the other abilities required of a successful restaurateur: purchasing, hiring, advertising, customer relations, and so on.

Running a business can be thought of as a juggling act. An entrepreneur has to keep a lot of balls in the air at the same time. The failure statistics show that if he or she lets just one ball drop too hard, the whole enterprise can crash. Unfortunately, most people aren't good at everything. They have real talent in one or two areas, are fair at one or two others, and don't know a thing about the rest.

In other words, small business failures are very largely a result of the poor management abilities of entrepreneurs and their management teams.

The Financial Backer's Perception

The people who read business plans, our target audience, are painfully aware of the dismal record of start-ups. They may have invested money in failed ventures in the past and are not anxious to do so again. In particular, they're aware that the primary reason behind small business success or failure is the ability of the management team. Therefore, investors carefully scrutinize the background and experiences of those proposing businesses.

It's often said that investments are never made in small businesses, they're made in small business owners. That statement has two implications, one having to do with credit worthiness and the other having to do with competence.

In the case of a loan, a bank will never advance money to a new business without the personal guarantee of the owner. The owner has to be financially reputable, and his or her guarantee must be collateralized with some marketable asset.

Further, the financial backer has to be convinced of the competence of the entrepreneur. The investor is trusting his or her money to that competence and needs a high level of confidence that it's there.

Backers are particularly attuned to the concept of *balance* within a management team. They recognize that few people are good at everything it takes to run a business. So they look for teams whose members cover all critical areas.

For example, suppose a talented engineer is proposing a business based on a high-tech product she's invented. Backers are unlikely to approve a plan put forward by the engineer alone. She will have to show plans to either hire or recruit someone in marketing, someone in finance, someone in production, and so on, as they'll be needed in the development of the business.

Professional Help

A related issue is the entrepreneur's recognition that he or she needs adequate professional help in running the business. Every enterprise needs the assistance of four professionals from time to time:

An accountant

A lawyer

A banker

An insurance agent

The accountant is needed on a regular basis to tell us where we are financially. The lawyer is needed when we get started to set us up in good legal form, and occasionally if we get into trouble. We need a banker to finance the ups and downs of normal business operations. And we need appropriate insurance coverage to avoid being put out of business by some unplanned, chance occurrence. Of course, if the business is large enough to have a professional controller, we don't need an outside accountant except as an auditor.

In a sense, these professionals are part of the management team. An entrepreneur should identify each and establish a relationship with them while preparing his or her plan. Their names and credentials should be briefly included in the business plan. The banker, of course, may be the target of the plan and then wouldn't be identified in it.

HOW TO WRITE THE MANAGEMENT SECTION

Remember that the primary objective of a business plan is to sell the target audience on the business idea. Given what we've been saying, it should be apparent that a big part of the sales job is presenting the competence and talent of the entrepreneur(s) and the completeness of the management group. We do that by writing about the individuals concerned:

Personal background and status

Employment history

Experience in the industry

Experience in small business

Management experience

Education

Motivation

Health and energy

We don't have to discuss every person in equal depth. Clearly, the equity participants are the most important, especially with respect to their current family and financial status. With respect to employees, we can limit ourselves to what they bring to the workplace.

A résumé contains a great deal of the information being considered here, but for key people it's better to write a brief narrative description supported by a résumé. The narrative gives the thread of the person's story, while the résumé provides detail such as exact dates, addresses, and titles. Résumés can be included as supporting appendices.

Let's consider what we might want to tell a reader in each of the areas listed above. It's important to understand that you must never lie about anything in your background. Banks and investors can and do check up on the things people say in business plans and loan applications. To be caught in a significant falsehood is fatal. However, the truth can be told more or less attractively, and knowing what to emphasize and what to leave out can make a big difference.

Personal Background and Status

The bank wants to lend to people, not companies. Therefore, the loan committee has to be given a brief glimpse into the personal lives of key individuals. We want to convince the decision makers that those people are serious, level-headed folks with every intention of sticking with this business venture and repaying the bank's loan.

Important members of the team should be presented as well-rounded individuals. Our goal is to give the impression of stability and wholesomeness. Someone with a family who takes an active part in their community is generally best. Involvement in church and civic groups reads well.

Banks also like to lend to people who've lived in the area for a while. If you've lived in the community for ten years, or if you've lived nearby, in the same general area, for a long time, mention that. It's better than just having blown in from the other side of the world.

Avoid things that will worry a banker. For example, if your hobby is skydiving, it's probably better not to mention it. A banker isn't as likely to be impressed by a skydiver's boldness as he is to be concerned that the fellow will be killed. Then, who'll pay off the loan?

Financial stability is important too. Individuals who have been prudent with their own money are likely to be careful with the bank's. Further, in most start-up situations, the bank will be looking for collateral from the entrepreneur's personal assets. The presentation of a solid financial position goes a long way in establishing an individual's credibility, especially in midlife. In other words, it's okay to be broke when you're young, but if you're middle-aged and haven't got a dime, the banker is going to wonder why.

Employment History

Investors want to know what kind of experiences and responsibilities the people who will be handling their money have had. A résumé will list the jobs and titles you've had in the past, but relevant experience should be pulled out and amplified. Positions of responsibility are important even if they're not in the field you're trying to go into.

A would-be entrepreneur need not have spent an entire career working in the same place, but a long history of short-term jobs doesn't look good, either. Try to deemphasize such a period in your life. For example, suppose you were trying to find yourself in the period from 1990 until 1996 and bummed around the country working as a short-order cook or sweeping up in fast-food joints. If you have to mention that period at all, say something like:

> 1990–96 Entry-level positions in the
> food service industry

Such a statement is technically true and reads a lot better than listing the details. If you're asked about the period, you can explain it in as favorable a light as possible. It's usually easier to do that in person than in writing. Just remember, never lie.

Experience in the Industry

Some investors view industry experience as an absolute requirement. Even if your business idea is a good one, backers may feel that you're unlikely to know what you're getting yourself into if you haven't spent at least some time working in the field.

This generally makes sense. If you're proposing a start-up and you've never worked in that field before, it's a good idea to get some experience working for someone else before you take the plunge in your own business. It's also a good idea to have done that before you present your plan to a potential backer.

A related concept involves going into business in a field in which you've previously participated as a hobbyist. Imagine, for example, an amateur photographer wanting to open a professional studio. The amateur is sure he knows everything he needs to know about photography. The audience, however, will want to know what he knows about the business of photography. The two aren't the same.

Experience in the proposed field should be presented in as much detail as is reasonable. This is your best argument for why you'll be successful in the proposed business. You know what it's all about, and have proven that you're good at it, for yourself or for someone else. Bankers like to ask, "What makes you think you can do this?" The best answer is, "I've done it before."

Having tried it before and failed isn't necessarily fatal either. In that case, be sure you demonstrate that you learned something about why you weren't successful the first time and how you'll use that knowledge in the future.

Unfortunately, relevant industry experience isn't always possible. When that's the situation, you have to build a case on either related experience or on having done enough research to know what you're getting into. Although it's more difficult, it can be done. In such cases, your business plan is more important than ever, because it has to demonstrate that you know enough about this line of business to make a go of it without relying on your working background.

Experience in Small Business

Backers know that the world of small business and entrepreneurship is considerably different from that of the big corporation or government service. If you've worked in small companies before, say so, because the exposure will be a point in your favor.

Management Experience

Management experience is important. Business owners spend a great deal of time supervising their employees as well as teaching those employees how to do things right. Most of us have some rough edges when we start managing others and make some pretty significant mistakes early on. It's better to make those mistakes on someone else's payroll.

Training others is an important element of entrepreneurship. As a result, some exposure to teaching or training is generally considered an asset.

In general, it's a good idea to tell your readers the following things about your management experience:

How many years you were in management roles

How many people you supervised

How big your budget was

What part of the overall organization was your responsibility

Education

Statistics show successful entrepreneurs tend to be moderately but not extensively educated. The most typical success profile includes a bachelor's degree and perhaps a master's degree. No college degree can be a detriment, as can a string of master's degrees or a PhD. People tend to think that those with extensive higher educations are not in touch with the real world. On the other hand, no education beyond high school may imply a lack of sophistication in the eyes of some readers. Generally, the older and more experienced you are, the less important your educational credentials become.

The best education is, of course, relevant to the proposed endeavor. If you're opening a restaurant, it helps to have a degree or certificate in culinary arts. A business education is always an asset.

In most cases, education isn't something we can do much about in the short term. An entrepreneur might take a course or two in night school before opening his or her business, but that's about all. It's generally best to state your educational credentials in a simple, straightforward way, and let it go at that. Expand and amplify only if the education is particularly relevant to your business.

Motivation

If your plan is for a start-up, it's important to give the reader some idea of why you're trying to start your own business. You do most of this in person rather than in the written plan.

It's generally best to state your reasons in terms of an interest or excitement about the business and what it does for its customers. Don't state your motivation in terms of personal goals relating to finances or independence.

For example, it's okay to say: "I want to open a restaurant because I've always been fascinated by food and cooking and I enjoy dealing with people." It's not a good idea to say: "I've always wanted to be my own boss and achieve financial independence, and a restaurant looks like a good way to do it."

Independence and money are good secondary reasons for doing something, but your backer wants your primary drive to come from a love of what you're doing. People who are fascinated by their work are better at it and are more likely to succeed.

Health and Energy

Running your own business can be a tough, punishing grind, especially in the first few years. People will want to be assured that they invest in entrepreneurs who are physically up to the challenge. Someone with a debilitating, chronic illness is a poor risk.

Entrepreneurs should simply state that they're energetic, healthy people. A great deal of amplification isn't necessary. For example, don't get into how many miles a week you jog or how often you play tennis. Do say that you're healthy and stay in good shape through exercise.

Be Short and Concise

Organize all this information into a short, succinct statement. A page for each person is generally the limit. However, for most people a half page is enough. A longer statement may bore your reader and can look like you're on an ego trip. Putting descriptions like this together takes some careful thinking.

The personal statements in the plan itself are short and concise. However, be ready to talk at length on the subject in person. Financial backers will want to get to know you quite well. Have a lot of thinking in backup.

ORGANIZATION AND RESPONSIBILITIES

The Organization Chart

An organization chart is an effective way to describe most enterprises. Its importance increases as the complexity of the business increases. For example, a small retail establishment run by a proprietor and a few employees has little need for a formal organization chart. On the other hand, a start-up manufacturing company of some size has to have a way to spell out who will be responsible for what functions and how the functions will relate to one another. The organization chart provides a simple graphic vehicle for specifying those relationships.

Companies are generally organized along functional, product, or geographic lines. A functional organization means individuals or groups are assigned to accomplish certain business functions such as marketing, production, or accounting. Those groups accomplish their functions for all of the products and services offered by the company.

A product-oriented organization implies that people are responsible for particular product lines, and within those product lines, they accomplish all of the required functions.

A geographic organization is appropriate when operations are to be spread out over considerable distances, and it doesn't make sense to try to manage from afar. Widely dispersed selling and distribution operations are typically organized geographically.

A business plan for all but the simplest enterprises should include a chart showing the company's organization based on either functional, product, or geographic lines. Most small to moderate-sized firms use a functional organization. The standard chart breaks the company into operating groups and clearly depicts reporting relationships. The conventional box-and-line diagram works well for virtually all businesses (see Figure 6.1).

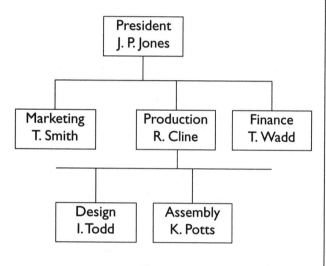

Figure 6.1

It's important to understand that at the time of start-up, an organization may not have many people and may not look much like what it is intended to become a year or two later. In the early days, entrepreneurs often do nearly everything themselves. Later, as their businesses grow, they bring in others to take over some of the responsibilities.

A business plan has to show this transition in organization. It must reflect how things will work on day one as well as how the company will get things done two or three years later.

The best way to do that is to design the organization as you expect it to be sometime in the future. That creates more boxes on the chart than there are people initially in the company. So when starting out, the same name goes in several boxes.

This approach allows you to design job descriptions and relationships at an early stage of planning. If growth occurs as planned, you bring new people into the boxes as they're needed. If you find the organization isn't working well and needs to be changed, that can be done as time goes by.

Balance

At this point it's important to show that the management team is balanced and that there are no necessary skills and abilities left uncovered. For example, three brilliant engineers with a great new invention don't make a good management team. They may have tremendous expertise in research and production, but they'll be perceived as lacking important skills such as marketing, finance, and personnel management. As a result, backers won't invest until they broaden the team to include expertise in those areas.

That broadening can be accomplished through partners, employees, or consultants, but it has to be there.

Duties and Responsibilities

The duties and responsibilities of every member of the management team have to be specified in detail. These duties should tie to the jobs indicated on the organization chart, and relate to the background descriptions of the individuals involved. The organization should always try to build on people's strengths and minimize the effect of their weaknesses or lack of experience. For example, if one individual has a long and successful background in sales, we shouldn't put him or her in charge of finance (except, perhaps, as is temporarily necessary in the beginning).

Duties should be spelled out very carefully. A good plan is clear on who does what, who reports to whom, and who has final authority for which decisions. Don't gloss over these points; they're more important than they appear.

People going into business together often say things like "Well, we've been friends for years, we'll work things out as we go along." That's a recipe for trouble later on and perhaps the loss of the friendship! Resentments build up quickly if one party comes to think he or she is contributing more to the business than the other and the difference isn't reflected in ownership or compensation. Here's a story to illustrate the point.

Sally and Geraldine decided to open a flower shop. They agreed that Sally would buy the flowers, Gerri would arrange them, and both would participate in selling. Everything went fine until the toilet needed cleaning.

A month later Sally and Gerri decided they wanted a new delivery truck. Sally wanted it to be yellow, while Gerri preferred blue. They nearly dissolved the partnership before settling on green. It's amazing what people will fight about if no agreements have been made in advance.

Financial backers are aware that problems like these arise in business ventures. They want to be convinced that you've done everything possible to make sure such disputes don't damage your business after they've lent you money. One good way to convince backers that this won't happen to you is to have a well-thought-out organizational section in your plan. We'll discuss these ideas more in Chapter 11.

THE STAFFING PLAN

The staffing plan is a tabular representation of the kinds and numbers of people the business plans to hire in the foreseeable future. It lays out in an easy-to-follow format the number of people the firm will add and when they will be needed. Down the side of a chart, list all the job titles you'll need over the next few years. Across the top lay out time periods into the future. Use months in the first year and shift to quarters and then years as you move out in time. For each type of person, place an X where you'll hire that individual.

STAFFING PLAN																		
	Year 1												Year 2				YR 3	YR 4	YR 5
	J	F	M	A	M	J	J	A	S	O	N	D	1Q	2Q	3Q	4Q			
Controller									X										
Personnel Manager																	X		
VP Manufacturing														X					
Sales Manager						X													

STAFFING PLAN																				
	Year 1												Year 2				YR 3	YR 4	YR 5
	J	F	M	A	M	J	J	A	S	O	N	D	1Q	2Q	3Q	4Q			
Production Workers				3	3	3	7	7	7	8	8	9	9	12	15	18	22	30	45	75
Accounting Clerks	1	1	1	1	1	1	1	1	1	1	2	2	2	2	3	3	4	5	7

The format can be modified slightly where we have a number of people in a particular job title. Simply indicate the number of people on board at any time. Above is an example for production workers and accounting clerks.

Notice that total headcount in any period is available by just adding down the columns.

Salary and wage expenses can easily be calculated, too. Just multiply the headcount figure in any time period by the estimated average earnings of the people in that category. For example, suppose the average production worker makes $15 an hour. That's $15 × 40 hours = $600 per week. There are 4.3 weeks in a month and 13 weeks in a quarter. Then wage expense in production in November of the first year is 9 × $600 × 4.3 = $23,220. Similarly, in the third quarter of the second year it's 18 × $600 × 13 = $140,400.

When we do our financial projections, we'll have to add something for fringe benefits and overtime, but the approach should be clear.

It's extremely important that the dollar figures in the financial pages tie to the staffing projections made here through calculations like the ones just illustrated. If they don't, you're in real trouble with your audience. The credibility of the whole plan can be jeopardized if it's internally inconsistent.

Management's Salaries

Financial backers will generally want to know what entrepreneurs plan to pay themselves and key team members, especially in the early years of the business's operation. Many deals have failed because bankers and other investors felt that the entrepreneurs were taking too much out of the business for current living expenses.

Investors generally expect an entrepreneur to personally subsist on as little as possible while the business is getting off the ground. The fact that you're doing that needs to be demonstrated.

There are two concerns in investors' minds here. First, they don't want you spending their investment on lavish living. Remember that if they put money into the business and you draw out a salary, it's reasonable to imagine that you are at least in part living on their funds even if money from sales is also flowing through the business. The second concern is just the reverse of the first. Your backer doesn't want you to starve yourself and your family so badly that you have to abandon the business.

The best way to demonstrate that you're living between these limits is to prepare a personal budget. It should show your monthly expenses and any other sources of income you and your family have. Keep the document in your backup package. You can use it to justify how much you need to take out of the business.

Policies and Human Resource Strategies

If your plan anticipates hiring a large number of people, you should make a brief statement about how you plan to attract, select, hire, and retain employees. Do you plan to pay above average wages or get by paying as little as possible? Will there be an incentive or profit sharing plan? Will management be autocratic or participative? Will you lay people off as necessary or try to provide job security? Will you try to foster a family spirit among your employees or will they just work for you?

In a business plan's marketing section, the planner convince the audience that a real opportunity exists and that the proposed enterprise can capitalize on it. There's no rigid format for this presentation, since what must be considered varies from business to business. There are, however, a number of issues that should always be discussed.

The marketing section begins with a description of the product or service being offered and ties that to a detailed analysis of the market and the company's approach to it. This product-market analysis leads to a long-term revenue forecast of at least three but probably five years. Such a forecast provides estimates of unit sales by product and type as well as of total revenue dollars.

The market analysis also produces the **detailed** sales forecast (the sales plan) for the next (first) year of operation. This plan is different from the longer-term revenue forecast in that it is operational rather than strategic. The sales plan focuses on exactly what we intend to sell to which customers in the short run. It also includes information on pricing and *who* is going to sell the product. The pricing information will establish gross profitability while the question of who will do the selling leads to plans for managing and compensating the sales force. Because of the level of detail in the sales plan, much of it can be excluded from the plan document itself and held as backup and/or included in the planner's presentation to his or her audience.

In the marketing area, the plan must be both strategic and operational. It must contain a broad argument that convinces readers that the opportunity is worthwhile, and at the same time it has to give a detailed explanation of how the business will survive in the next (first) year.

In the remainder of this chapter, we'll discuss how to structure arguments and presentations on a variety of issues that must be addressed in the marketing/sales section of a perfect business plan. The chapter ends with a few issues that are important to the planning process but which are often misunderstood or ignored.

THE IMPORTANCE OF THE MARKETING SECTION TO THE AUDIENCE

The marketing and sales section is the foundation of any business plan. Nothing else in the document will make up for a marketing and sales section that fails to convince its readers that a viable market exists and that the product or service being proposed will sell therein.

The planner's personal credibility is most vulnerable in this area. Statements about demand and the willingness of customers to buy a product are usually filled with opinion, clouded by personal experiences, and frequently contested by the plan's readers. These issues can be vague and subjective, and most points are almost impossible to prove. Even competent entrepreneurs can be shot down if they fail to demonstrate a thorough knowledge of the market in which they propose to operate.

Look back at Chapter 3. Every one of the target audiences lists the market and the business's approach to it as a hot button. Your plan and presentation have to be clear, concise, and based on concrete fact and logic. If you project sales of $2 million, you have to be able to defend that number, telling why it isn't $1.5 million or $2.5 million.

In what follows, we'll lay out ways in which a plan can be presented to maximize the planner's credibility with the audience.

The Central Position of the Revenue Forecast in Planning

In planning it's important to keep in mind how the revenue forecast and our analysis of product and market fit into the plan and the processes of the business. It simply doesn't make sense to spend much time on the other parts of the plan until we have a fairly good handle on a revenue forecast.

It should be clear that there isn't a business unless somebody has sold or is about to sell something. That statement doesn't necessarily mean that sales is the most important function in a business. Rather, it means that sales is one of several indispensable elements, and in a sense it comes first. The first here isn't even chronological, because product development must generally precede sales by some time.

Sales and marketing are first because if people aren't willing to pay money to satisfy a need, the product will just be a nifty gadget and

never a business. Furthermore, people have to be willing to pay enough to cover costs, and they have to sign up in numbers that will generate enough profit to make it all worthwhile.

This may all seem obvious, but it's a concept that often gets obscured and muddied as people become embroiled in the planning process. Product function and quality are only of value to the extent that the product can be sold at profitable prices and quantities. More to the point of this chapter, market share and revenue volume are only of value if they lead to a favorable bottom line. When planning for sales, executives and entrepreneurs tend to concentrate on volume and forget the complexities of pricing and cost that link sales to profit. Being fuzzy about that link is a common downfall of business plans when it comes to gaining credibility with their audiences.

The Basis for the Rest of the Plan

In planning, the idea that sales and marketing come first has a particular significance. Revenue is at the top of the Income Statement, but more importantly the revenue forecast forms the basis for nearly all of the other activity contemplated by the plan.

The revenue forecast translated into physical units dictates the level of activity that most of the departments in the company will have to support. Clearly, the sales forecast dictates how big the production department will have to be. This is true of both new and existing businesses, but it is most obvious in organizations that are expected to undergo large changes in size in the near future. For a new business the unit sales forecast tells how large a factory will have to be built as well as what size and kind of labor force will have to be hired. For existing businesses that won't change much; the impact may be limited to fine-tuning the size of the direct labor force.

The translation of revenue into physical activity is a planning step that is often missed. It's easy to understand that the sales level implies factory production, but it is also easy to miss the fact that it also dictates how many people will be needed in peripheral areas like accounting and purchasing. In order to get at this last idea, the planner has to break the sales forecast into orders, and consider their complexity, that is, on the average how many line items in each. This leads to an estimate of how many transactions will have to be processed in accounting and how long each will take in the billing department. That, along with a standard for the number of transactions per day that can be processed by an average employee, leads to the correct staffing levels. Similar thinking applied to the amount of raw material needed will project the cost of purchasing and the accounts payable department.

Clearly this kind of thinking will be simple and approximate for a small business just getting started and more complex and detailed for an existing company contemplating expansion. Nevertheless, in either case we have to think hard about how much we intend to sell and then determine the level of support we'll need.

HOW TO WRITE THE MARKETING AND SALES SECTION

The marketing section of a good business plan begins with a description of the product, analyzes the market, and builds to a long-term revenue forecast. The detailed short-term (the next year) sales plan is separate and comes after the product-market discussion. The written development of product-market-revenue should take readers from concept to numbers and make them believers all the way.

Generating credibility depends on connecting one stage in the argument to the next with a believable link. Often the link is a numerical assumption that can be supported in its reasonability by reference to history or to the experience of similar businesses. What follows is a series of topics which form stepping-stones along which the successful plan moves its audience.

Product or Service Description

Every plan must contain a description of the product or service offered. Even if the organization is an ongoing business, the planner must not assume that the audience is totally familiar with the product. A brief description followed by a statement of what changes, if any, are expected to take place during the planning period is appropriate. If the product is new to the audience, a more detailed description is in order. This is especially true for new venture plans.

Perspective

It is frequently important to include more than one perspective in the initial description of a product or service. A key distinction can be that of a user as opposed to that of the producer. For example:

User perspective: This telephone will store up to 100 frequently dialed numbers.

Producer perspective: The addition of a $2 microchip allows this phone to store up to 100 numbers with no significant increase in failure rate.

Think about your product, and decide if more than one perspective is relevant. If so, be sure your description covers them all. For example, a hotel or restaurant might cater to both business travelers and tourists. Describe the features that appeal to each.

Differentiation

Most businesses provide products and services that are available from other sources. Therefore, a good description must include information on how the product or service is differentiated from that of the competition. The product description shouldn't simply be just the item being sold. It should include the item and everything offered to support it. That can mean price, service, training, variety, delivery, credit, or any other feature associated with the purchase.

Audiences won't sign up for a plan that they think is selling a "me too" product or service. They have to be convinced that the product is effectively differentiated. To do that, the planner must describe the offering as better, faster, cheaper, or in some way superior to the rest of the market. Furthermore, the differentiation has to be credible and demonstrable.

By credible we mean that the reader has to accept that the proposed differentiation will actually make a difference to a buyer. Let's consider an oversimplified example to illustrate the point. Suppose a plan proposes to sell bicycles, and differentiates the product by offering a selection of 25 colors. It would be hard to convince a reader that bicyclists are color sensitive enough for that to make a difference. Further, a sharp business person would insist that retailers wouldn't want to stock that many colors. These objections would block the acceptance of the plan. On the other hand, a bicycle that's substantially lighter in weight than others in its price class is likely to convince even the most skeptical analyst.

The written argument must establish a differentiation rationale that generally involves finding a market need that is not currently satisfied and showing that some feature of your product meets that need. Here's another example:

Suppose we sell a high-speed printer for use in data-processing departments where printed output is crucial to the customer's business operations. That is, a down printer causes a substantial work stoppage. If our printer isn't much different than anyone else's, how can we establish a significant differentiation? If we notice that the industry standard service contract guarantees a technician on site within five hours of an equipment failure, our product can be differentiated effectively by offering a two-hour response time. This shortens the customer's downtime, and we can generally charge extra for it.

Demonstrable differentiation means that our plan reader is convinced that buyers will accept the differentiating feature. Suppose we offer a durable product based on the claim that it's more reliable than the competition. That's a tough sell, because without some substantiation the buyer can't know the product is more reliable until it's owned for a while. In that case, an independent lab report might make the difference.

The audience will raise every possible objection to the product marketing rationale. This is a healthy process, because planners often lose sight of their ultimate objective, to sell at a profit. The planner gets caught up in the product's features and the intricacies of the organization, and tends to overlook the shortcomings of the product/business. The key to successful planning is to think through all the objections a reader may come up with and answer as many as possible in the plan itself. The process is similar to what a good salesperson goes through. He or she thinks out answers to customer objections ahead of time and is ready to counter as soon as they arise.

Remember that plan readers are very sharp businesspeople. They'll pick up on logical loopholes and omissions, especially in the marketing and revenue area.

Market Description

The market must be described in terms of its size, history, recent growth trends, expected future growth, and geography. The reader will also want to know who the customers are and why they participate in the market. Are there significant barriers to entry; are there significant economies of scale? Is there any expectation of major change? What are the established methods of distribution and sales? What is the normal method of advertising and promotion?

A great deal of information for these questions is available from trade publications and market research sources. Market research is discussed later in this chapter.

For smaller, simpler businesses, the issue becomes one of common sense. If you're proposing a restaurant, the reader will want to know what kind of people in the area will be attracted to it and why. You'll also want to demonstrate that there are enough potential customers in the area to make it worthwhile. For example, a fancy, expensive restaurant in a blue-collar neighborhood probably isn't a good idea; an inexpensive family-style place is.

General Discussion

The market description should flow more or less as follows:

1. Description of the customer need.

2. A statement about the general characteristics of the customers, and an identification of major customers if they are a limited group.

3. A brief description of the major competitors (a detailed competitive analysis comes later) and their relative positions.

4. A statement of the target market within the overall industry if appropriate. That is, are we aiming for a particular submarket, such as buyers of imported beer.

5. A brief history of the industry and the major players.

6. A description of how the industry operates: What are the sales and advertising practices?

   Is there a driving force that determines the nature of the business? For example:

   > Computers—technology
   > Groceries—distribution
   > Steel—cost of manufacture
   > Broadcast—federal licensing

   Is entry into the market easy or hard?

   Are there economies of scale?

   Do customers buy based on price, quality, brand loyalty?

7. A statement about industry growth in the past and future expectations.

8. A statement about relevant government regulations.

9. Any other significant information.

The above outline should be followed and adapted as necessary to the particular business.

The product must be shown to fit into the market described. How it fits in is an important point that cannot be overlooked.

Niche Plans

An industry *niche* is defined by a range of product characteristics in which there is relatively little competition. It is a hole in the market in which the dominant firms choose not to play. A business can participate in an industry either broadly or as a niche player.

As an illustration, let's reconsider the example we discussed briefly in Chapter 5, a company that makes shoes for people with extremely wide feet. Major shoe companies might feel that there isn't enough business in those unusual sizes to justify manufacturing and marketing them. A firm specializing in wide shoes could operate an effective business in that segment. We call this a *niche*, meaning a small, separable space in the larger market.

Niche strategies are fairly common among smaller companies. It is an effective way to compete in a world dominated by huge players. Niche profit margins can be quite good. The niche business will spend less of its resources fighting the competition, because it effectively has a small monopoly, and will be able to earn a high profit margin on a limited volume.

There are enough niche businesses around to make it worth discussing their peculiar planning problems.

The first thing a niche plan has to do is convince the audience that the niche exists and that a customer need is either unserved or poorly served by existing suppliers in the field. Research and expert opinions can help in the argument. Next, one has to demonstrate that the niche will continue. Audiences will be concerned that today's niche opportunity will disappear tomorrow either because customers change their habits or because other firms begin to compete. The reader must believe that the niche is not a transient phenomenon, and that larger firms will not move in.

This argument leads to a problem. Niches generally exist because they don't contain enough business to attract dominant firms. This says that although a niche represents a promising market for a new or small firm, the prospects for long-term growth are limited. It is unusual to see a niche business bigger than $200 million.

Further, if a niche player is too successful, it will attract the attention of larger companies. In our example, if making wide shoes turns out to be very profitable, a major manufacturer might decide to do it too. That would put the original niche player at a disadvantage, because it wouldn't have the resources to compete head to head with a major company.

This creates a planning dilemma for at least two of the three types of target audiences. Both venture capitalists and corporate top managements require strong growth projections to achieve their goals, and that's usually unrealistic in the long run for niche businesses. However, it may or may not preclude the plan's acceptance, as audiences can sometimes be convinced to accept niche plans in spite of their growth limitations.

A venture capitalist may not see the problem as fatal if there is enough growth potential to cash out of the business before it levels off (see Chapter 3). That requires a careful study of what is possible before the niche is exhausted.

Corporate executives sometimes accept niche plans based on the expectation that the division will expand outside of the niche in three to five years. The venture may be viewed as a cheap foothold in a promising market that the company would like to be in.

We can summarize by saying that constructing a plan for a niche business involves putting together an argument that establishes the niche and then minimizes the effect of its limitations. This can be done by showing that the audience's goals can be achieved within the limitation or by showing that the limitation can be overcome.

Market Research

Reference to reputable market research is an excellent way to bolster the credibility of a business plan. It lends an air of sophistication and professionalism that's hard to achieve otherwise.

For our purposes, there are two kinds of market research. The first is background information about an industry and its competitive conditions including trend projections. For most industries this is available from your own study of trade journals, books, and articles. It can sometimes be found in prepackaged form from market research firms (at a cost) or at the library. Such material is an essential ingredient for virtually any business plan. Jumping into an industry without surveying what's going on is like diving into a swimming pool without checking to see if

it's full of water. Plan audiences won't do that and they will insist that planners do their homework on the industry.

A plan's market description should also be supported by reputable market research sources whenever possible. These references lend credibility to the business analysis being presented. It's very difficult to get audience acceptance if statements about the market are made simply from the experience of the person presenting the case. Even if his or her expertise is accepted, an author is perceived as having too much of an interest in his or her own plan to be impartial in the market analysis. An independent reference is generally required.

A second kind of research consists of studies commissioned for a specific purpose, usually to justify what is being proposed in the plan. These can, of course, be very effective in convincing an audience but are generally quite expensive. Whenever possible, it's a good idea to find out what kind of backup data your audience will be looking for regarding your market. In other words, don't spend research money without having a high level of assurance that it will make a difference to your audience.

Competitors

The general market description briefly summarizes the competitive situation, but it's important to go beyond that and provide the reader with a complete description of all the competitors. Readers want to know who the competitors are, what their strengths and weaknesses are, how their products differ from yours, what their market shares are, and so on.

This information is presented in a *competitive analysis*, an approximately one-page summary of each significant competitor. The information provided should include an informative narrative and as much of the following as can be gathered:

Name (also name of parent if a division)

Annual revenues in this market

Profitability

Market share

Distinctive product characteristics, strengths/weaknesses

Major market strengths

Major market weaknesses

Product price/quality vs. own

Perceived strategy

Recent and expected growth

Recent win/loss performance against them

Many experienced planners provide this information in detail on separate backup pages and then summarize it in tabular form in the main plan. A wide spreadsheet with competitors listed down the side in descending order of market share and the above categories shown across the top enables the reader to take in the entire market at a glance. Don't forget to include your own company in the appropriate place among the competitors.

Promotion and Advertising

The plan must include a statement on the business's approach to sales promotion and advertising. It should discuss the methods to be employed and the media used. The approach should be contrasted with what is standard for the industry, and any deviations should be explained and rationalized.

Larger, more complex businesses should present a table in the plan document showing expected advertising and promotional expenditures broken out by media. If the business is not new, promotional spending should be contrasted with what was done in previous years.

The success or failure of any previous promotional efforts should be analyzed as well. The idea is to present an in-depth analysis of what the company has gotten for its promotional dollar and then to propose a new strategy based on the historical experience of cost effectiveness.

The size of this section depends on the advertising intensity of the business. A soft drink manufacturer would have a very sophisticated presentation, while a maker of industrial equipment would propose some ads in trade journals and a number of trade shows. If advertising is an important part of similar businesses, you'd better present a sophisticated analysis of how you plan to spend your promotional dollars. If not, you can get away with a brief discussion.

It's a good idea to give the reader an idea of the message content of the advertising. What will the ads look like, what will they say? The plan should show the audience that the planner has analyzed the cost effectiveness of the promotional dollar and has made an informed judgment about future spending. Another important detail will be whether or not you'll be using an advertising agency or doing the job yourself. Agencies can be very expensive. Sometimes they're worth the money and sometimes you can do just as well yourself. Find out what other businesses do before committing.

Once you're in business, you may find that you need to change the level of advertising either up or down. Don't write your business plan in such a way that your advertising effort becomes a contractual element in the agreement between you and your backer. Retain the ability to change your own advertising.

Market Share

Once the product, market, and competitors have been described, the plan can begin to talk about the strategy to gain market share. Be careful in this area. Credibility can slip in market share discussions if you don't know exactly what you're talking about. Plans for existing firms often state the company's current and planned market share with no support. However, beginning entrepreneurs who simply say, "We'll have a 6% share by next year," often invite questions on how they're going to make this happen. It's much better to avoid the probing questions by answering them before they're asked.

A good business plan will always include a description of how the targeted share is to be achieved, be it through price, superior product, better service, or enhanced selling effort. The following question must also be answered: What are the competitors going to be doing while we take share away from them? What will be their response?

These arguments should be as quantitative as possible, for example, "A 5% price advantage over ABC is expected to result in an increase in volume of 50,000 units per year for a revenue increase of $4M, which will lead to a market share increase of one half percent." Or, "The addition of 15 salespeople producing an average of $1.5M each will yield additional revenues of $22.5M for a 3% increase in market share." A quantitative presentation allows the reader to vary the assumptions and test the impact on the bottom line without discrediting the entire plan.

Tie Share Growth to Revenue and Market Growth

If your plan makes a statement about future market share, the reader is virtually certain to ask a question about the total market's expected growth rate. If possible, your response should be supported by reference to outside sources such as trade associations or research firms.

The company and the market's projected growth rates must be consistently linked through the share projection. Suppose our current share is 5% and the plan forecasts a 20% revenue growth. Suppose we also want to project a 10% share growth; that is, we want next year's share to be 5.5%. The market then must be growing at a rate of 9%.

The arithmetic can be a little confusing if you're not familiar with it. Imagine we're selling $1M in a $20M market for a 5% share. A 20% growth in revenue says that we will sell $1.2M next year. That number has to be 5.5% of the new market size:

New Market = $1.2M / .055 = $21.8M

So the market growth rate is:

$$\left(\frac{\text{New Market}}{\text{Old Market}}\right) - 1.0 = \frac{21.8}{20.0} - 1.0$$

$$= 1.09 - 1.0$$

$$= .09$$

$$= 9\%$$

Revenue growth, market growth, and current versus projected market share must always be quantified. A quantification that is not arithmetically consistent as shown here will be attacked and will weaken the plan's credibility.

Be Sure Your Arithmetic Hangs Together

It's very important that a business plan never make a mistake or an omission in a calculation like this, because it can undermine a great deal of the argument. For example, suppose a planner predicts a 20% revenue growth for the company and then states that projected market share is 5.5%, just as we've done here. However, suppose the planner doesn't think about the connection between those figures and the market growth rate and makes no statement about the latter, perhaps because he or she just doesn't know what it is. Now suppose that a member of the audience knows that the market is growing at only 5%. Further suppose that he or she makes the calculation above showing the implied rate of 9%.

This signals to the audience that the entire plan is on shaky ground. If the implied market growth rate isn't there, it's likely that the company's promised growth can't be achieved. Doubt and disbelief about the planner and his or her ideas are introduced into the audience, and these may never be overcome. What can be worse is that a further element of doubt is created about the planner's professional competence. "How could he or she make a mistake like that?" the audience will ask.

MARKETING PLAN/STRATEGY

A qualitative statement describing the firm's overall approach to the market must be made in the marketing section. There is no prescribed format for such a statement. It needs to cover whatever is important to the business in question. The important issues are:

What is the basis on which we compete?
Price
Quality
Technical sophistication
Service
Convenience

How do we get our message to the market?
Advertising
Promotion
Word of mouth

How do we approach the customer?
Sales staff
Independent sales representatives
Telemarketing
Referrals

How do we stack up against the competition?
Leader or follower
Innovator or copier

Do we have a particular attitude or philosophy about customers and the marketplace?

Are there any major changes in the market in the future?
Government intervention
New competitors entering the field (especially big companies with deep pockets)
New technology
Changes in customers

What are the major threats and opportunities in the marketplace at present?

What kind of growth are we planning relative to that of the market; what are our current and projected shares?

Are there any major changes planned in our thrust or approach?

Once again, the idea is to sell the audience on the depth and competence of the analysis.

In this regard it is wise to try to find out if there are any issues that the audience feels are particularly important in the current market. Be sure to discuss those issues in depth. You don't necessarily have to agree with the audience's opinion but it is fatal to omit or give short shrift to what the reviewer thinks is a key issue. Doing that will give the impression that the planner lacks a thorough understanding of the business. To disagree is okay, to be unaware is not.

It's generally harder for a business to achieve increased revenue through share growth than through taking a constant share of an increasing market. A statement should address how the overall marketing strategy will achieve the target share. Is the company going to sell based on product quality, price, superior sales and service, a niche market where there is little competition, or some combination of these or other points? The marketing strategy description is crucial. To achieve credibility, the plan has to describe some convincing reason that customers will forsake the competition. Even if the price is lower or the product is better, there has to be a marketing strategy to tell people about it.

Location

In most retail businesses, location is a key element of the enterprise's marketing strategy. If this is the case, the business plan must present a thorough analysis of why the location selected will contribute to making the business work. This generally calls for an examination of how the business relates to its customers. At one extreme a shop may require that people walk by in order to become customers. That is, few people go looking for it. A cookie shop in a retail mall is an example. Such a business must be located in the midst of high walk-by traffic.

Another type of business draws people as a destination. A furniture store is a good example. Most customers are willing to make a specific trip when they're interested in buying furniture. In such a business, walk-by traffic isn't important but reasonably easy access is. A furniture store isn't likely to do well if it's hard to get to or far from population centers.

Of course, some businesses aren't location sensitive at all. If you travel to your customers, they really don't care where your office is. Think of a plumber, an electrician, or a maid service.

Location also has a cost element. The best locations cost the most money. Rents are high in regional malls where retail traffic is heavy, while a store by the side of a country road is dirt cheap. Projected sales figures based on the traffic at the location you've chosen must justify its rent.

In addition to describing the relation of customers to the location, a business plan has to tell a lot about the physical nature of the place of business:

Exactly where is it located

The building's physical characteristics (a floor plan is sometimes included)

Whether renovations are intended and their cost

Whether the facility will be leased or owned

What else is in the area

Anything else that's relevant

Because location is so important to so many businesses, we've included an appendix to this chapter discussing the idea of site selection in more detail. Also see Chapter 10, where we use a technique called break-even analysis to assist in selecting a retail location.

Pricing

A plan should contain a statement about a business's pricing policies, especially where pricing is an element of marketing strategy. In many businesses, the effective average price that the business plans to receive is not its published list price. In other words, it is not uncommon to set a price with the intention of selling most of one's product at "sale" or discount levels.

The relationship of prices to those of competitors must also be established. Does the business set prices above the competition because of some premium offered to the customer or below the competition to try to gain market share?

It is also important to establish the relationship between price and cost. It's a common planning error to expect to receive a list price that provides an adequate margin over cost only to find that the average unit sells at a discount, which leaves the company unable to cover overhead. This is especially important where there are multiple product lines each of which has different planned profitability. Price and cost assumptions have to be explicit in the plan, and they must be used as input to the financial projections.

Revenue Levels

The marketing section should culminate with revenue broken out by product, region, and customer class. If the company is not new, each calculation should be compared with last year, and a brief narrative given explaining the progress from the past into the future. The presentation should summarize the overall revenue projection and not be overly detailed. The idea is to provide a summary page in which the reader can see the rationalization for the general revenue level at a glance.

The revenue projection is calculated out for several years. Readers want to know where you think you're going in five years as well as next year. However, the later years don't have to be as detailed as the first year, which must tie exactly to the detailed sales plan.

THE SALES PLAN

Up until now we've talked about marketing rather than sales. The marketing section emphasizes broad, strategic issues and develops the underlying basis for the business. It culminates in a forecast of revenue levels. The sales plan supports the first year of that revenue forecast with tactical detail. It forecasts who is going to sell what to whom, for how much and when. It is fully broken out by product and includes units and prices as well as total dollars. It should also include the commission plan, which tells how much the salesperson will get paid for each sale.

Brand-new ventures that have no history behind them may not have a very detailed sales plan. Certainly, the comparisons with earlier years won't be there. Nevertheless, entrepreneurs should try to put together enough detail to spell out who will sell what to which customers, for how much, where, and when. Existing businesses should definitely build up a detailed sales forecast.

The entire sales plan usually contains too much detail to be included in the plan document itself. It's usually better to include a few of the exhibits and explanations while holding most of the detail in reserve for your presentation or as backup.

Do not, however, minimize the sales plan's importance because of this recommendation not to include it in the primary document! If you get to the final round with your audience, they're almost sure to ask you to justify and support your revenue forecasts. Pulling out the kind of detail described below will do wonders for your credibility. It shows the audience that you're a careful, meticulous businessperson and that you have thought through where your sales are coming from. Most of the time, the audience won't want to crawl through the detail with you once they've seen that you've got it. They'll just accept that you've done your homework and let it go at that.

The Detailed Forecast

The sales plan consists of several pages of charts showing the planned shipments for the year. These should be broken down by product and by sales management responsibility, but if other breakdowns are important to the nature of the business, such as customer classes, they should be included as well.

The presentation should clearly establish the number of units to be shipped and the assumed average price of each. These will allow you to arrive at the revenue forecast. The pricing assumption needs to be explicit and compared with previous years. The plan must be clear about whether changes in the revenue level are due to price or volume changes or a combination of both. The pricing assumption determines the gross margin from the forecast revenue and must not be vaguely stated in the plan document.

Convincing Presentations

The sales plan is an important credibility-gaining part of the revenue forecast. It should establish a quantitative link between the revenue forecast and sales effort. It should also recognize that all salespeople are not equally productive and that, up to a limit, productivity generally increases with experience.

When you present a plan, a few quantitative charts can make all the difference in the world in terms of acceptance of the forecast. Here's a simple example of a presentation technique that works:

First, present a typical relationship between a salesperson's experience and sales performance in the industry. Use a chart something like the following stated in thousands of dollars:

($000)

Years Experience:	1	2	3	4	5	10
Sales Per Year:	100	500	800	1,100	1,400	1,500

Then, list salespeople by experience, being sure to adjust for exceptional performers or difficult conditions (see page 67).

Tom and Linda are exceptional performers or have particularly fertile territories. Joe, on the other hand, may have an unusually difficult territory. His customers may be spread over a large area requiring that he spend more time traveling than the others. The comparison with last year is an important test of reasonability. A downward trend is generally not acceptable without good reason, such as the loss of a major customer or the discontinuation of a product line.

Presentations like this do wonders for credibility. They give an air of precision and reliability to the whole sales and revenue forecasting exercise. However, the assumptions must be supportable. That means that one must be able to demonstrate from company history or data from a similar business that people gain effectiveness with experience roughly in accordance with the first chart.

Sales District X
($000)

	Years	Expected Sales	Adjust	Fcstd Sales	Last Year
Joe	2	$ 500	—	$ 500	$ 322
Tom	4	1,100	200	1,300	1,204
Linda	8	1,400	500	1,900	1,920
Harry	10	1,500	(100)	1,400	1,456
New Hire	1	100	—	100	—
Total				$5,200	$4,902

Western Region
($M)

Product	Next year	Last year	% Change	Comments
A	$ 500	$ 450	11%	Normal growth
B	800	950	(6%)	XYZ, a major customer closed
C	700	500	40%	Opening new district, adding three salespeople
Total	$2,000	$1,900	5%	

The productivity analysis should be provided for every sales district and then consolidated for region and overall totals. *However,* this level of detail is generally not included in the plan document. It is used in calculating the overall sales numbers and shown in the plan presentation as evidence of the planner's method and meticulous attention to detail.

Supporting detail, such as the sales buildup, should be provided in an appendix. It is important to let the audience know that the detailed backup exists, and that the appendix is available to interested readers upon request. The presentation should give them a sample of what it contains whether they ask for it or not. Be careful, however, not to give so much detail that the audience becomes bored with the presentation.

Analysis vs. History

Sales projections should be analyzed by product and region versus last year's performance. Deviations, good or bad, must then be analyzed and explained. Presentation in chart form is generally very effective. For example:

If you're a new venture and don't have a last year, do the chart just showing projected revenues and comment on the differences you expect to find between regions.

It is important to provide projections and charts that approach the revenue from several directions. It should be built by region, by customer or customer class, and by product. These should be compared with last year's totals, and all should arrive at the same total number.

This multidirectional approach gives a well-rounded, complete feeling to the forecast. The reader gets a sense that nothing has been left out or omitted, and that the planners have thought through the market thoroughly.

THE IMPORTANCE OF FORECASTING PRODUCT MIX

The sales plan should include a unit forecast based on the product mix defined in the plan. It is a common error to forecast in dollars and allow some administrative group to break the dollars into units based on history or some other criteria. This absolves the sales department of much of its planning responsibility and makes the plan significantly less valuable as a control device after the fact. A new venture plan that does this will be considered naïve.

An example may clarify the issue. Suppose we have two products, A and B, as follows:

	A	B
Price	$10,000	$5,000
Cost	6,000	4,000
Margin	$4,000	$1,000

Notice that A has a gross profit margin which is 40% of sales while B's is only 20%. Now, suppose we have a goal of selling $1 million with a gross profit of 35% or $350,000. That profit requirement specifies exactly how many As and how many Bs we have to sell to achieve the plan. In other words, achieving the plan doesn't just require selling $1 million of product. If we sell all Bs, we'll miss the bottom line substantially even though we make the sales goal.

Forecast Detail and Sales Compensation

Couching sales goals in terms of total revenue only can build a troublesome downside bias into the plan. There is a tendency for salespeople to push low-margin products which are often easier to move. This achieves the revenue plan but not the profit plan. To prevent this, order goals must be broken out by product, and the sales department held to making the piecemeal forecast, not just the overall revenue. Selling behavior is managed with the sales incentive plan by lowering commissions on low-margin products and raising them on the goods that contribute most to the bottom line.

Suppose we have a product that comes in three versions: Economy, Family, and Sporty, each with a different profit contribution per dollar of sales. The Economy model is usually the lowest profit model, while the Sporty makes us a bundle. The Family version is somewhere in between.

The easiest sale will usually be the Economy model. It's the best buy relative to product cost, and customers usually recognize that, at least intuitively. The sales department must have an incentive to move the customer up the line rather than to just take Economy orders. There are two ways to do that. The first is to measure sales management's performance on meeting the revenue goal by product line and not just in total. That means that if a sales department achieves its revenue quota, but all the sales are in the Economy line, the sales manager doesn't get his or her bonus. To get his or her entire bonus the sales force has to achieve a quota in each category. Here we can see why this kind of product line detail is essential to the planning process. If we leave it out, we give up an important handle with which to manage the sales force.

However, managing the manager isn't generally enough to move sales into the higher margin lines. There's an old barb in management circles that says, "If you want a salesman to do anything, you have to pay him for it." Salespeople are motivated by dollars and cents. In order to get sales into the higher margin lines, the commission plan has to be structured to do so. That is, commissions have to be highest in the Sporty line, lower but still good in the Family line, and quite poor in the Economy line. A salesperson should not be able to survive selling in the Economy line only.

Simpler Start-Ups

It's worth reiterating the comment made at the beginning of Part 2. Simpler businesses and many start-ups will be dealing with a lower level of detail than some of the discussions presented here. Use these basic ideas to construct a plan that makes sense for your business. See the examples in Appendix E for more guidance.

APPENDICES

Appendix 7A

THE COMMISSION PLAN

The commission or compensation ("comp") plan is an integral part of the marketing and sales plan. It is often packaged separately from the rest of the business plan because of the sensitive nature of personal compensation. Sales compensation is the payment for the labor services of salespersons. New venture plans usually give the commission issue only cursory treatment, which doesn't create a problem while sales remain modest. However, when sales are substantial and product lines become complex, commissions are an important factor in planning and guiding the company.

Different Rates on Different Products

The goal of the commission plan is to motivate the sales force to sell in the best interest of the company. In that respect, all sales are not of equal value. There are several reasons why the sale of one product in the company's line may be preferred to another. Here are a few:

- Higher profit margins after consideration of all costs and expenses.

- Temporarily overstocked inventories need to be reduced on specific lines.

- Customers sometimes resist new products as unknown or untried, even though the company needs to launch them.

- A new product that is enthusiastically accepted can draw sales away from old products more quickly than anticipated, leaving unsold inventory that must be disposed of.

We direct sales into the more desirable lines by putting higher commission rates on those lines. It is a fundamental mistake to believe that salespeople will sell where we want them to for any reason other than they will make more money by doing so.

The Backward Bending Supply Curve of Labor

For sales compensation, it's our goal to draw as much effort as possible out of our salespeople, especially the good ones. Commissions are the price we pay for the labor offered; a higher commission rate essentially means a higher price per hour for effort expended.

We need to borrow a concept from economics to illustrate a basic characteristic of human nature. For most commodities, the supply curve looks like that shown in Figure 7.1. A higher price means a higher quantity offered. The line slopes upward to the right and does so without limit. The supply of labor services, however, doesn't behave like that. The supply curve for labor generally looks like that shown in Figure 7.2. As the price increases, the amount of labor offered increases for a while, but after a point further price increases lead to a reduction in the quantity offered. This is called the backward bending supply curve of labor, and it means that if you pay someone who controls his or her own hours too well, he or she will quit early.

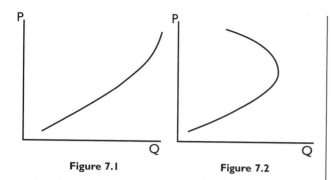

Figure 7.1   Figure 7.2

The curve bends backward because, unlike most economic goods, the supply of labor is limited; there are only about 15 hours in a day in which a person can work. Further, working involves a tradeoff. The more one works, the less leisure time one has. In essence, if you pay a person highly, there comes a time when he has enough money and opts to take some time off. This is exactly what we don't want our best salespeople to do.

There are generally two ways to manage the backward bending curve. The first is to keep the sales force hungry by constructing the comp plan in such a way that salespeople are always operating below the point where the curve bends back. The problem with this approach is that under these conditions the best people will tend to leave for more money elsewhere. The second way is by use of *accelerators*. Accelerators involve paying a higher rate for sales over quota. In other words, as we start to approach the backward bending area of the curve, the rate of pay gets higher. This tends to push the point at which the curve bends back higher. Accelerators often get larger as performance gets better. For example, if the normal commission rate is 6%, we might pay 8% for sales between 100 and 150% of quota and 10% for sales over 150% of quota.

Commission plans are also designed to manage one other quirk of human nature, procrastination. Customers tend to put off closing deals. The longer a deal is put off, the less likely it is to happen. Salespeople are given an incentive to close deals in a timely manner by establishing quarterly bonuses as part of the comp plan. We divide the yearly quota into quarters, and give a bonus for making each quarter's number within the quarter, but not if it is caught up after the quarter is over. Similarly, we give a year-end bonus to keep those who are behind interested.

An Example

Let's take the product line we mentioned earlier. We had Sporty, Family, and Economy models that decreased in profitability from good to poor. Suppose we want to establish a commission plan that will pay a salesperson achieving quota $75,000 per year where $20,000 is base salary and the rest is commission and bonus. We expect that person to sell $1,000,000 in merchandise and want the sales to be about 10% in the Economy line, 60% in the Family line, and 30% in the Sporty line.

We'll assign commission rates of 2%, 4%, and 6% to Economy, Family, and Sporty, respectively, and pay quarterly quota bonuses of $2,000 and an annual quota bonus of $3,000 if each quota is made in the right product lines. Then if sales turn out as expected, our target salesperson will earn the following:

Line	Sales	Rate	Commission
Sporty	$300,000	6%	$18,000
Family	600,000	4%	24,000
Economy	100,000	2%	2,000
Total Commission	$1,000,000		$44,000
Quarterly Bonus			8,000
Annual Bonus			3,000
Base Salary			20,000
Total			$75,000

Now let's introduce the idea of an accelerator. Assume the plan will pay 125% of the base commission rate for sales between 100 and 150% of quota and 150% of the base rate for sales over 150% of quota. However, the accelerator will not apply to the Economy line because we don't want to incentivize those sales. Suppose a salesperson had additional sales of $100,000 in the Family line and $200,000 in the Sporty line. That salesperson would then get additional commissions as follows:

Family Line
$$\$100{,}000 \times 4\% \times 1.25 = \$5{,}000$$

Sporty Line
$$\$150{,}000 \times 6\% \times 1.25 = \$11{,}250$$
$$\underline{\$\ 50{,}000 \times 6\% \times 1.50 = \$\ 4{,}500}$$
$$\$20{,}750$$

Quota is, of course, defined as the million-dollar sales goal broken into the three product lines as above. It is extremely important to set quota so that the average salesperson hits it. If we set quota too high, the sales force won't make enough money. If that happens, they'll tend to quit and go to the competition. On the other hand, if quota is too low everyone will be into the accelerator range, and we'll overpay the salespeople. This is an unnecessary expense and may cause them to reduce their efforts. When making up a comp plan, its always a good idea to evaluate the compensation results of several levels of performance above and below quota to make sure the plan is paying what we want it to.

Appendix 7B

ACCURACY AND DETAIL— TOO MUCH AND TOO LITTLE

A plan is an attempt to model a business on paper. A model is an abstraction of reality, and a logical question arises as to the level of detail that should be included in that representation of the real world.

It would never be reasonable to attempt to plan in the detail on which a business is actually run. For example, when a business buys office supplies, it places orders and keeps records that enumerate how many boxes of paper clips and pads of paper were acquired and the prices of each. It would be foolish to attempt to plan those details. A plan simply includes several thousand dollars of expense for generic office supplies and entirely ignores the existence of records of the purchases. On the other hand, it would be entirely appropriate to forecast inventory purchases of key, high-value components of product, and to model the interplay of order, delivery, and use through a projection of inventory levels for each part. The question is, where should we plan in detail and where should we use a rough estimate?

There are really two questions involved. First, which processes should be included in the plan and which should be ignored? And second, at what level of detail should the included processes be forecast?

Accuracy—The Process Issue

Here's a simple example of the process question. Suppose we know that in our business a certain percentage of product is returned. Returns are credited to the customer's account, while the goods are reworked at some cost and then placed back in inventory.

There are two ways to reflect this situation in a plan. If we want to include the details of the return process, we will forecast gross sales as well as returns and have a specific line item for rework expense in the income statement. We'll also have an inventory account for rework in progress and a detailed budget for the department that does the rework. Further, we'll have to include some words on the return/rework process in the plan's verbal sections.

Alternatively, we can just forecast net sales and add a percentage to overall cost to reflect rework expenses.

Accuracy—The Detail Issue

The level of detail question works like this: Suppose a sales manager has a department with 25 people in it. The salespeople earn a base salary plus commission and have substantial travel and entertainment expenses. When we forecast this department's expenses, should we list every individual and add up his or her exact salary, taking into account next year's expected raises, or just look at the running rate of payroll, compute an average per person, and project based on the number of people we plan to have on board? Further, how should we project commissions and travel and entertainment? We could make a separate projection for each salesperson based on past performance, or base our forecast on an average per body in the field.

Implications

As might be expected, there aren't any "right" answers to these questions. The correct level of representation and detail depends on the situation and the importance of the process to the overall business. There are, however, some general truths and observations that can be made which help in selecting the right levels.

The organization's business plan evolves from the revenue forecast, which is a projection of sales effectiveness and customer response. In other words, the revenue forecast is a forecast of human behavior. Like any projection of human events, it is inherently inaccurate. Most businesses are looking at plus or minus 10% to 20% in sales forecasting accuracy. In new businesses, the range is more like plus or minus 50%. In other words, if the driver, revenue, is only accurate to within 20%, it doesn't make much sense to forecast items within the plan down to the penny or even to the dollar. It also doesn't make sense to model noncritical processes.

The Obscure Plan—Too Much Detail

Too much detail is a common error. Once a revenue forecast is established, people tend to treat it like a rock upon which to erect a structure of excruciating detail. This has become especially true since the advent of personal computers. Planners can produce reams of paper packed with four-decimal detail at the touch of a keyboard. This isn't especially harmful except to the extent that the computer-generated detail obscures what's really going on or contains programming errors that aren't detected because of the complexity of the algorithms and the mountainous output.

The point is that the revenue forecast rock is often shifting sand and the detail is useless if not counterproductive. Neophyte planners draw comfort from plans containing great detail. They feel that if one works hard enough on something it will contain great quality. The implication is that detail, hard work, and quality all go together and that one implies the other. In fact, the opposite is often true. Too much detail or inclusion of the wrong processes can obscure the result and produce a plan that's impossible to follow or outright wrong.

Business plans are often put together to serve as a guide in improving an organization's profitability. It is not uncommon to see a highly motivated manager and his or her staff present a plan to dramatically improve the bottom line, which turns on an immediate cut in expenses in the neighborhood of 50%. The plan is always supported by reams of computer output.

A financial person in the audience generally says, "Wait a minute, in the short run you've only got one reduceable expense of any size— people. A 50% cut in total expense means you'd have to fire 75% of your people. Can you do that and stay in business?" The answer is, of course, no, but why hadn't these bright people seen it? The reason is that the forest had largely become obscured by the trees. Their planning process had become so complicated that they made a multitude of small unrealistic assumptions and failed to see them adding up to one big unmakable plan. They lost the ability to step back and take an overview look at the plan, to see the gross implications of the detail.

Too Little Detail—Credibility

On the other hand, too little detail leads to a loss of credibility. It gives the impression that the planner hasn't thought things through and that the plan does not represent a cohesive business that will stand on its own feet and make a profit. A revenue projection, for example, drawn out of the blue without detailed supporting assumptions will not be accepted by a sophisticated audience, in spite of the fact that they believe a market exists. More about that particular problem later.

The selection of the right amount of detail is a key element in getting the plan accepted. To achieve credibility, a plan must be understandable without being confusing or appearing vacuous. In addition, if it is to serve as a useful control device after it is accepted, a plan must model the business in a way in which it can be used as a yardstick against which to measure actual results.

An Example

Consider the example above involving sales returns and rework activity. Under what conditions should the return/rework process be included explicitly in the plan? The answer to that question depends on the importance of the process to the success of the business. Suppose we have a business in which production is fairly routine and product quality is not a problem. Customers return one or two percent of sales each year, but the reasons generally relate more to the customer than to the product. This situation exists in established businesses that have been operating with a stable product line for a long time. Under this scenario, we probably wouldn't want to explicitly model the return process. We'd go with the net approach outlined. That doesn't mean that we ignore the existence of returns. We just model it in a summary fashion.

But what if we're looking at a new product in a high-tech field. Product quality is still an unknown, and monitoring returns could be a key method of controlling production effectiveness. Here, an explicit inclusion of a returns forecast and an estimate of rework expense could be a crucial element in the success of the business. If a quality-control problem arises on the factory floor that results in higher than expected failures in the field, management will become aware of its existence and magnitude much sooner if the return process is explicitly included in the plan. In this case, the number and dollar magnitude of returns will immediately show up as a deviation between plan and actual and the rework cost center will be immediately over budget.

If we'd taken the simpler approach in such a situation, the problem would have shown up as an unfavorable variance at the gross-margin level and would have taken substantial financial detective work to isolate. In fact, management might not have seen the problem at all, because the variance at gross margin due to returns might have been obscured by other variances. In this way, a poorly specified plan can allow a problem to go undetected for a long time. In this example, it is clearly appropriate to model the return process because it is critical to the success of the business.

Revenue Detail

The accuracy/detail question has an important application in sales forecasting. In business planning a question often arises as to how many ways should the sales forecast be cut up. That is, how many categories of revenue should be forecast and tracked. Consider a typical example:

Example—Compounding Categories

Suppose a company sells a basic product in several variations that compound one another. Let's consider a product everyone is familiar with. Imagine a basic bicycle that can be purchased with narrow, medium, or wide wheels. It also comes in three colors and can be fitted with a racing seat or a comfort seat, racing or touring handlebars, and five, ten, or fifteen gears. The number of different possible configurations is:

Wheels		Colors		Seats		Handlbrs		Gears		
3	×	3	×	2	×	2	×	3	=	108

If on top of that, there are, say, four sales regions with three districts in each, there are 1,296 different categories of revenue. Let's also assume that, in this example, the 108 different "products" don't differ significantly in cost.

The question is, should we construct a plan that includes explicit assumptions for 1,296 categories of revenue? The answer is generally no. Even though modern computer power will allow us to do it easily, that much detail will probably be counterproductive. Note also that many of the categories will usually be zero. We wouldn't expect to see the comfort seat combined with racing handlebars very often.

What Makes Sense for the Business

In cases like this, we have to abstract and condense along lines that make sense for the business. Clearly, the twelve sales districts have to be separately planned, because they involve separate management responsibilities. But the 108 products need to be condensed down to a handful. In this case, categorizing the bicycles as Racing, Touring, or Off Road, and forecasting these by sales district, would probably be appropriate. The sales reporting system can be set up to capture the additional detail, but there is rarely a need to weigh down the plan with it.

Essential Detail

The case just described should be contrasted with the following, in which maintaining product detail is essential.

We expanded the example we looked at when we were discussing the commission plan. In that example we had a product with three models, Economy, Family, and Sporty. Suppose the cost of each is a different percentage of its revenue, and we're forecasting sales levels as follows ($ in thousands):

	Family		Sporty		Economy		Total	
	$	%	$	%	$	%	$	%
Revenue	50	100	15	100	35	100	100	100
Cost	40	80	5	33	30	86	75	75
Gross Margin	10	20	10	67	5	14	25	25

Notice the difference in profit contribution along with the difference in position in the line. The biggest seller is the Family model, but the Sporty model contributes as much profit. The Economy model contributes a minimal profit on an intermediate level of sales. The differences in profitability are a result of different unit production costs and of different customer price tolerances in the three markets.

It is often tempting to forecast revenue and cost at the Total level only, especially when the product mix is subject to a great deal of uncertainty. That temptation must always be resisted. The Total Only approach abstracts away from the crucial fact that the business is made up of three distinct markets. The company would probably like to sell all Sporties because of the high profit margin, but the market might require a presence across all three to participate in any one. A plan that abstracts away from this will lose its ability to depict the essence of the business. It will also lose much of its value as a control device. Often, operating problems will appear as a deviation from plan on the total gross-margin level with or without deviation at the revenue level. The plan provides no insight into what to do if no projections were made of volume and cost effectiveness within each market segment.

A detailed plan also provides an important element in managing the sales department.

In summary, planned revenue should be segregated to reflect significant market, cost,

or management boundaries. The pressure to further subdivide should be resisted.

Appendix 7C

SELECTING YOUR LOCATION

There's an old saying in retailing and commercial real estate circles that goes: The three most important things in determining a business's success are location, location, and location. Is this true? Well, it often is, but sometimes it isn't. While location is absolutely critical to some businesses, it's less important to others. A good location generally means one that's convenient to get to and has high customer traffic. But it's important to understand that better locations usually cost more money to rent or own. An entrepreneur has to balance a location's quality against its cost to arrive at the best decision for his or her business.

Location Analysis—A Science or an Art?

People often talk about location analysis as if it were an exact science. They speak as if there were some secret formula that, once applied, guarantees selection of the perfect spot for a business. In reality, there's no such formula. Location analysis is a matter of sifting and organizing a great deal of data and then making an informed decision. In the end, it comes down to personal judgment. Of course, experience helps, and people who specialize in commercial real estate tend to have insights developed over the years that beginners lack.

In what follows, we won't be presenting "the answer" to the location dilemma. Rather, we'll point out a number of things that should be considered and weighed carefully in the decision.

The Nature of Location

Location really has two separate dimensions. First, it's important to consider the community in which a business is located. This gets at the question of whether or not the people and businesses there have a demand for the product or service which our business offers. For example, you wouldn't want to put a high-tech computer store in a low-income, rural, or blue-collar community.

The second issue involves location within the community. That is, once we've determined that a market for our product or service exists in an area, the question of exactly where we put it has to be answered. We want to locate somewhere within the community that will maximize our attractiveness to customers. That issue is very related to exactly what our product or service is.

Site and situs are other words that refer to the location issue.

Types of Business

Not all businesses are equally location sensitive. Suppose you're a chimney sweep. People don't care where your office is because they generally never go there. They just need to know you're in the area and will come when they call you. The same is true for a great many service businesses. Employment agencies, maid services, and plumbers, for example, don't depend on a specific location within a town. They do, however, have to be sensitive to the community's overall demand for their product or service. A maid service, for example, won't do well in an industrial area or in a low-income residential district. A fast food restaurant, on the other hand, is dependent not only on how many potential pizza or hamburger eaters there are in town, but also on how conveniently it can be gotten to.

Community

Choosing a viable community for a business involves taking a hard look at population, demographics, and competition.

The first step is determining if enough potential customers, people, or businesses depending on what you sell, live in an area which you can reasonably expect to service.

First, decide how far people will drive to get the kind of thing you sell. For example, for fast food it might be five miles; for bedspreads and draperies it might be twenty or thirty.

Next, look at some potential sites and draw circles on a map of that radius around them. Examine who is in the circle. The real question is: how many people who can be expected to buy from you are within that range?

In order to answer that question, you have to develop a customer profile for your business. A profile is a listing of the important characteristics of a buying unit, usually a household. These include age, family size, income, and so on. A profile might look something like this:

Age	30–45
Family size	4–5
Income	$40,000–$60,000
Education	High school graduate, some college
Children's age	Teens

Next, you have to get some idea as to whether the people in your area match the profile. Demographic information for census tracts is available in larger public libraries. The town hall or county seat may have some information as well. Call before you drive there.

Be careful of subtle traps. Not everything shows up in the profiles. Consider, for example, the difference between a university town and one supported by an auto assembly plant. Ages, family sizes, and incomes might be fairly similar, but other basic characteristics will probably be very different. A fast food restaurant might do well in either place, but what about an art gallery, a bicycle shop, or a health food store? These would probably do better in the college town. On the other hand, what about an auto parts store, a motorcycle shop, or a body builder's gym? Our bet would be the blue-collar environment.

Competition has to be considered in addition to the customer base. How many similar businesses are already there? A town may be able to support several fast food operations, but two health food outlets will probably kill each other.

To make the community decision, look at profiles, competition, and demographics, but also walk around a lot with your eyes open.

Site Location Within a Community

The final location question involves choosing a specific site within a community. The first thing to address here is the importance of your location to your customer. If your business is such that your customer doesn't come to you, then exact location may not be too important. Many service businesses are like that. They depend on advertising and telephone contact to reach the customer; then the service is brought to the customer's home or place of business. On the other hand, location is important to a majority of retail businesses.

Retail location revolves around the idea of traffic, walk-by and/or drive-by. Traffic is the reason for the success of many stores in modern shopping malls. The mall draws a great deal of traffic based on their large anchor stores as well as the sheer number of smaller establishments. Small stores that wouldn't have a chance in outside locations can do well in malls because of all the customers walking by. That is, people don't go to the mall specifically to visit the small store, but they do stop in and buy as they walk past.

A location must be visible and accessible. If you're on a road with high traffic, but it's difficult to get off the road and into the store, the traffic won't do you much good. The speed of drive-by traffic is important here. Being visible from cars doing 55 mph isn't nearly as good as being visible from cars doing 25 mph.

There are two issues involved in traffic: quantity and quality. Quantity is a matter of count: how many people walk by or drive by in a day. You can figure that out by standing in front of a location and counting for a few days. Be sure to do it on different days of the week. Weekday count is likely to be different from weekend. You may want to hire a reliable teenager to do it for you.

Quality is more difficult to determine and harder to pin down. It's related to the fact that not all passersby are potential customers at the time they're passing or at all. The concept is best illustrated by an example:

An entrepreneur we know opened a decorator art gallery in a suburban strip center. He located between three established businesses: an upscale restaurant, a women's spa, and a large supermarket. He thought success was guaranteed because of the traffic to these other establishments. In particular, he reasoned that women do most home decorating, that they would be going in and out of the spa and the supermarket and would stop in his store.

Our friend got a real shock when he found that women going to the spa tended to change into exercise clothes at home, drive to the spa, park, and run almost head down from their cars to the studio. They returned the same way. No way were they going shopping in their gym clothes!

Supermarket shoppers behaved similarly, but probably for different reasons. A woman on her way to the grocery store is a woman with a mission! Once she's parked in the supermarket's lot, she tends to go directly there and then directly home. There's no time to shop for decorations while the ice cream's melting.

The point of our story is that traffic made up of people who aren't potential customers doesn't count. Walk-in customers for an art gallery or a gift shop need to come from people who are leisurely cruising around if they're not specifically shopping for those items.

Assessing the quality of traffic is a tough judgmental call, but it needs to be done if you're going to maximize your probability of success.

Realtors

An entrepreneur looking for a site should generally consult a commercial realtor in the community. He or she should also get a banker's thoughts on the issue.

A caution is appropriate with respect to realtors. Be sure to contact an *experienced commercial* realtor rather than someone in residential sales. Be careful, because commission-driven salespeople will try to get your business even if they have very little commercial experience. A realtor who sells houses is likely to know absolutely nothing about selecting business property.

OPERATIONS: PRODUCTION, EQUIPMENT, AND RESEARCH

Every business sells some product or service. The business plan must describe how that product or service is acquired or produced and made ready for sale. The plan's readers need to be convinced that the people running the show have the expertise to deliver whatever it is that the business provides to its customers.

The depth required in this area is probably the most variable element in business planning. In some businesses, operations are simple and obvious, while in others they are complex and contain a multitude of potentially fatal problems.

REQUIREMENTS OF DIFFERENT BUSINESSES

The different requirements involved in presenting operations for various business types are probably best illustrated by considering retailing and manufacturing.

The operation of a retail establishment is conceptually straightforward and simple to grasp. This statement doesn't mean that the retail business is easy or requires less work than other businesses. It simply means that the mechanics are easy to understand. The retailer purchases product from a manufacturer or distributor, stocks and displays that product, and sells it to customers who walk in the door. Getting customers to come in and convincing them of the product's merits may be quite difficult, but those are marketing issues.

Operations for a retail business simply involve buying the product, transporting it, storing it, selling it, and delivering it. Describing these things in the business plan is fairly easy and doesn't take up a great deal of space. It also doesn't present much risk of confusing or misleading the reader. Further, it isn't hard to convince readers that an entrepreneur can do it. To put it another way, in retailing, the risk is generally perceived to be in the marketing area, not in operations.

NOTE: Inventory management and distribution can be very complex for large multistore businesses like the big discount chains. Here we're focusing on relatively small stores.

Now, consider a business that manufactures a complex technical product like a semiconductor or a computer. Here the product's quality and reliability depend on how it's put together in the factory. The process of construction can be technically so complex that it is incomprehensible to someone not trained in the field. In such a plan, the description of operations is much more difficult and involved. It's also more important to the success of the business.

Readers understand that a substantial part of the business's risk lies in how operations are organized and handled. For example, if the factory has a quality problem, product may fail when customers use it. That can result in the eventual failure of the business even if the product is well conceived, sales and marketing are sound, and a definite market exists.

Readers have to be convinced that the entrepreneurs know what they're doing in terms of operations. The task of convincing can be difficult, if the readers lack the technical knowledge to really understand the process.

The Attitude of Plan Readers

In spite of the critical nature of operations in some businesses, there is a definite tendency for audiences to accept what is presented in the plan. In the majority of cases, people will believe that an entrepreneur with appropriate credentials can put together an operation that will produce the product or service being proposed. This is even true when members of the audience don't really understand the technology of the business themselves. In fact, in such cases it can be more effective to describe the credentials of those responsible for operations than the operations themselves.

This doesn't mean that the operational planning doesn't have to be done. Financial backers want their entrepreneurs to go through the detailed exercise of planning operations. They just don't want to get too deeply into the nitty-gritty themselves. A convincing business plan should therefore have the complete detail of operations available in backup, but it's usually not necessary to put too much of that material in the plan document itself.

Business plan reviewers understand that doing the detailed planning gives entrepreneurs a better understanding of what they're getting into and provides an invaluable blueprint for implementation once they've gotten started. The detailed material has to be there, but in the background.

The Danger of Being Too Technical in the Plan

The folklore of business planning is full of stories about the failure of high-tech proposals put together for venture capital audiences by engineers and scientists with brilliant ideas. The moral of these tales is that although a particular idea was great, the plan was rejected because it either failed to adequately treat marketing and finance issues, or it was essentially a technical treatise that was incomprehensible to the readers.

Both of these mistakes are real dangers when plans are written by people who don't have much business experience and are caught up in the technology of what they do. Attention to the guidance offered by this book will avoid the first error, but the second remains an important pitfall that only you can prevent.

It's tempting to let the operations section of the plan become a technical treatise on production, research, and/or development. Technically oriented entrepreneurs understand product and technology and enjoy talking about them.

An overly complex or incomprehensible chapter on product development is a detriment to any plan even if the rest of the plan is well done. People will reject a plan they find intricate and confusing even when the underlying idea is sound. Remember the advice of Chapter 3: write *for your audience, not for yourself.* Emphasize the things that turn your audience on, not the things that turn you on. Keep in mind that plan readers are rarely excited by intensely technical discussions.

Choosing Your Level of Detail

The amount of detail required in the operations section depends on the type of business you're trying to describe. In this book we present two sample plans. The operations illustrated vary in complexity from very simple to quite involved. We have a sample plan for a retail store and a high-tech service organization in Appendix E. These illustrations should guide you in establishing the general level of effort and depth you should provide as you work through your business plan.

HOW TO WRITE THE OPERATIONS SECTION

The following pages will provide some guidance on writing about things that should be covered under operations for any type of business. Regardless of the nature of your enterprise, you have to say something about each of the following:

> Materials and labor
> Processes
> Facilities
> Equipment

In addition, you *may* want to say something about:

> Milestones
> Proprietary items
> Research
> Development
> Service
> External influences

Divide your operations section into a series of subsections, one for each of the topics above that you feel is important. Include others as appropriate. If you're thinking of starting a service business, see Chapter 9 for some special issues that should also be included. Let's consider each of the topics listed in turn.

Inputs—Material

Finding sources of product or raw material is a crucial step in getting ready to go into any business. The consequences of not having your supplies in place when you open the doors are disastrous. Imagine, for example, setting up a retail clothing store. Suppose you've planned a grand opening and spent a great deal of money on fixtures and the opening day festivities, and then have nothing to sell because your supplier couldn't deliver your product on time.

NOTE: *Inputs* and *outputs* are common terms meaning what goes into and what comes out of a process. In a business context, inputs are generally materials and labor, while output refers to the business's product or service.

Buying wholesale products, commercial supplies, and raw materials isn't generally as easy as walking into a retail store and buying consumer goods. Vendors often won't sell to just anyone. You may have to establish yourself as an approved distributor or at least a competent reseller to obtain certain products. Timing can also be a problem. Vendors often require that orders be placed weeks or months before goods are actually shipped. If you want credit from a supplier, you definitely have to start making your arrangements early.

The quality of your inputs has a direct impact on the perceived quality of your own output. That's certainly true in retailing where name brands sell more easily than unknowns, but it's also true when what you're buying is just one input among many.

Plan reviewers want to know that you've established relationships with your suppliers and that there's a high level of assurance that you'll be able to get what you need to establish or continue your business. They also want to be told about the terms of your agreements and the quality and reliability of what you plan to buy. When inputs are commodities that can be purchased on the spot, like food for a restaurant, your audience needs to be told that, too.

Pricing is an important feature of the relationship with suppliers. You need to tell your reader whether you expect to pay standard prices or receive special discounts as a result of quantity or some other criteria. The pricing of input should be factored into your financial projections, and the link between those estimates and the price assumptions you're making should be plain to the reader.

It's also a good idea to tell the audience why you chose one supplier over others. Acceptable reasons include price, quality, delivery, reputation, and credit terms.

In some cases a business will have substantial latitude with respect to buying inputs that are already made or buying materials and making the input product themselves. Certain electronics components, for example, can be purchased preassembled or in pieces. Similarly, a building contractor could subcontract work to a plumbing company or hire its own plumbers and do the work itself. These options should be discussed in the plan.

In general, a business plan should list all of the firm's significant suppliers, discuss the arrangement with each, and describe anything that might be considered unusual.

Inputs—Labor

Some businesses have specialized requirements for the people they hire, while others just need warm bodies with little unusual talent or skill. Consider the differences between opening a retail store and a factory. You can be fairly sure you can get reliable sales clerks and people to handle inventory, since those jobs don't require any unusual skills or training. As a result, retail staffing generally isn't an important planning issue. You can dismiss it in a line or two.

Staffing a factory is quite another story. Depending on the product, a factory may require engineers, machinists, electrical workers, and any number of other specialists.

The planning issue turns on whether you'll be able to get the kinds of people you need to run your business in the place you've chosen at a reasonable cost. There are two questions that need to be answered: are the people with the required skills in the neighborhood already, and, if so, are they already working for someone else whom they'd be reluctant to leave?

If you're proposing a business that's big and complex enough to need specialized labor, your plan's audience wants to hear how you'll get it. That generally takes a little research on your part. Look into the average educational level in the area, the number of other businesses that use your kind of labor, and the unemployment rate. Look at census information, which is often available at the county seat or town hall. Also ask the Chamber of Commerce about what kind of talent is around.

It might be tempting to put a high-tech business requiring sophisticated engineering and marketing talent in a depressed rural area because great facilities are available at bargain prices. The problem is that there may not be any place nearby where well-paid professionals would be willing to live. That means they won't come to work for your business without excessive financial compensation.

An area full of the right people can be a problem if they're already working for someone else and would have to be lured away at premium prices. You don't want to jump into an intensely competitive market for labor if you can help it.

If professional talent isn't in your area, it will have to be relocated in order to work for you. It's customary for employers to pay for such moves. A good rule of thumb on relocating employees is that the move costs about a year's salary. That can be a big unplanned expense.

The staffing plan we talked about in Chapter 6 should be presented here as well. It represents a time-phased hiring plan showing what kinds of personnel you'll need and when you'll have to have them. In short, the people reading your plan have to be convinced that the business will be able to get those human resources at the times indicated.

Facilities

Regardless of whether a business is complex or simple, its plan should have a thorough description of the facility it is to occupy. A number of specific issues need to be addressed.

Space. The square-foot space requirements of the business should be described for the near term and the longer run. The current or planned facility is then discussed in terms of how well it meets those requirements. An important issue is always whether or not the present facility is expandable to meet projected future needs.

Location. The facility's location should be analyzed with respect to the following:

- Its impact on customers and marketing. (If this has been covered in the marketing section, it need not be treated again here.)

- Its accessibility for delivery of inputs and equipment and for shipment of output.

- Its accessibility to the labor force.

The pattern of road, rail, and air transportation can be very important, depending on the size and bulk of products and inputs.

It's important to show that the location works for the particular business being planned and that no major problems are reasonably anticipated.

Layout. How operations are laid out within the proposed facility should be discussed in some detail. A floor plan is generally appropriate for any business that isn't strictly an office or an outside operation. The layout should indicate flows of product and people, specific work areas, inventory spaces, and anything else relevant to the workings of the business.

Acquisition. The plan should indicate whether the company plans to purchase or lease the property. The details of either type of contract should be indicated. If a property is to be purchased, readers will want to know the price and how it's to be financed. If it's leased, they'll need to be made aware of the rents, term, and any other conditions or restrictions that come with the agreement. They'll also want to know if there are provisions for assignment, sublet, or outright breaking of the lease. (If the business fails, people want to know if there's a way out of the lease obligation.) Leases vary on just what the tenant is responsible for. In most commercial leases, the tenant pays for property tax, insurance, and normal maintenance. All that needs to be understood and figured into the cost estimates.

Retail leases are often "percentage leases." That means a base rent is paid to the landlord plus a percent of gross sales over some specified amount. For example, a small shop might pay $1,000 per month plus 2% of sales over $100,000 per year. Be sure to include the cost of that percentage in your planning.

Operating Costs. Operating costs include the things mentioned above, as well as heat, light, phone, water, and general upkeep. These costs should be thought out and included in your financial projections.

Costs of Getting Started. Most business facilities, leased or owned, aren't suitable for use as acquired. Renovations are often necessary, and the place nearly always has to be reconfigured for the specific needs of your business. In real estate terminology, you have to put in *fixtures* appropriate for your business. Such additions can range anywhere from installing basics like electrical wiring, heating, or air conditioning to putting shelves and counters in retail spaces.

The cost of fixtures and reconfiguration is not insignificant and needs to be treated at least briefly in the plan. This is an area that's easy to overlook or underestimate. Planners should get firm estimates of the work to be done from reputable contractors and reflect those costs in their business plans. The discussion need not be overly detailed, but readers will want to know if you've anticipated these costs.

Capital Equipment

Most businesses need a certain amount of equipment to operate. *Capital equipment* refers to large, more or less permanent items that the business retains and uses for a number of years. Capital items need not be immovable or permanently stuck to the ground. Thus capital equipment includes vehicles as well as machines, computers, and certain changes and additions to the facility. The cost of heavy equipment includes the cost of freight and installation at your site. It may be worth mentioning that equipment never includes inventories held for sale, that is, anything that you intend to sell to a customer later.

A list of capital equipment required in the near future is an indispensable part of any business plan. Such a list is necessary in plans for existing businesses as well as for start-ups. The list includes the name and description of each piece of equipment, a short explanation of why it's necessary, and its estimated cost.

The cost of the equipment and its depreciation must be included and properly accounted for in the plan's financial projections.

A well-thought-out equipment list is *absolutely essential* to a business plan. It's also one of the things people like to argue about. Investors will want to be convinced that you can't get by without this or that, and that you can't do with a smaller model of something to save a little money. Prepare the list concisely, but be ready to go into excruciating detail on what you need.

Processes

Processes refer to the things that are physically done by the business in the preparation of the product or service being offered. The number of processes required and their complexity vary a great deal between businesses.

In manufacturing, the most basic processes include *fabrication* (in which parts are made from raw materials), *assembly*, *test*, and *inspection*. There can be any number of other processes and subprocesses depending on the nature of the product. Machining, welding, wiring, heating, molding, and drying are just a few.

In a restaurant, food preparation and table service are the two basic processes. However, food preparation can be divided into procedures for each course, for meats, for fish, for vegetables, etc. Service can be similarly divided depending upon how fancy the establishment is.

In a retail store, the main processes are the receipt and stocking of merchandise and sales. The system of inventory control can also be thought of as a process.

With respect to processes within operations, a business plan has to give its readers a sense of what's going on without becoming embroiled in minutiae. The writer must determine how precise this part of the plan will be, as different businesses call for substantially different levels of descriptive detail.

A manufacturing plan should list the factory's major processes and show diagrammatically how work flows from one place to another. It should also describe in detail processes that are unusual or are particular risk areas. A plan for a restaurant should describe the division of responsibilities in the kitchen and dining room, but only briefly. A detailed treatment would only be appropriate if there was something quite unusual being proposed. A retail store's plan might describe inventory control, but would probably do little beyond that because the processes are so obvious.

Manufacturing

Plans for manufacturing companies require a few special considerations. First, the plan must tell whether production is accomplished through a process or a *job shop operation*. In this context, the word process means that product is continually produced. Oil refining is a classic example of process production, although items like automobiles can also be produced in a process. In a job shop operation, on the other hand, a work order is placed for a particular quantity of a particular product. That lot of goods moves through the various steps in the factory until it emerges as finished product.

Second, it's important to know whether a product is built to order or for inventory. Built to order product requires a customer commitment in hand before production begins, and there is often some customization involved. Items that are built for inventory are standard and are built based on the company's planned sales rather than on firm orders.

Proprietary Information

Some businesses depend on proprietary inputs, which can be tangible or intangible. For example, a particular product may be patented and available to no one else. On the other hand, some member of the team may have certain knowledge or skills that are critical and unavailable from others.

Proprietary items are important to backers because they're generally necessary for the success of the venture, and their loss could sink the business. In such cases, the plan needs to explain how the item of value is being protected.

Patents on products and processes are the most common form of protection. The plan should describe the nature of the patented item and give the expiration of the patent. If the proprietary information is knowledge in someone's mind, the ties holding that person to the business should be discussed.

In short, the plan should convince the reader that the enterprise has a firm hold on whatever proprietary items it needs, and that the risks of losing those items are small.

Research and Development

Research means searching for something that hasn't yet been created. In other words, inventing something. Industrial research usually involves trying to come up with things that people are fairly confident can be invented. For example, suppose a need is identified for a computer with performance characteristics that are different from those currently available. Engineers think that existing equipment can be adapted to meet the need but aren't sure how to do it. Inventing that new machine is research.

Development means taking an existing product or idea and working it into the business. In the example of the previous paragraph, suppose the engineers were able to build a working prototype computer in the laboratory, thereby proving the idea was sound. Development means taking that model and designing it to be producible in the factory at a reasonable cost.

However, development is more general than just working with things that come out of the laboratory. For example, a retail store's

installation of new checkout scanners can be thought of as development, as can the addition of enhanced inventory control procedures.

If the business being planned expects substantial research and/or development in the near future, those details should be discussed in the plan document. The discussion is especially important if the anticipated results are crucial to the success of the business. This situation arises frequently in proposals for high-tech ventures where someone has an idea for a new product and wants to start a business to develop and market it.

Research Is Risky

Business plans that depend on the successful outcome of research are considered very risky by financial backers, who usually decline to participate. Research is a risky proposition for two reasons. First, there is no assurance that whatever product is being researched will ever emerge. If it doesn't, the business is a failure and all investments are lost. Second, even if the research is eventually successful, it's questionable whether it can be done (developed and produced) in the projected time and with the funds estimated in the plan. This second objection is particularly vital. Research projects are notorious for running over budget and taking substantially longer than planned. Unanticipated problems always seem to arise, which take extra time and money to fix.

There's less risk when a prototype needs to be developed into something marketable. However, even then the estimated time and budget in the business plan are far from assured, and investors may shy away. As we said in Chapter 3, investors like existing products with proven markets.

Research projects may be funded by certain aggressive venture capital firms if the anticipated rewards are high enough. In recent years, computers, electronics, and biotechnology have attracted substantial research funding.

If the business you're proposing requires some research or development, it's a good idea to explain away the risks in your plan. You should convince the reader that the development schedule is manageable and that you understand the risks involved. It's also important to anticipate what will happen if the research and development don't go as planned. In that case, try to show that the business won't fail; perhaps it will just be delayed. Also try to assure the reader that you won't need extra money. Investors hate being asked for more financing when there's still nothing to show for their initial investment.

Milestones (PERT)

If the business is relatively complex, it's a good idea to include some kind of time-phased implementation plan for setting up operations. Such a schedule would project the dates by which facilities will be acquired, renovations completed, equipment delivered and installed, key people hired, etc. These events are called *milestones*.

PERT is a well-known graphical technique for portraying such a time-phased plan and displaying the appropriate milestones. The letters stand for Program Evaluation and Review Technique. The PERT system has the advantage of showing the order in which events must be completed. It also shows that some events must be done before others and illustrates where bottlenecks are likely to occur. Here's a simple example:

Suppose we are going to start a manufacturing business. A factory must be acquired and renovated and equipment has to be ordered and installed. Many other things will need to be done at the same time, but we'll limit our attention to these. A PERT representation looks like:

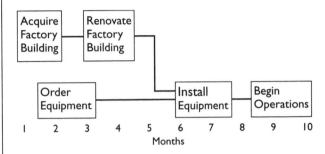

The diagram is essentially a flow chart moving from left to right. Time in months is displayed along the bottom. The lines of flow indicate which items have to be done ahead of other items. In this simple example, there are two activities going on, the building and the equipment that goes in it. The key to the method is that an item can't be completed until all the lines going into it are completed. Thus, it is apparent that the equipment can't be installed until the factory is acquired and renovated. That's fairly obvious in this case, but in more complex procedures it can be difficult to see where things get bottled up. A PERT chart allows us to identify key milestones as the events in the boxes. These are scheduled in accordance with the time line along the bottom.

The technique also provides a convenient method for keeping track of progress. As milestones are actually accomplished, the dates of completion are written on the chart. Subsequent events can be rescheduled by looking at the elapsed time required for each and sliding subsequent portions of the chart to the left or right along the time line.

Service and Support

In some businesses, after-sales service and support are important. This is especially true of more complex, technical products. Customers who buy computers, copying machines, or automobiles need to have someone to call when the products break and for periodic maintenance. There's little or no ongoing service implied in the sale of clothing or furniture or in any food service business.

In extreme cases, such as the sale of larger computers and automobiles, service becomes a more or less separate business operating in conjunction with the sales operation. Indeed, service can sometimes generate more profit than the original sales business, especially after there are a large number of units in use.

If service is important, the plan should say so and describe how that service is to be accomplished. Some businesses contract it out to maintenance organizations who do nothing but service. Others establish their own maintenance departments. These can be local or geographically dispersed so that service personnel are located near customers using the product.

Important service issues include pricing, parts inventories, travel expense, dispatch, and training. Chapter 9 is devoted to the special problems of service businesses, and the second sample plan in Appendix E describes a complex service company. If service and support are a substantial part of the business you're proposing, you should study that material carefully.

External Influences

In many businesses there are important issues outside of competition that influence performance. A business plan should demonstrate that the author is aware of these forces and has a plan to cope with them. Typical external influences include the following:

Government Regulation. The government operates on federal, state, and local levels to regulate and control business activity. The EPA has extensive antipollution regulations. States dictate who has to carry how much health insurance for employees. Towns and counties have zoning and sign ordinances. Any relevant regulations that will impact your business or are likely to do so in the future should be discussed in the plan.

Technological Change. Business methods have to change when the technology of the industry changes. Those that don't will be left behind when better or cheaper products are produced. A discussion of changing technology in the industry is often appropriate in a well-written plan.

Changing Customer Patterns. Will customers continue to buy and use the company's product as they do today for an existing company or as they are expected to do initially for a new company? An analysis of the changing patterns of demand is often a valuable addition to a business plan.

SPECIAL CONSIDERATIONS FOR A SERVICE BUSINESS

INTRODUCTION

A *service business* is one in which the customer purchases personal services from the vendor. There may be some sale of product involved, but the primary reason for the sale is the service. Auto repair is a good example. When you get your car fixed you pay for parts, but the shop is primarily in business to sell labor. Contrast that with a restaurant. There you're buying a product, the food, even though preparation and table service are a large part of what you're paying for. Clearly, the distinction is a matter of degree, since most services provide some product and most products contain some labor which can be thought of as service. In this chapter, we're concerned with businesses in which the emphasis is on the labor side. These businesses include:

Maintenance and repair

Consulting

Health care

Janitorial and cleaning

Some construction businesses

    Plumbing

    Electrical

From a planning perspective, service businesses have many of the same marketing and financial problems that other businesses have. However, there are a number of distinct issues that must be discussed in a plan for a service business that don't occur in businesses that sell product. The most important is pricing, which is unex-pectedly more involved than in the case of product.

Your Place or Mine?—Field Service or Bring It In

The location where the service is provided is an important distinction in the operation of service businesses. In some cases it makes sense for the customer to come to a central servicing location, while in others the service provider must travel to the customer. The difference generally hinges on the movability of whatever is being serviced. Automobiles and people (as in health care) are serviced at central locations. Houses are serviced where they stand. The distinction is important because it has a great deal to do with how the servicing organization is set up and the cost of the service.

The Nature of Your Service Business

A business plan for a service business should describe the nature of the operation in detail. It should tell what the service is, how it's delivered, who will do it, what special qualifications are required to provide it, what equipment is required, and during what hours it will be performed. Finally, the plan should show the detail behind the pricing calculation.

PRICING A SERVICE

Entrepreneurs are often ignorant of the calculations needed to price services correctly. As a result, improper pricing is a common cause of failure in service-oriented start-ups. Therefore, it is important that plans for service businesses examine the pricing calculation in some detail. Readers will want to be assured that you're charging enough to cover all your costs but not so much that you'll be uncompetitive.

Service rates seem high to most people. An auto mechanic's labor is charged at $60 to $80 an hour, while repair time on a large computer is billed at well over $100 an hour. Contract programmers are billed at more than $150 an hour. This seems a little outrageous considering that the repair person probably makes only from $30,000 to $50,000 per year—that's somewhere from $14 to $24 an hour—and programmers rarely make over $80,000, about $40 an hour.

In order to understand what's going on, we'll walk through the price calculation for a typical service. We'll assume a maintenance/repair service that's done at the customer's site on a technically complex piece of equipment.

Billable Hours

The pricing exercise begins with the concept of billable hours. That's an estimate of the total number of hours in a year that an average service person will spend working on equipment, in other words, "hands on" service time for which the customer can be billed.

We start with the total number of available working hours in a year, not counting overtime. That's 40 hours a week, 52 weeks a year, or 2,080 hours a year. Next, we reduce that by several factors.

Assume an average employee gets two and a half weeks per year of vacation—that's 100 hours. Next, assume five sick days each year—

that's 40 hours. And there are usually ten paid holidays for another 80 hours. Finally, we have to recognize that the service employee does a certain amount of paperwork, assume about two hours for each of the 47 working weeks we have left—that's another 94 hours.

We'll also assume that in order to stay technically current, we have to send the service person for training by the manufacturer of the product for approximately two weeks out of each year. That takes out another 80 hours.

After calculating what's left, we reduce the remainder by an efficiency factor. That allows for breaks, going to the bathroom, and anything else that employees do that isn't strictly work. Ten percent is an average estimate for that sort of thing.

Finally, since service is performed at customer sites, we'll assume that the service person travels one half hour for every hour spent working on equipment. That means we reduce the time available by one third to allow for travel. For the moment we'll assume there isn't any dead time, that is, time sitting around waiting for calls.

All this summarizes as follows for a single service person:

Total Annually Available Hours			2,080
Less:	Vacation	100	
	Sick	40	
	Holidays	80	
	Paperwork	94	
	Training	80	394
Net available hours			1,686
	Efficiency		× .9
Net working hours			1,517
	Travel factor		× .67
Annual Billable Hours			1,016

Cost of Service

Next, we have to consider the cost of service. Remember that the billable hours just calculated have to cover all costs if service is our only business. For the sake of illustration we'll assume that this is the case, and that any parts we sell will just cover their own cost. We'll also assume that we're running ten technicians out of a single office staffed by one manager, one inventory control person, and one clerical/dispatch person.

Assume the technicians each earn $35,000 a year, the manager makes $60,000, and the inventory and clerical people make $25,000 each. All wages are accompanied by benefits of 20%. Total annual wage expense is then:

Ten technicians @ $35,000	$350,000
Two office workers	50,000
Manager	60,000
	$460,000
Benefits @ 20%	92,000
Total	$552,000

We'll also make some reasonable assumptions about the office expenses for an operation of this size:

Rent	$36,000	per year
Utilities	$ 8,000	"
Dispatch phone	$15,000	"
Supplies	$ 6,000	"
Depreciation	$ 3,000	"
	$68,000	per year

Assume the cost of technical training is about $3,000 per person man week, including travel and lodging. For ten technicians at two weeks a year, that's $60,000.

We'll assume that each technician drives about 25,000 miles a year in a truck that costs $30,000. Assume the trucks are fully depreciated over four years on the straight-line basis. Operating a truck costs about $.35 a mile for gas, oil, tires, repairs, and insurance. That's $8,750 per year. In addition, each truck depreciates by another $7,500 per year, so the total expense is $16,250 per year for each of ten trucks. The total vehicular cost is then $162,500.

Summarizing the cost we have:

Salaries and wages	$552,000
Office	68,000
Training	60,000
Vehicles	162,500
Total Cost	$842,500

The Rate Per Hour

Now, each technician had 1,016 billable hours, so the organization has a total of 10,160 billable hours. Therefore, the organization's cost per hour of providing service is:

$842,500 / 10,160 hours = $82.92 per hour

If our goal is a reasonable pre-tax profit of 15%, we have to gross that figure up as follows:

$82.92 / .85 = $97.55

This figure is the rate at which we have to bill customers. Notice that the service technician's wage rate is only $16.83 per hour ($35,000 / 2080 hours).

Modifying the Rate for Different Businesses

The calculation above can easily be modified to reflect different sorts of businesses. If the customer comes to you, you don't have travel. If your employees drive their own cars, you may only have to pay a mileage rate. In some businesses, you can get away without paying for travel time at all. In a local maid service, for example, you just tell the employee where to show up. If you use part-time employees, you may not have to deal with as many benefits, vacations, or holidays.

On the other hand, some businesses may have additional cost and time elements. If expensive equipment is required, it will involve substantial additional depreciation expense. If you're pricing your own time as a consultant, you'd better include some nonbillable time for marketing and selling your services. Advertising and marketing costs often have to be added as well.

An important factor can be dead time, that is, time spent waiting for calls. This can be especially important in a start-up. The billing rate just calculated won't cover cost and profit if the provider isn't working full-time. Unfortunately, raising the rate too much can make it uncompetitive.

Comparing Your Rate with Others

Once you've come up with your rate, you have to look around at what the competition is charging. Plan readers will want to know that your rate isn't going to be uncompetitive. If rivals are charging substantially less, it may not bode well for your business. Here are some potential reasons:

- A competitor may be pricing service at a loss to attract other business.

- A competitor may be pricing low because it's slowly going out of business, but it may kill you in the market until it's gone.

- The market may be overpopulated with sellers, causing intense price competition. Think twice about entering such a business.

- A competitor may be more effective or more efficient than you are—another red flag.

Your pricing versus the competition's needs to be rationalized in the business plan. Backers must be convinced that the entrepreneur has looked at the market and made an informed judgment about the viability of his or her service business.

OTHER FACTORS TO CONSIDER

There are a number of other issues that should be considered in planning a service business. The characteristics of particular businesses will dictate whether each should be discussed in the business plan.

Customer Density in the Service Area

A service business should define exactly how wide an area it plans to cover. For most businesses, that's dictated by a reasonable driving time for either the customer to come to the service or for the provider to go to the customer. Draw a circle on a map of that radius. Then decide whether there are enough customers within that area to support the business. Further, how many providers are likely to be required to service the area.

Personal services like health care are related to the population within the circle and to the average age of people in the population. Equipment-related services depend on how much equipment is in the area and how often it fails or needs to be maintained. A plan needs to demonstrate that there will be enough demand in the service area to support the business.

Mean Time Between Failure— MTBF

Manufacturers of technical equipment usually keep records of how often it fails and needs service. They calculate a statistic, the Mean Time Between Failure, as a means of predicting service force requirements. If the number of pieces of equipment in an area is known as well as the MTBF, the number of calls can be predicted. If we also know the average time it takes to complete a call as well as the average travel time, we can estimate the employees required to provide service in the area. See Appendix E for a detailed example of such a business.

Windshield Time and Customer Density

Travel time is often humorously called "windshield time" in service businesses, and is related to the density of customers in an area. Generally, rural areas where people and businesses are separated by large distances require more travel time than urban areas. This is, of course, only important if the service is to go to the customer rather than vice versa. Density impacts pricing as well as staffing requirements, so there may be different pricing calculations for the city and for the country.

Sophisticated service providers that operate in a number of different locations often use a graph called a requirements curve that relates customer density to an administrative cost factor and determines efficiency as customers get farther apart. (See Figure 9.1.)

To use it, you find the relative efficiency factor for the customer density in the proposed area and add an additional efficiency multiplier to the pricing calculation described above.

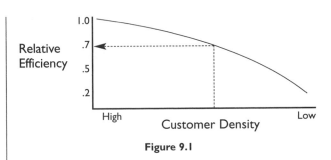

Figure 9.1

Another way to treat outlying customers is to charge incrementally for travel time as the customer's location lies beyond a certain radius from the service office.

SERVICE CONTRACTS VS. TIME AND MATERIALS

A service contract is an arrangement in which the provider agrees to fix anything that goes wrong over a period of time for a specific fee. Buying an extended warranty on a car or TV is a kind of service contract. An HMO is a service contract for health care services. The key point is that the customer pays whether service is needed or not, and the provider supplies as much service as the customer needs. It's a lot like an insurance policy, except that in traditional insurance, the contract isn't with the service provider, but with a third party, the insurance company.

Service without a contract is called time and materials, because the customer pays for the providers' time and the materials used. It's a call-when-you-need-us type of arrangement.

This distinction should be thoroughly discussed in the business plan. Providers usually like service contracts because they tend to stabilize income. They also provide for periodic maintenance, which is sometimes ignored by time and materials customers.

Response Time

In some service businesses the time it takes to get to where the service will be performed is very important. Response time is obviously important in an ambulance service, but it can be critical for things like computer repair, too. When a business computer goes down, the whole firm may be seriously crippled, and can even come to a stop. In such instances, the time it takes the repairperson to arrive is no joke. Business plans for services should address this issue if it is important to customers.

The problem for the service provider is that guaranteeing a quick response requires maintaining a higher staffing level than it otherwise would. It generally implies that some service people will be idle some of the time, and that, of course, costs money.

The solution is often a separate contract for customers who want quicker service, for which they agree to pay more. Generally, the only way a customer can be sure of getting very fast response is to sign a service agreement specifying a minimum time.

The planned average response time and any special deals offered should be discussed in the plan in detail. In particular, the audience needs to be convinced that the response time claimed can be consistently met.

CHAPTER 10

BREAK-EVEN ANALYSIS

Break-even analysis is a way of looking at costs to determine the volume a business must do in order to break even in terms of profit and loss. In other words, it answers the question "How much do we have to sell to just keep our heads above water?" A simple extension reveals how much more business is required to make any particular level of profit or return on investment.

A break-even analysis is a requirement for virtually any business plan, especially if it's for a new venture. Readers expect to see the analysis and will be disappointed with the entrepreneur who doesn't provide it.

Break-even planning does two things. First, it forces entrepreneurs to come to a better understanding of the financial workings of their businesses. Going through the process makes them aware of just how important the next sale is and how many sales they need to stay in the black. Second, since break even shows the minimum sales level a business can live with, it can often reveal whether a proposal is viable. We'll end this chapter with an example that uses break even to evaluate a retail location.

FIXED AND VARIABLE COSTS

When we conduct a break-even analysis, the first thing we do is look at our monthly budget and separate all our costs into two categories, fixed and variable. *A fixed cost* is one that doesn't change as the level of sales changes. A variable cost does change as our sales change. Fixed costs are often called *overhead*.

Here's a simple example. Suppose Sally Jones starts a business in which she makes and sells potholders. First, she rents a space and hires some employees to sew the material into product. Imagine for the sake of illustration that the workers are part-timers who get paid only for the hours they work. Sally also buys some sewing machines and a delivery truck. Next, she buys material and begins to produce product. Suppose in her first month Sally makes and sells 10,000 potholders, but in the second month she sells only 5,000. The fixed/variable cost distinction hinges on which costs are the same in months one and two and which are different.

The rent Sally pays for the space she's using clearly won't change from month one to month two, so that's a fixed cost. However, the cost of materials and labor will be half as much in the second month, so those are variable costs. Other fixed costs would include the depreciation on the truck and the sewing machines and the phone bill. Other variable costs might be inbound freight on the material and gas to run the delivery truck. If Sally had hired a full-time production supervisor who was on the payroll all the time, that person's wage would be a fixed cost.

Many costs don't fit neatly into either category. Take the truck as an example. Depreciation and insurance are clearly fixed costs, but gas and oil may be variable if she makes fewer deliveries in slow months. *However*, if she makes an equal number of smaller deliveries in slow months, gas and oil will be the same as in busy months, and should be thought of as a fixed cost. Heat and light in the workshop may have the same problem. If the shop employs fewer people in slow months but is open all day every day, heat and light will be the same as in busy months, and can be thought of as fixed. But if in slow periods, Sally only opens half as many days as usual and runs a full crew, heat and light will be less than in busy periods. They would then be more properly considered variable costs.

Regardless of such problems, break-even analysis requires that all costs be separated into either the fixed or variable categories. Sometimes a single cost element is separated into a fixed portion and a variable portion for the analysis.

BREAK-EVEN DIAGRAMS

Fixed and variable costs can be represented graphically. Plot cost along the vertical axis and sales along the horizontal axis (see Figure 10.1).

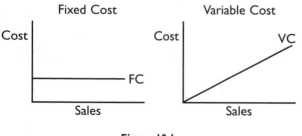

Figure 10.1

Fixed cost is constant as sales increase, while variable cost increases with sales.

The two diagrams are generally combined by plotting variable cost on top of fixed cost. The resulting line is then total cost.

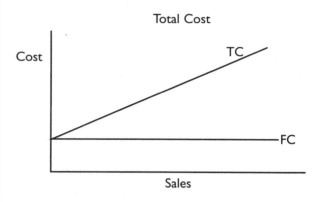

Figure 10.2

Figure 10.2 portrays the business's cost picture. The income that comes from sales is called revenue and is shown as a forty-five-degree line, that is, a line that increases dollar for dollar as sales increase.

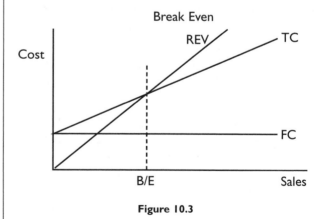

Figure 10.3

Break even is the point at which income equals outgo, where total revenue equals total cost. In Figure 10.3 it's the point where the Total Cost line and the Revenue line intersect. The break-even sales volume is directly below that point on the horizontal axis.

CALCULATING BREAK EVEN

The diagram makes it easy to understand the break-even concept, but is awkward to work with. In practice, it's better to figure out the break-even volume arithmetically.

Contribution

Every time a sale is made, some variable cost is incurred. Generally the selling price is substantially above variable cost. If it isn't, the business is in big trouble! The amount by which price exceeds variable cost is called the *contribution* made by the sale. For example, suppose Sally Jones's potholder factory can make a box of potholders for $7 in labor and material, her only variable costs. Assume also that Sally can sell that box of potholders to retail stores for $10. The contribution on that sale is $3, which means the sale *contributes* $3 toward Sally's profit and fixed costs (overhead).

Contribution is generally expressed as a percentage of sales. In the case just described, the contribution of $3 is 30% of the $10 sale. Expressed as a percent, the figure is called the *contribution margin*. If a business sells a number of products at different prices and contribution margins, an average value is used for the percent margin.

The Break-Even Calculation

The break-even calculation is really quite simple. It asks how many sales have to be made each month to contribute enough money to pay for all the fixed costs. In the example above, suppose Sally's fixed costs were known to be $1,800 per month. If each unit sold contributes $3, she must sell 600 units ($1,800 / $3) to break even. Since each unit sells for $10, break even sales in dollar terms are $6,000 ($10 × 600).

However, there's an easier way to the same result. Just take the total fixed cost and divide it by the contribution margin expressed in decimal form:

$$\$1,800 / .30 = \$6,000$$

This calculation essentially says: How many dollars that contribute 30 cents each does it take to make $1,800?

USING BREAK-EVEN ANALYSIS—A RETAIL LOCATION

Suppose an entrepreneur is contemplating opening a store in a particular location. However, he isn't sure the traffic will support the business. Break-even analysis can help to solve the problem.

In a store, fixed costs would typically include rent, utilities, property taxes, depreciation, and the salaries of salespeople and management. The entrepreneur also must include his or her salary if he or she intends to work there. With respect to a store, rent can be a little tricky. It's basically a fixed cost because the store can sell more or less product and the rent generally stays the same. However, most retail leases charge a percentage of sales over a certain amount in addition to a base rent. These are called percentage leases. In such a case, only the base rent is a fixed cost; the percent is a variable cost. To keep our example simple, we'll assume we pay only a base rent. A store's other variable costs generally include only the wholesale cost of goods and freight.

Suppose, on the average, the store buys goods for 45% of the price which includes the cost of freight. That is, for every dollar of sales the retailer pays the wholesaler 45 cents. Then variable cost is 45% of sales and the contribution margin is 55%. In other words, out of every dollar of sales we get to keep 55 cents to contribute to profit and overhead. Further, suppose the store's total overhead, or fixed cost, is $4,000 a month.

Begin the analysis by finding the break-even volume. How much does the store need to sell to have total revenue just equal total cost?

If 55 cents of each dollar of sales is a contribution to overhead, how many of those dollars must be sold to just cover the $4,000? In other words, how many "55 cent dollars" are there in $4,000? The answer is obtained by dividing $4,000 by .55:

$$\$4,000 \; / \; .55 = \$7,272.73$$

The store has to sell $7,272.73 to just break even. This won't give the owner any profit or return on investment, but he or she won't be losing money either. We'll round the number to $7,300 for convenience in the rest of our work.

Required Traffic Count from Break-Even Volume

Now let's work backwards to traffic count. Suppose it's known that the average sale in a store of this kind is $25. That means in order to break even, the business must make at least ($7,300 / $25 =) 292 sales transactions during the month. By watching similar stores, the entrepreneur can figure out that one walk-in customer out of three buys something. That means (292 × 3 =) 876 walk-ins a month. Next, suppose he or she observes other stores and notices that about one person in twenty walking by comes in. That would imply that somewhere in the neighborhood

of (876 × 20 =) 17,520 walk-bys are needed a month. If the store is open seven days a week, that means the location must provide at least (17,520 / 30 =) 584 walk-bys in an average day to survive. To make a profit will take more.

How does the entrepreneur tell if a location will provide that kind of traffic? Obviously, by having someone stand there and count for a few days. The basic economics of commercial real estate is that you pay a higher rent for higher traffic, so your break-even point is higher as well.

WRITING UP THE BREAK-EVEN ANALYSIS IN A BUSINESS PLAN

This example shows the kind of break-even calculations that can be used to support a business plan. After going through the calculation and arriving at the break-even volume, use it to demonstrate the viability of the business. In our example, the store owner would go through the calculation and then say to his or her backers, "Look, I need only 584 walk-bys a day, and my research shows that there are actually more than 1,500. That implies the store is almost certain to succeed in the proposed location!"

Numerical demonstrations like this are *tremendous credibility builders*. If it's done well, the audience comes away with the feeling that the entrepreneur is thorough, precise, and astute, and that he or she has made every effort to research the venture before starting.

The use of numbers is particularly important. Every figure in this presentation can be challenged and easily adjusted to see if the projection remains viable under a less favorable assumption. For example, a potential backer might challenge the entrepreneur by saying that the assumption of a 55% contribution margin is too high. The backer might claim that 55% reflects sales at list price, but that many sales will have to be made at a discount, so an average margin of 45% is more realistic. It's easy to work through the numbers and see what the traffic implication of the lower margin is. Had the entrepreneur constructed the argument in less precise terms by saying, for example, that traffic was "good" or "high," there would be no way to effectively refute the objection.

The break-even analysis is particularly good material for inclusion both in the plan document and in the entrepreneur's presentation.

EXTENDING BREAK EVEN TO INCLUDE PROFIT AND RETURN ON INVESTMENT

It's relatively easy to extend the break-even technique to project the level of sales required to achieve a given level of profitability or Return on Investment (ROI). All that's necessary is to treat any profit requirement as an additional fixed cost and go through the calculation exactly as before.

Consider Sally Jones's potholder factory again as an example. Suppose Sally had spent a total of $25,000 on her delivery truck, her sewing machines, and anything else she needed to get set up in business. In other words, her investment in the business was $25,000. Suppose she wants to earn at least a 12% return on those invested funds (ROI). What level of sales is required to achieve that goal?

First, we'll assume that Sally is in the 33% tax bracket, including federal and state taxes. ROI goals are usually stated in after-tax terms, so we have to figure out what pre-tax return will result in a 12% after-tax return. Since a 33% tax rate implies that the taxpayer gets to keep 67% of each dollar of net income, we're asking what return times .67 equals 12%. We get this by simply dividing 12% by .67:

$$12\% \ / \ .67 = 18\%$$

This says that Sally must have a pre-tax profit that is 18% of her investment of $25,000:

$$\$25,000 \times .18 = \$4,500$$

However, that is an annual requirement. The additional monthly profit required is one twelfth of that, or $375.

Sally's fixed costs are $1,800 per month. Adding the required profit gives $2,175. Her contribution margin is still 30%, so the volume required to earn the goal is:

$$\$2,175 \ / \ .3 = \$7,250$$

In other words, in order to be financially successful, Sally must sell at least $7,250 a month or $87,000 per year. That's a lot of potholders!

PLANNING LEGAL FORM AND OWNERSHIP

The legal form under which a business is organized affects liability, taxation, and its ability to raise money. With proper planning, the legal form also provides a framework for agreements aimed at resolving disputes among owners and governing what happens when one leaves or dies. That makes legal form and certain contracts between owners important elements of business planning. Despite that importance, however, form and inter-owner agreements are generally not covered in detail in the plan document itself. With respect to form, it's usually sufficient to include a brief statement about it in the plan's operations section. Inter-owner contracts are subtler.

Agreements between owners cover two issues: (1) who does what jobs and how much does each person receive, and (2) what happens when there's a dispute among owners or one dies or wants to leave. The first issue, who does what, is implicit in the staffing section of the plan that gives everyone's background, qualifications, and assigns titles and job responsibilities.

The second, what happens when owners have serious disagreements, is something entrepreneurs would rather not bring up with the business's financial backers unless asked about it. Obviously, it will worry backers if they think the entrepreneurs expect to have serious enough disputes to sink the company. On the other hand, everyone knows people can disagree, so backers may want to know you've thought about the issue. Hence it's a good

idea to downplay preparations for resolving disputes but to be able to show you've got them if they're needed. That's done by mentioning inter-owner contracts briefly in the plan and keeping details in backup material that's available if needed.

In short, we can say that form and contracts are less of a *plan* issue than they are a *planning* issue. In any event, they need to be considered carefully when businesses are started. It's especially important to look forward in time and think about the form that makes the most sense in the long run as the enterprise develops into what we expect it to become. To do that, we need a working knowledge of the implications of each legal form of business organization.

BASIC LEGAL FORMS

Loosely speaking, businesses can be organized into one of three legal forms:

> Sole proprietorships
>
> Partnerships
>
> Corporations

There are variations on the partnership and corporate forms, which we'll discuss after covering the basics.

We say these are legal forms because they define the legal rights and responsibilities of the business and its owners to each other and to the rest of the world.

With respect to most of the issues we'll discuss initially, the sole proprietor and partnership forms are very similar. A sole proprietor is a business with an owner, and a partnership is simply a proprietorship in which there's more than one owner. For now we'll combine the two under a proprietorship heading and discuss the distinguishing characteristics of partnerships later.

PROPRIETORSHIP AND CORPORATE FORMS— BASIC DIFFERENCES

Before going further, let's be sure we understand exactly what proprietorships and corporations are. In a proprietorship, owners *are* their businesses. For example, if Harry Smith owns HS Auto Repair, HS is simply Harry *doing business as* HS Auto Repair. Doing business as is usually abbreviated dba or d/b/a. Hence on legal documents, the business might be referred to as Harry Smith dba HS Auto Repair. This means that any legal or tax matters about the business are *personal* to Harry.

In the corporate form, a separate legal entity is interposed between a business and its owner(s). The corporation operates the business and in turn is owned by stockholders. So if Harry Smith owns all of the stock of HS Auto Repair, Inc., he owns a corporation that runs the business in the eyes of the law. This is true even if Harry is the only employee and does all the work himself.

A corporation is a separate entity under the law. It has its own rights and responsibilities, generally pay its own taxes, and can sue or be sued. There are three areas in which proprietorships and corporations differ. They are

(1) the liability of owners for the torts and debts of the business, (2) taxation, and (3) raising money. We'll discuss each along with some issues involving employees.

NOTE: A *tort* is a legal wrong or injury done by one party to another. In this context it is an injury done by a business to a person or another business. For example, a defective product may injure a consumer resulting in a liability to compensate the victim for lost income and medical expenses as well as for pain and suffering.

Limited Liability of Owners

In the proprietorship form, owners are entirely responsible for the business's debts and any damage it does. That means the owners' personal assets can be taken to satisfy business liabilities. For example, if Harry Smith, dba HS Auto Repair, fixed someone's brakes incorrectly causing an automobile accident, the victims could sue Harry for his life savings as well as the assets in his business. The same is true if the business defaults on a loan.

In the corporate form, liability *theoretically* belongs to the corporation and does not extend to stockholders beyond their investments in its stock. In other words, if a corporation owes more than it can pay, the personal assets of the stockholders can't be touched. All they can lose is the money they invested in the stock, which may become valueless. This idea is called *limited liability* and is one of the main attractions of the corporate form.

Limited Liability in Owner-Operated Businesses
Unfortunately, limited liability doesn't always work for owner-operated businesses. Let's explore why.

Companies generally create liabilities that exceed their assets by borrowing money they can't repay and by losing lawsuits. When owner-operated firms borrow, lenders circumvent limited liability by demanding *personal guarantees* from the owners before making loans to their companies. Personal guarantees are side agreements that make owners personally responsible for repayment should their businesses fail to meet loan obligations. The device destroys the value of limited liability in the context of small business loans.

To illustrate damages to another party, suppose Harry Smith's HS Auto Repair *Inc.* (now a corporation) negligently repairs brakes causing an accident. The injured party would sue *both* the corporation *and* the individual who did the work. It is a fundamental legal principle that one cannot avoid liability for one's own torts. Harry would be liable if he worked on the car himself, and might be liable for an employee's work based on negligent hiring (of an unqualified mechanic).

Hence, limited liability is often a myth for owner-operated companies even though it's real for stockholders who don't participate in the businesses. That means if Harry's sister had stock in the company but didn't help to manage it or sign a loan guarantee, she's unlikely to be liable in either situation.

We're not saying that limited liability never works in small, owner-operated companies. Rather, we're saying that it can often be problematic, and the advice of an attorney is strongly recommended.

Piercing the Corporate Veil

The corporate form requires that certain formalities be observed and that business assets be kept separate from those of owners.

The formalities largely involve holding regular, documented meetings of the board of directors, and recording the board's concurrence on major decisions.

The separation of assets is especially important with respect to money. An owner can't treat the business's bank account as if it contained personal funds. For example, an owner should never use the company's checking account to pay personal living or entertainment expenses or to buy personal assets like furniture or cars.

Limited liability may be lost if either of these rules has been broken. That is, a creditor or an injured party may be successful in claiming that the firm's corporate character is a sham, and the business is really a proprietorship. The argument is called *piercing the corporate veil*. If a court makes that finding, the business owner is exposed to unlimited liability.

All this makes the choice of business form an important planning issue. It's generally cheaper and administratively easier to run a proprietorship than a corporation. Hence if the nature of the business is such that liabilities are unlikely, or if limited liability is likely to be circumvented, forming a corporation may not be worth the trouble and expense it takes. It's also possible to purchase commercial liability insurance that will take the place of limited liability with respect to damages, but not with respect to loans.

Taxation

Traditional corporations and proprietorships are taxed very differently. Proprietorships are *pass-through* tax entities. That means earnings are simply passed through the business to its owners in proportion to their interests, and are taxed as personal income at *personal rates*.

In a traditional (C-type) corporation, the government recognizes the company as a separate legal entity and taxes its earnings at corporate rates. What's left, the firm's Earnings After Tax (EAT), can either be retained in the business or paid to shareholders in the form of dividends. To the extent that earnings are paid out as dividends, they become personal income to stockholders, which is taxed as personal imcome.

Hence, corporate earnings may be taxed twice, once as corporate income and a second time as personal rates. The phenomenon is called the double taxation of (corporate) earnings and is a major disadvantage of the corporate form. (We'll see shortly that certain corporate forms avoid double taxation.)

The Tax on Retained Earnings

From what we've just said it would seem that no one would ever choose the traditional corporate form because it implies double taxation. But that isn't always the case. When a firm plans to retain all or most of its earnings—which is usually done to help the company grow—the tax rates have to be examined to determine the best strategy.

In a proprietorship, personal taxes on pass-through income must be paid even if those earnings are kept in the business. For example, suppose a firm earns $1,000 with which the owner buys business equipment. Assuming a top tax rate of 35%, he or she has to pay as much as $350 in personal tax on those earnings even though he or she never had personal use of the money.

In the corporate form, earnings retained in the company are taxed at corporate rates but escape double taxation because they're not paid out as dividends. That means the corporate form is preferable if the applicable corporate rate is lower than the rate the owner will pay on incremental personal income. That's quite possible because corporate rates are as low as 15% if the firm isn't making much money.

In general, good planning implies choosing the corporate form when a high-income owner has a company with good growth potential that's likely to retain earnings indefinitely.

Salary vs. Profit

When business owners work in their own corporations, they generally pay themselves salaries. They're simultaneously employees and stockholders. It's important not to confuse owners' salaries with corporate earnings, which are subject to double taxation if paid as dividends. As long as salaries are reasonable for the work done, the IRS will treat them as tax deductible expenses to the corporation and personal income to the employee/owner subject only to personal tax.

This means it's often possible to plan the distribution of earnings to avoid double taxation entirely. Since there's a broad range of reasonable salaries for the jobs owners typically do, it's usually possible for them to pay themselves salaries to the extent they want to bring money home and retain the remaining earnings in the business. In that way, each portion is taxed only once.

Raising Money

Another important distinction between the proprietorship and corporate forms involves the ability to raise substantial sums of money, usually for startup or expansion. Corporations and proprietorships can both raise money by borrowing, but only corporations can sell stock.

Lending to Small or New Businesses

Recall from Chapter 3 that lenders are reluctant to advance money to small or new firms because so many fail, leading to the loss of a lender's investment. It's important to realize that lenders don't get a big reward for making a successful business loan. They just get their money back with interest. Hence loans to small or new firms are high-risk, low-reward propositions, and lenders tend to decline the business unless loans are supported with *collateral*.

Collateral refers to assets that secure loans. They're pledged to lenders and can be sold to satisfy debts if borrowers fail to pay. Since small businesses and their owners usually don't have much collateral, they have a hard time borrowing, even if business prospects look good. This is generally true whether businesses are proprietorships or corporations.

Corporate Stock

Investing in a small business through ownership of corporate stock presents a very different opportunity. A person who invests in the stock of a risky firm has a good chance of losing an investment, but also has a chance of getting rich if the firm does well and the stock's price goes up. In other words, the risk and reward picture is more balanced. A substantial risk of loss is offset by the chance of a big gain making the investment opportunity more attractive.

The result is that many people who won't lend to risky firms will buy their stock. This has an important planning implication because stock is only available in the corporate form. It means a company that expects to need cash for start up, expansion, equipment, or research generally must organize as a corporation.

Motivating Employees Through Stock Options

Stock also creates a device called the *stock option*, which can help to motivate key employees. A stock option is the right to purchase shares at a designated price during a specified period at the end of which the option expires. Then, if the stock's price exceeds the price named in the option before it expires, the option owner can buy shares below market price and immediately sell at a profit.

For example, a firm whose stock is selling for $30 might issue an employee an option to buy 1,000 shares at $60 that expires in five years. The options have no immediate value, because their exercise price ($60) is above the stock's market value. But suppose the stock's price rises to $90 within the five-year period. The employee can then buy 1,000 shares at $60, and immediately sell at $90, making a profit of $30 per share for a total gain of $30,000.

Companies give selected employees stock options as part of their compensation. Employees who receive options are generally willing to work for lower salaries than they otherwise would because the benefits from options can be much greater than the salary foregone.

Companies like paying employees with options because they don't cost anything when issued, and the practice can attract talented people to companies that otherwise couldn't afford them.

Fringe Benefits

In addition to wages, most businesses pay employees with fringe benefits, the most important of which are health and life insurance. Benefits are tax deductible to the business, and are not treated as taxable income to employees.

However, in a proprietorship, or any business form characterized by pass-through taxation, owners working in the business DO have to pay income tax on the value of fringe benefits they receive. In a traditional, C-type corporation, on the other hand, employees who are also stockholders (owners) are treated strictly as employees with respect to fringe benefits and escape personal tax on their value.

This rule seems to argue strongly in favor of the corporate form, but there's an additional complication. As a general rule, the fringe benefits given to owners have to be made available to the majority of employees. That means entrepreneurs can't pay themselves tax-free benefits without offering the same benefits to most of their employees, which is something many small companies can't afford to do.

HYBRID FORMS: S-TYPE CORPORATIONS AND LLCS— THE BEST OF BOTH WORLDS?

In smaller businesses, the most significant advantage of the corporate form is usually the ability to raise money through the sale of stock, while its biggest disadvantage is the double taxation of earnings. (Recall that limited liability is often problematic in small, owner-operated companies.)

However, the government favors small business formation because new businesses create jobs. So, congress and state lawmakers have created several hybrid forms of business organization that offer the best of both worlds for some

companies. Two of the best known are the S-type corporation and the Limited Liability Company, generally called an LLC. The S-type has been around for many years, but the LLC is relatively new. The new LLC form has some technical advantages that have led to its virtually replacing the S-type in most states.

Both forms are corporations in that they offer limited liability and the ability to sell ownership interests (stock), but they are generally set up as pass-through tax entities, so their earnings are not subject to corporate income tax. Earnings flow directly to the personal income of owners, and are taxed only once at personal rates.

In these organizational forms, the company itself files only an *information tax return*, which doesn't require a payment. Rather it shows the business's taxable profit and identifies its owners and their shares. That enables the IRS to determine whether those owners have declared the company's income on their personal tax returns. Essentially, the tax system treats S-type corporations and LLCs as partnerships, which also pay no tax, distribute earnings among the partners as personal income, and file information returns.

NOTE: The owners of S-type corporations and LLCs can elect to be taxed as regular corporations. This can save on taxes in certain unusual situations. The vast majority of S-types and LLCs elect pass-through tax treatment.

The Differences Between S-Types and LLCs
Some differences between S-types and LLCs are largely a matter of terminology. The owners of an LLC are called members rather than stockholders, the term used for both C and S corporations. Members have ownership interests rather than shares of stock.

S-types, however, have some restrictions on ownership that can be big negatives. The most significant is that all of the shareholders must be people. That means an S-type generally can't be owned by another corporation, a partnership, or a trust. This makes it impossible to use the form when two businesses want to form a joint venture in order to do something together. In addition, S-types can have no more than 75 shareholders, all of whom must be U.S. citizens or residents. The 75-person limit clearly restricts the form's ability to raise money by selling stock. LLCs don't have either of those limitations.

S-types also require that profits be distributed to owners strictly according to their ownership shares. That seriously limits flexibility in planning. For example, suppose Harry and Sally start a business that they agree in the long run will be owned equally. But they want Sally to receive 75% of the first year's profits, perhaps because she did most of the setup work. That can't be done in a straightforward manner in an S-type, but it's a simple matter of writing the plan into the operating agreement in an LLC.

On the other hand, stock options are not available under the LLC form, while they are in S-types.

PARTNERSHIPS

Partnerships are essentially sole proprietorships with more than one proprietor. The distinguishing features of partnerships largely have to do with relationships among the partners rather than relationships between the organization and the outside world. We'll discuss several important issues briefly.

Partnership Agreements

The heart of a partnership legally and operationally is the partnership agreement. The *partnership agreement* is a contract between the partners that spells out how large each of their interests is, what their duties are, and how earnings are to be distributed.

Virtually anything can be put into a partnership agreement. The issues addressed typically include guidelines for day-to-day operations, management practices for disputes, conditions for adding new partners, and rules for paying out the share of a partner who departs or dies.

It's important to create a formal, written partnership agreement when the business is started or early in its life. Oral agreements are legal, but are difficult to enforce when disputes arise.

Liability

Partnerships, like sole proprietorships, are characterized by unlimited liability. Recall that that means the personal assets of owners can be taken to satisfy business liabilities. However, the idea can be more frightening in a partnership, because partners are jointly and severally liable for the firm's obligations.

Jointly and severally is a legal term that means all of the liable parties can be sued for the full amount of the claim regardless of their individual faults. For example, suppose Joan and John are jointly and severally liable for an injury that was 90% Joan's fault. Further suppose that she doesn't have any money, but John is well off. Joint and several liability means John can be forced to pay the entire claim.

In a general partnership (the most common kind) any partner can bind the partnership into a contract or a debt without the knowledge or permission of the other partners. And, the partnership as a whole is liable if any partner commits an act that injures someone or damages property while he or she is on partnership business.

Since partners are jointly and severally liable for the liabilities of the partnership, the personal assets of any partner can be taken to satisfy any claim after the partnership's assets are exhausted. To make matters worse, the party with the claim doesn't even have to exhaust the assets of the guilty partner first. He or she can go after the partner whose assets are easiest to access.

Taxation

A partnership is a pass-through entity for federal tax purposes. It files only an information return, passing its earnings through to the personal returns of the partners. Earnings are taxed as personal income to partners even if those earnings are retained in the business and not actually paid to the partners.

Formation and Termination

A partnership is formed when two or more people begin doing business together without incorporating or forming an LLC or creating some other form. This is an important point! If you start doing business together without saying anything about legal form, the law assumes you're a partnership. It also assumes you're equal partners regardless of how much each of you contributed to the enterprise. And it subjects you to the risks of joint and several liabilities. Given these rules, it's easy to see why a written partnership agreement is

important if you don't contribute and participate in the business equally.

Termination

Ending a partnership can be tricky. Obviously, it can be done by agreement, but in about half the states partnerships are automatically dissolved when a partner withdraws or dies unless the partnership agreement says otherwise.

Automatic dissolution can be a problem if the remaining partners want to stay in business, because they have to distribute assets to the withdrawing partner or heirs immediately and then reform the business. The difficulty is that the withdrawing partner's share is usually tied up in illiquid assets, that is, assets that cannot easily be turned into cash. These are usually used in the business, such as a production machine. That means paying the departing person his or her share can require borrowing money or partially liquidating the business.

The problem is avoidable if the partnership agreement stipulates that the partnership is to continue upon the withdrawal or death of a partner, and specifies a rationale for determining the value of the departing person's share and a method of payment. We'll discuss this idea more later.

SPECIAL FORMS

The majority of businesses are organized as either sole proprietorships, partnerships, corporations, or LLCs. There are, however, other forms for special situations.

Limited Partnerships

We've already discussed the general partnership form in which all partners participate in the business and have unlimited liability. In a *limited partnership*, the *limited* partners do not participate in running the business, and do enjoy limited liability. However, there must be at least one general partner who runs the enterprise and is subject to unlimited liability.

Limited partnerships are usually formed to invest in real estate. The limited partners contribute money that the general partner invests and manages. As long as limited partners remain *passive investors*, they can lose no more than their investments. However, any management activity on their part can subject them to unlimited liability.

Professional Organizations

Special rules apply to businesses organized to provide professional services like medical doctors, lawyers, and accountants. As a general rule, such organizations can't be standard corporations or LLCs, which might limit the liability of the service providers. Historically, they had to be general partnerships.

In recent years there's been a trend toward creating new forms for professionals that have more flexibility and put some boundaries on the totally unlimited liability associated with partnerships. The forms allowed vary by state, so it's imperative to get local legal advice before trying to set one up. The new forms include the Professional Corporation (PC), which is called a Professional Service Corporation in some states, the Limited Liability Partnership (LLP), and the Professional Limited Liability Company (PLLC).

As a general rule, the new forms have at least two distinguishing features. First, all of the owners have to be professionals licensed to provide the service offered. For example, only

lawyers can be partners in a law firm. Second, the new forms attempt to limit the liability of service providers for the malpractice of other providers in the same firm. For example, if one member of a group of surgeons injures a patient, other members may not be liable if they had nothing to do with the injury.

Insurance

We've said a good deal about personal liability in this section, making the point that it often cannot be avoided through organizational form. It's generally a good idea to insure against that kind of liability. Most of us are familiar with the idea of malpractice *insurance* carried by doctors and lawyers. A similar form of liability insurance is available to other businesses.

ISSUES BETWEEN OWNERS

Whenever more than one person owns a business, there's a chance they'll disagree to the point that they become unable to work together. People often overlook this possibility when starting businesses, and fail to make enforceable agreements about their relationships and how the firm's value is to be divided if they separate.

It's important to keep in mind that we're talking about relatively small businesses in this section. Since there's more than one owner they'll be partnerships or *closely held* corporations (which may be C- or S-types or LLCs).

Closely held corporations have three characteristics: (1) there are a small number of shareholders, (2) there's no market for the stock, and (3) shareholders controlling a majority of the stock participate in management. It's also common that all of the shareholders work in the business for their livelihood.

Notice that the second point locks shareholders who hold *minority interests* into the company, because they can't sell their stock and recover their investments.

NOTE: A minority shareholder's interest is too small to influence or control corporate decisions. Majority shareholders either own or belong to a group whose members together own an interest large enough to control the firm. Contrast this with a stock investment in a large, publicly traded company. If you're unhappy with the firm, you just sell your stock on the open market and generally recover its market value.

Partners are in the same situation because partnership interests can't be transferred to outsiders without the permission of the other partners, all of whom generally work in the business.

All this can set up a very difficult situation for a shareholder or partner with a minority interest in the company. Here's an example.

The Dilemma of the Minority Interest

Suppose Tom, Dick, and Harry each contribute $50,000 toward starting a new construction business agreeing that they all have equal interests either as partners or shareholders. Also suppose they all work in the business, drawing all of its earnings in the form of equal salaries.

Now, assume that after a few years, Tom and Dick decide that Harry isn't pulling his weight, and that they'd like to get rid of him. Their reasons may be real or phony, and Harry probably doesn't agree that he's a drag on the others, but that doesn't matter. What can Tom and Dick do if they don't want to come up

with the cash to buy out Harry's interest at a fair price?

Unfortunately for Harry, he holds a minority position relative to Tom and Dick acting together. As majority owners they have the ability to eliminate Harry's job or cut his salary while refusing to buy out his interest at a reasonable price. The practice is called a squeeze-out. The majority owners squeeze an unwanted minority interest out of the business.

The Legal Position of the Squeezed-Out Minority

Under legal theory and precedent, majorities shouldn't be able to squeeze out minorities in either partnerships or closely held corporations. (The reasoning doesn't apply to larger publicly traded corporations.) That's because all partners have a fiduciary responsibility to other partners, and majority owners of closely held corporations owe a similar fiduciary duty to minority shareholders. *A fiduciary relationship* is one of special trust and confidence in which one party puts himself or herself in the hands of the other who has superior power or knowledge. For example, lawyers and bankers are fiduciaries for their clients. A fiduciary is ethically and legally bound to treat the other party fairly.

Hence, Tom and Dick shouldn't be able to take advantage of Harry the way they have in our example. But as a practical matter they often can. If Tom and Dick can show a reasonably valid *business purpose* for their actions, a court may let them get away with squeezing Harry out, although they may be forced to pay him more or less fairly for his share of the business. To use the power of the court system, however, Harry would have to sue Tom and Dick, which is likely to be expensive and time-consuming.

Minority Shareholders Who Don't Work in the Closely Held Corporation

Minority shareholders who don't earn their livings in their closely held companies can also have problems. In that situation, the majority shareholders who do work at the firm can pay all of its earnings to themselves in salary leaving nothing for dividends. That means passive investors who don't participate in management don't get any return on their investments, but can't get their money out, because there's no market for the stock.

Who Holds the Minority Interest

Our example illustrates that caution and planning are appropriate when someone accepts a minority position. But it's important to notice that it may be difficult to predict who will wind up in such a position. When Tom, Dick, and Harry started their business they were probably all friends and had no idea that two of them would take sides against the third. That happens all the time. It isn't even unusual to see family members squeezed out by other family members.

STRATEGY FOR MINIMIZING THE EFFECT OF DISPUTES AMONG OWNERS

The fundamental planning approach to minimizing the consequences of the problems we've just discussed is to agree in *writing* on:

1. Who has what management responsibilities (jobs)

2. What each person's compensation will be

3. A set of rules stipulating how a departing owner will be paid

The documents that carry such agreements have different names in different organizational forms. In partnerships, they're partnership agreements. In corporations they're *bylaws*. And in LLCs they're *operating agreements*. It's also advisable for the stockholders in the corporate forms to sign *pre-incorporation agreements* stipulating essentially the same things before starting.

The third issue, the departure of an owner, can be incorporated in these documents or can stand alone as a separate *buy-sell agreement* that dictates the terms under which the remaining owners will buy out the interest of a departing owner. We'll discuss buy-sell agreements in more detail shortly.

Cautions for Partnerships

Partnerships in all states except Louisiana are governed by a version of the Uniform Partnership Act (UPA). The act provides a set of default rules that come into effect when there's no partnership agreement. In effect, if you don't have an agreement on an issue, the law makes one for you. It's important to understand that if people work together without any agreement as to form and have a dispute, the law assumes they're a partnership subject to the UPA. Oral partnership agreements are legal, but difficult to enforce as details are hard to prove. Here are a few issues on which people are likely to want to vary their agreements from the terms of the UPA.

Under the UPA, partners are equal with respect to their management interests and shares of profit. Disputes are settled by simple majority votes. But partners don't always set themselves up as equals. Some may make larger investments, spend more time in the business, or have greater experience than others. Under those conditions partners may agree that some have larger interests than others.

Under the UPA, partners aren't paid salaries but depend on the distribution of earnings for their compensation. Clearly, this may not make sense when partners of differing ability and experience work in the same enterprise or some spend more time there than others.

Under the UPA, the departure, death, or disability of a partner generally requires dissolution of the partnership and a winding up of its business. This is in marked contrast to the corporate form, which continues after the death of any number of stockholders. The remaining partners are free to reform and start again, but reforming can be a costly administrative nuisance. Most partners would rather have their organizations continue and pay departing partners or their heirs reasonable values for their interests.

BUY-SELL AGREEMENTS

A buy-sell agreement is a crucial planning document that will usually avoid the crippling effects of disputes among owners. It provides for the departure of an owner who is disgruntled, doesn't get along with other owners, dies, or just wants to leave.

The agreement is signed by all owners and specifies a method for determining the price remaining owners *must* pay an owner who leaves for a share of the firm. It should also call out a plan for the payment of that value if cash isn't immediately available. The buy-sell can also limit an owner's ability to sell his or her interest to parties other than the other owners.

A buy-sell is also important to outside investors, because disputes between owners, who are likely to be key executives, can cripple the company. For example, banks don't want to lend to businesses that can be stopped in their tracks because the owners can't get along and no one is willing or able to leave.

Valuing the Interest of a Departing Owner

The heart of a buy-sell agreement is the specification of a method for determining a business's overall value, which leads to the price a departing owner will receive for his or her share.

Agreements should be done early in the lives of businesses (preferably before they're started) when the owners don't know who's likely to leave. Unfortunately that makes it virtually impossible to put a monetary value on the business in the buy-sell document. Hence agreements usually specify valuation formulas or the use of professional business appraisers (found in the phone book or through your CPA). It's a good idea to write the buy-sell to require at least two appraisals and to stipulate a method of reconciling the results.

It helps to understand the process if you're familiar with the standard approaches to valuation:

Book Value. A firm's book value is the accounting value of assets minus liabilities. It's rarely a satisfactory method of valuation, because it just shows the depreciated value of the amounts paid for assets less what the business currently owes. The value of a viable business comes from combining assets with the knowledge and skill of people to earn money and is generally much higher than book value.

Multiples. Certain standard multiples are available by industry that can be applied to recent earnings to approximate the company's value. For example, the starting point for valuation in purchase negotiations is often ten to fifteen times recent annual profits.

Capitalization of Expected Earnings. This is the most theoretically sound method, but it's only applicable where a stable history of positive earnings is available. The approach assumes the earnings will continue for a long time, and uses financial mathematics and a relevant interest rate to come up with a present value that's financially equivalent to the expected stream of income. The method can also incorporate an anticipated growth rate in the future earnings stream.

The Value of Similar Businesses. Sometimes it's possible to determine the value of a business based on the values of comparable businesses, which are known because they've been sold recently.

The most difficult businesses to value propose new products that have good prospects, but lack proven records of sales or earnings. They're especially problematic if research or development is required before the products can be brought to market.

It is important that buy-sell contracts *require* that an agreement on value be reached, perhaps through arbitration. Arbitration is a dispute resolution method in which two sides present their views to an impartial third party, the arbitrator, who decides the issue. The parties must have contracted to submit the dispute to binding arbitration beforehand and agree to accept the result.

Avoiding Unknown Owners

Another important aspect of buy-sell agreements concerns the death of stockholders in the corporate forms. When that happens, the deceased owner's spouse or children can wind up owning a share of the businesses. That can be a disaster if the heirs aren't familiar with the business but want to be involved anyway. A similar situation arises if a stockholder sells his or her shares to an outsider who may be unknown to the other stockholders. Note that this doesn't happen in partnerships because the admission of a new partner requires the consent of the other partners.

Regardless of whether an owner dies or sells his or her stock, someone new and unknown is injected into the group of owners. Problems usually arise with respect to decisions that require the unanimous or nearly unanimous approval of the shareholders. In those cases the new owners, even if they hold only minority interests, can stop the strategic plans of the original owners cold.

NOTE: The bylaws of most companies require that at least a super-majority of shareholders approve certain strategic decisions such as mergers, acquisitions, and major expansions as well as the sale of significant parts of the business. (A super-majority is some percentage substantially more than half, such as 75% or 80%.) In smaller companies unanimous approval is often required.

Buy-sell agreements get around the problem by requiring that the deceased or departing owner's shares be offered for sale to the existing shareholders or to the company itself before they can be inherited or sold to someone else. We say the existing owners are given *a right of first refusal* with respect to the transferred shares. Obviously, a method for determining the price of the shares must also be specified.

Paying for a Deceased Owner's Share

When an owner dies there generally isn't enough ready cash in the business or in the hands of the other owners to buy the deceased person's share from his or her heirs. The best way around the problem is to have the company purchase life insurance on all of its owners with significant interests in the firm in amounts sufficient to buy out those interests. Then, when a death occurs, the company itself buys the deceased person's share and the other owners' interests are increased proportionately to their ownership before the death.

WHAT PLANNERS SHOULD KNOW ABOUT E-COMMERCE

WHAT IS E-COMMERCE?

In a broad sense e-commerce is any business situation in which transactions or information transfer are enabled by electronic technology. This includes a lot of things we don't usually think of when we hear the term. Examples include checkout lines at the supermarket and real estate brokers whose listings are accessible on web sites. An increasing number of traditional businesses have web sites that provide potential customers with information about themselves and serve as a form of advertising.

Technology in Brick-and-Mortar Businesses

In terms of business planning, this simply means that today many traditional, off-line firms (called brick-and-mortar business in the jargon of e-commerce) have elements of technology imbedded in the way they do things, and those elements have to be understood and described in business plans. That's usually done in the operations and/or marketing sections. Additionally, the costs of that technology must be reflected in the financial projections. *This is a very important point; no one should plan any business without careful consideration of how it will use modern electronic technology to be competitive.*

Defining E-Commerce More Narrowly

Despite the technically broad definition of e-commerce we've just given, the term is generally used to refer to businesses that sell their products and services online, that is, through the Internet. Such firms are generally called dotcoms for the .com suffix that terminates the names (addresses) of their web sites.

It's worth noticing that some dotcoms started on or because of the Internet, while others are there because they have to be. Bookstores provide a good example. Amazon.com originated as a result of the Web and became a major force in literary retailing. Barnes&Noble.com is the online response of the leading brick-and-mortar book retailer to the challenge posed by Amazon. Both are e-commerce dotcoms, but Barnes&Noble.com is operated alongside the company's traditional stores, while Amazon.com is strictly an e-commerce organization.

E-COMMERCE AND BUSINESS PLANNING

It's important to understand at the outset of our discussion that e-commerce doesn't fundamentally change business planning. All of the things we've said about the structure of a plan document, target audiences, the need to connect the market idea with a customer need, the product's ability to satisfy that need, the business's approach to bringing those things together, and financial projections are just as significant for e-commerce enterprises as they are for traditional businesses.

The difference is that e-commerce attracts customers, sells them products and services, takes orders, and receives payment through a new medium, the Internet. That change in approach gives rise to new requirements for knowledge and equipment (hardware and software), a new approach to marketing and advertising, a new vocabulary of technology-related terms, and a new set of problems, also technology related.

That means an e-commerce plan has to demonstrate that the entrepreneurs not only understand their products, but that they also understand how to use the Internet to sell those products. That has to be accomplished within the general business planning framework we've been talking about all along.

The Business Model Concept

The term business model has become a part of the vocabulary of business planning and strategy, largely during the Internet era. The idea isn't limited to e-commerce, but it tends to be used there more than elsewhere.

A company's *business model* is a concise statement of how it markets, produces, and distributes what it sells and the resulting financial relationships between revenue, cost, and profits.

For example, suppose a construction company operates in a suburb of a large city selling upscale homes to affluent, professional families. Also suppose it incurs material, labor, and subcontracting costs of about 55% of revenue, spends about 10% on advertising, pays 5% of revenue in interest on construction loans, and has other overhead expenses of about 15%. Its business model would include at least the following:

- Its target market as professional families with high incomes

- Its suburban location

- The key characteristics of the houses it sells

The following are percentage relationships between revenue and cost, expenses, and profits:

Revenue	100%
Cost	55
Gross margin	45
Expenses	
Advertising	10
Overhead	15
Interest	5
Total expenses	30
Profit before tax	15

A business model is essentially a very summarized business plan. It contains a notion of the firm's approach to its market, the key elements through which it brings value to its customers, and a statement of the financial results those ideas are expected to produce.

The idea is best understood by thinking through an e-commerce example. Consider an online bookstore. The product is books, which are obviously available at traditional bookstores. Hence the business model has to make the point that an online store offers valuable advantages such as wider selection, rapid delivery, shop-at-home convenience, etc. Then it has to briefly describe how online sales and delivery are accomplished, and make a statement about the resulting financial picture. The difference between this and the business plan is a matter of detail along with supporting documentation and assumptions.

Because of the emergence of the term business model, largely in the high-tech field, an e-commerce business plan should include a statement of the proposed firm's model. It's a good idea to put it immediately behind the executive summary, which contains some of the same information (see Chapter 5).

DISTINGUISHING ISSUES IN E-COMMERCE

In the remainder of this chapter we'll outline the major issues and requirements that differentiate e-commerce enterprises from brick-and-mortar businesses. As a general rule all such issues should be presented and discussed in the body of the business plan and their costs should be reflected in the plan's financial projections. Some items have analogs in traditional business and some do not.

BUSINESS SETUP

Doing business on the web requires a web site, which is analogous to a store or office in brick-and-mortar businesses. The site consists of a series of images called web pages, which appear on the customer's computer screen when he or she visits via the Internet. An e-commerce web site generally does at least three things:

- It tells the customer about the product or service offered.

- It shows an inventory of items or services available for sale.

- It takes customer orders or provides contact information.

Domain Names, Registration, and Web Hosts

Customers access web sites by typing the web site's name, which is also its web address, into a web browser on their computers. *A web browser* is a computer program through which a user accesses the Internet. Every web site has to have a unique address, called a domain name, which leads browsers to its location on the Web. Domain names are of the form *www.examplename.com*.

In order to get started in business, you choose a domain name and contact a broker called a registrar who will see if anyone else already owns that name. If not, you can register your name for a small fee. Registrars are accredited by the Internet Corporation for Assigned Names and Numbers (ICANN). If the name you want is already in use, you have to pick another unless the person who owns it isn't using it and is willing to sell it, which sometimes happens.

After an e-business has a registered name, it contracts with a *web host* for access to the Internet. A web host is a company that maintains computer hardware that connects websites to the Internet for a fee. Your web site is actually a resident on your host's *servers*, even though you administer it from your place of business.

Hosting can be cheap or expensive depending on the capabilities offered. The capacity of a site's connection to transfer data from the Internet to your business is an important feature called *bandwidth*. The more bandwidth the host provides, the more orders your business can handle, and the more you'll pay for the connection.

Designing and Building a Web Site—Technically

Designing and building a web site is a specialized form of computer programming, which most people can't do themselves. Indeed, building a sophisticated commercial web site takes a great deal of expertise. That fact has led to the emergence of an army of freelance web site designers, many of whom work out of their homes. They're easy to find in local advertising and the phone book. Most are reasonably priced and will put together a good site for a few thousand dollars. They will also help with domain name registration and finding suitable hosting arrangements.

ATTRACTING AND SERVICING CUSTOMERS

The first and usually biggest challenge faced by e-businesses is getting customers to their web sites. Secondary challenges involve making sure the site is usable by a typical customer and providing customer service.

Search Engines

When people look for things on the web, they use *search engines*, which are themselves web sites that provide links to other sites based on *keyword* descriptions typed by the customer. The engines search the Web for sites that have something to do with what the customer says he or she wants, and then display links to those sites on the screen. Unfortunately this can result in a list that contains hundreds if not thousands of sites.

A key to e-commerce success is getting your site to appear near the top of those lists. This involves understanding how the search engines work and putting key words and descriptions in your site that attract them. This is something else a professional web site designer should be able to do. Unfortunately, the logic various search engines use changes from time to time, so it's important to choose a designer who is familiar with the latest search-engine technology.

Search engines display search results on the left side of the screen and *sponsored links* on the right. A sponsored link is basically advertising on the search engine. An e-business can get its name on the first pages of search results (on the right) by paying the engine to list it there under sponsored links.

Advertising on the Web— Banner Ads

Banner ads are found on virtually every commercial web site of any size. You can advertise on someone else's web site for a fee, and may be able to pick up some extra income by letting others advertise on your site. Ads are usually placed among sites in related fields. For example, a rental car company might buy a banner ad on a travel agency's web site.

Advertising in Other Media

Some Web-based businesses advertise in newspapers, on TV, and in the Yellow Pages. Those advertisements may provide traditional contact information such as location and phone number as well as a web site address.

Site Layout and Design— User Interface

User interface refers to the ease with which a customer can get around (navigate) a site, find what he or she wants, and place an order.

It's important because e-commerce is entirely self-service; there's no sales clerk to answer questions or direct customers to the right place. (Some sites have a customer-service capability, which we'll discuss shortly.)

This implies that an important element of e-commerce planning is putting yourself in the place of the customer and thinking through how he or she will get around your site. Don't forget to consider a typical customer's technical expertise in this context. It's also important to realize that what customers can see on their screens may be limited by their own computers and connections to the Net.

Along these lines, it's not a good idea to give a web designer a completely free hand in designing your site. They don't know your business or its customers, and need guidance on what's likely to work.

Customer Service

In traditional business, customer service is generally concerned with after-sale issues like billing and product performance. Additional considerations in e-commerce include navigating the web site, getting product information, and placing orders.

In traditional businesses, customers generally talk to customer service representatives (CSRs) either in person or on the phone. There are several options in e-commerce:

Phone. CSRs can be available at an 800 number posted on the web site. However, such numbers frequently become overloaded, especially at peak times, keeping customers from getting help. This leads to frustration with the business and e-commerce in general.

E-mail. An e-mail address for customer questions is often provided on commercial web sites. CSRs answer by return e-mail within a (hopefully) short time. This approach can also be frustrating if the response isn't prompt or doesn't answer the question in the customer's mind (which may not be what he or she wrote in the e-mail).

Chat rooms. Online chat rooms led by CSRs can provide interactive question-and-answer forums for customers.

Web pages. Web pages can provide answers to frequently asked questions (FAQs) or provide static information likely to be helpful to most customers. Web pages help but rarely eliminate the need for contact with a human CSR completely when customers have problems.

PAYMENT

Although a few e-businesses accept mailed checks and money orders, the vast majority of e-commerce sales are paid by credit card. Hence, you'll probably have to set up your e-business to accept credit card payments electronically. Unfortunately, taking credit cards on the Web exposes sellers to a higher risk of credit card fraud than exists in brick-and-mortar businesses. We'll look at the issue in some detail beginning with the mechanics of setting up a credit card system.

Arranging to Take Credit Cards in E-Commerce

First, we'll review how credit cards work. They're issued by banks, which advance funds to customers when they make purchases. The advances are loans to the customers paid directly to the selling merchants. It's important to understand that credit card companies like Visa and MasterCard don't lend money themselves. They just administer loans to cardholders made by various banks and apply the customers' payments to their accounts.

Hence, every cardholder has a bank that stands ready to lend him or her money to buy from any merchant that accepts its card. To receive the money, a merchant must also have an account at a bank in the system. The merchant's bank receives the money loaned to the customer by his or her bank and credits it to the merchant's account. The merchant's bank is called an *acquiring bank* and is the first of two relationships an e-business has to have to accept credit cards.

The second relationship is with a *payment gateway* that connects the e-commerce merchant to credit card processing networks. The function of the payment gateway is to provide authorization for the transaction immediately, while the customer is waiting. In other words it checks to see if the credit card number is valid and belongs to the named customer. It also makes sure the cardholder isn't over his or her credit limit.

In order to be accepted by credit card companies, an e-business has to have the computing hardware and software to transmit information to the credit card network and to store customer credit information at its own business. Both the transmission and storage of this data have to be *secure*, meaning information is protected from theft by unauthorized persons inside or outside the company. These are significant requirements that generally take an investment in equipment and software. That, in turn, means the business plan has to include funding for these resources when an e-commerce enterprise is begun.

E-Commerce and Credit Card Fraud

Credit card payments create a problem in e-commerce because they're always *card-not-present* transactions, meaning the credit card is not physically accessible to the merchant when the sale is made so he or she can't get a signature or demand customer identification. The result is that e-commerce transactions are more likely to be fraudulent than similar dealings in brick-and-mortar businesses. Generally, a thief needs only a valid credit card number and the associated expiration date to make a transaction. The incidence of fraud is as much as ten times higher in e-commerce than in traditional business.

This results in credit card fees that are as much as two thirds higher than those paid by traditional, offline businesses, and per-transaction costs that are as much as 75 cents higher.

Credit card companies have added a three-digit personal identification number (PIN) to the backs of cards, which merchants can demand before approving transactions. These make it harder for potential thieves to impersonate cardholders. However, scamming techniques have developed to get people's PINs, and not all merchants ask for them.

On top of all this, the financial burden of fraud is shifted from credit card companies to merchants in e-commerce, because transactions are card-not-present, and e-merchants can't produce signed receipts to support transactions. That means merchants rather than credit card companies absorb fraud-related losses.

Despite all of these problems, credit cards are the dominant form of payment in the industry, and e-commerce merchants have no choice but to accept them. In other words, taking credit cards is simply a must for e-commerce. You can't be in business without doing it.

SECURITY IN E-COMMERCE

Security in brick-and-mortar businesses tends to be centered on physical issues like theft of product, cash, and equipment. Theft of trade secrets and customer data, including credit information, is also a problem. Thefts can be by outsiders, employees, or customers. When outsiders steal it's generally called burglary; employee theft is called shrinkage, especially if it involves inventory, and customer theft is shoplifting. The usual approaches to security include security guards, alarm systems, cameras, and meticulous inventory control. E-businesses face all of the same issues except shoplifting, obviously, because customers don't have physical access to inventory.

But e-commerce has some additional, unique security problems that come from the fact that its portal on the world is a computer and the Internet. The areas of concern include theft of customer credit information in transit and hacker attacks on the company's computer system either to steal information or to maliciously disrupt operations.

Security in the Payment System

The use of credit cards in e-commerce implies a need for security in the payment system. The fraud we talked about in the last section involves a thief who already possesses an unsuspecting individual's credit card number and uses it to steal product. E-merchants also have to be concerned with criminals attacking their systems to obtain customer credit card numbers. That can happen in three places: when the customer transmits an order to the e-business, when credit information is sent to the payment processor, and when customer credit information is stored by the e-business. We'll briefly discuss protecting information when it's in transit and stored.

Information in Transit—Encryption

Information is most vulnerable when it's transmitted over the Internet. The biggest problem is the transmission of credit card numbers from the customer to the e-business and then from the e-business to the credit-authorizing network. The primary defense against theft in transit is encryption.

Encryption software encodes information before it's sent and decodes it when received. Obviously, both ends of the transmission have to have compatible software. Web browsers like Netscape Navigator and Microsoft Internet Explorer are equipped to handle encryption.

The most common and available encryption software is Secure Sockets Layer (SSL). The SSL system is secure because it employs a key at both ends. A receiving party can only decrypt a message if he has the appropriate receiving key. E-businesses provide their customers' computers with *public keys*, but keep corresponding *private keys*, which decrypt incoming information, to themselves.

Protecting the E-Business's System

People who break into computer systems, usually as thieves or vandals, are known as *hackers*. A hacker who accesses an e-business's system can steal information including customer credit card numbers and internal operating data. He or she can also implant viruses that damage systems and/or disrupt operations. The worst viruses actually destroy infected computers. There are several protections against invasion by malevolent hackers.

Password Protection. Passwords limit system access through the customer portal by requiring users to *log in* using secret codes called *passwords* before they can access information in their own accounts or utilize particular aspects of the site. For example, online law libraries allow paid subscribers to do online legal research from their own offices after identifying themselves with a password.

Passwords have at least two problems. First, many users don't keep them secret. Second, those that aren't encrypted in transmission can be intercepted and compromised.

Screening Routers. All computer networks have routers that direct electronic packets of information around those systems. Routers can be programmed to scan the information passing through them and block potentially hostile packets, making it more difficult to attack the system.

Proxy Servers. Proxy servers prevent outsiders from identifying individual computers within a business's system. That keeps the firm's internal network more secure from hackers on the outside.

Firewalls. A firewall is a computer placed between the Internet and a business's network. It examines incoming data for hostile or intrusive content. If questionable material is found, the firewall prevents it from accessing the system.

Every e-commerce business plan should contain a section in its operations chapter that discusses security. The description should include an argument addressing the adequacy of the system in terms of cost effectiveness, the tradeoff between the quality of security and its cost. The amount of money earmarked for security should also be identified in the plan's financial section. It's also a good idea to provide supporting detail on security and its cost in plan backup.

ORDER FILLING AND RETURNS

Order filling refers to everything that has to be done to get product to customers including taking and entering the order, picking it from inventory, packaging and addressing it correctly, and shipping it promptly. Returns involve receiving and processing items returned by customers and properly crediting their accounts.

Some of the biggest problems in e-commerce have come up in these areas. The first generation of e-businesses put most of their efforts into acquiring customers and neglected this admittedly unexciting field within day-to-day operations. The result was that a large number of customers became disgusted with e-commerce, and, for at least a while, shopped elsewhere. After that rocky start, businesses began to pay more attention to this kind of administration and made substantial improvements. However, the area remains problematic. The following characteristics of e-commerce make handling orders and returns difficult.

Customer Expectations. E-commerce customers have gotten used to and now demand precise delivery schedules and in-route package tracking as a matter of course. This differs markedly from offline businesses, which generally quote delivery dates within a range of weeks.

A Large Number of Small Shipments. Brick-and-mortar businesses make bulk shipments over long distances, break them up at regional distribution centers, and deliver large numbers of small orders to individual customers only in limited geographical areas. E-commerce enterprises, on the other hand, ship everything directly to customers. That means they deal with very large numbers of small orders, sent over long distances, usually using several carriers including FedEx, UPS, and the U.S. Postal Service. This is a much more difficult task than local delivery. The difficulty is compounded by the fact that each carrier uses a different tracking and billing system. All of this creates an administratively complex, error-prone organization. In this respect e-commerce is similar to the catalog sales business, and astute players have learned valuable lessons from that industry.

It is important that an e-commerce business plan address this area of operations in some detail.

Capacity Utilization. A large proportion of e-commerce businesses are seasonal in nature meaning sales are subject to large volume swings from one month to another. Surveys report that over half of e-commerce businesses see peak volumes four or more times larger than average volumes. This is a problem, because one of the most important value elements offered by e-commerce is prompt delivery.

Extreme seasonality coupled with a prompt service requirement implies many e-commerce enterprises need order-processing and shipping departments that can handle peak volumes just as quickly as they handle average or lower volumes. But that means those departments may be four or more times as large as the same departments in less seasonal businesses or businesses that can tolerate slower deliveries.

This is a costly issue that has yet to be solved. As many as half of e-businesses report losing money on order processing and shipping, and consider that area one of their biggest headaches. Although a total solution is unlikely, the issue should be addressed in business plans, at least to demonstrate that the entrepreneurs are aware of it and have given it consideration.

CONTINGENCY PLANS: WHAT TO DO IF THINGS DON'T GO ACCORDING TO PLAN

Business plan readers are generally sophisticated people who know that businesses, especially start-ups, rarely go as planned. A question frequently asked of the would-be entrepreneur is, what will you do if this or that doesn't happen as you expect? It's a good idea to provide a section in the plan document that shows that the planner has thought about the unexpected and knows what to do if things go awry.

A good contingency plan has two parts. First, it spells out the signals that indicate the business is off course, and, second, it lays out the actions needed to correct the problem. Even sophisticated managers have difficulty dealing with unexpected downturns. The problem is that people don't anticipate getting in trouble until they are in trouble, and by then it's often too late to rectify what's wrong. This is especially true in smaller businesses, where running out of cash is a major consideration.

This chapter discusses contingency planning, the art of anticipating problems, and working out solutions in advance. The key to success is not only having the solution thought out in advance, but also having the conviction to implement it at the right time.

The written business plan doesn't have to contain a great deal of detail in this area, but that detail must be in the head of the planner when he or she presents a case to an audience. For that reason, we cover the subject in quite a bit of detail.

RECOGNIZING A MISS

One of the most prevalent management shortcomings of modern times is the failure to recognize trouble before it's too late. Businesses generally operate according to some kind of plan, which may be implicit in the minds of the owners or explicitly written on paper. Failure to recognize trouble before it's too late means that planned performance is irretrievably lost by the time management takes any serious action to correct the problem. Of course, such misses come in all sizes and levels of seriousness from subpar profit performance to bankruptcy.

There are two fundamental reasons behind this phenomenon. The first is that the signals businesses give off when they're about to change are often vague and confusing. The second is that people have a hard time hearing news they don't like. For example, suppose sales start to fall off after a long period of steady growth. For the first month or two after the drop in sales begins, it's hard to be sure the trend is permanent and not just a temporary aberration. People tend to convince themselves the downturn is temporary, because that's what they want to believe. Entrepreneurial and sales-type personalities have a definite tendency to look on the bright side of things. That's a great trait most of the time, but it can be a real disaster when business is going down the drain.

Businesses get in trouble for a number of reasons. Here are a few of the more common:

Revenue. The total number of dollars coming in the door starts to decline. That can happen if competition heats up, prices fall, or market share erodes. It can also be the result of a decline in demand for the product.

Cash. Cash flow is the hard cash generated or used by the business. It's different from profit. For example, suppose you buy something for $.50 and sell it for $2.00. Your profit is the difference of $1.50, but if you replace the item in inventory you have to spend $.50 and your cash flow is only $1.00. If you sold the item on credit and have a receivable for $2.00, your profit is still $1.50, but your cash flow is minus $.50 until you collect the $2.00. Cash flow is explained in detail in Chapter 14. Cash flow can deteriorate even when accounting profits are good. That usually happens when receivables and inventory get out of control. It's easy to focus on developing product and making sales and forget those more mundane aspects of business operation. Cash flow also suffers when expenses are too high relative to sales, but then profit looks bad, too. In new and small businesses, it's usually a lack of cash that precipitates failure.

Costs/Expenses. When things are going well, every proposal seems like a good idea, and companies build elaborate spending structures. Then, if sales turn down, there's a profit and cash crunch from built-in spending patterns that are hard to change.

Development. Long-term success often hinges on the development of some product or process. However, development schedules are notorious for slipping (taking more time than planned). People have a tendency to believe that slips early or midway in the process can be made up later on. Unfortunately, that almost never happens. The problem is that when development schedules are created, time is generally allowed only for problems that can be anticipated. Of course, it's the unanticipated problems that kill us. Planners try to allow some contingency time for unknowns, but the pressures of business generally push for a quick completion. The result is that time for the unknowns is minimized.

People depend on making up early slips later on, and arrive at the end of the schedule woefully behind. That's often the first time top management hears there's a problem. Then the undeveloped product results in unmade sales and broken promises to customers. When those show up as poor financial results, people get alarmed, but by then it's a losing battle to catch up.

Customers. A company's image or reputation with customers can deteriorate for a number of reasons. Poor service or product performances are just two of the more common. It is an unfortunate truth that most unhappy customers don't complain; they just don't come back. Consider a dry cleaner whose service gets just a little sloppy. Customers don't leave immediately, they may come back five or six times, but their dissatisfaction builds up, and at some point they switch to another cleaner. People may start leaving several months after the service deteriorated, and the bewildered entrepreneur won't know why. By the time he or she feels the slowdown in business, considerable damage has been done.

The Importance of Timing

What we've really been talking about here are *time lags*. There's a lag between the time something bad starts to happen and the time it's recognized. If people aren't looking for problems, the time lag is much longer than if they're alert. There's another lag from the time of recognition until a corrective action is formulated. And there's a third lag between the time a corrective action is implemented and the time it takes effect. The three lags are additive; that's why it's so hard to recover from a missed business plan.

Here's an example. Suppose a company has a profit plan for the year to make pretax profits of $100 per month. Each month's income statement looks like this:

Sales	$1,000
Cost	600
Gross Margin	$ 400
Expense	300
PBT (profit before taxes)	$ 100

The annual profit goal is simply twelve of these months or $1,200.

Now suppose that in January sales materialize 10% below plan at $900 and continue that way. We'll assume cost remains the same percentage of the reduced revenue (60%). That means the income statement looks like this:

Sales	$900
Cost	540
Gross Margin	$360
Expense	300
PBT	$ 60

The business is operating at a profit level 40% below plan. It's tracking toward an annual profit of $720, a shortfall of $480. That probably isn't a life-threatening situation, but it's rather uncomfortable for management, who would like to catch up and make the annual profit forecast by year end. Suppose it takes four months for management to become convinced that the downturn is real and another

month to develop an action plan to do something about it. It's not uncommon in cases like this that the only thing that can be done about the problem is to reduce expenses. That generally involves a substantial cut in people. The costs involved in cutting people usually amount to at least a month of the savings (severance, outplacement, etc.). That adds another month to the effective time lag between problem and fix, for a total of six months. In that six-month lag, profits are behind by $240.

In order to catch up to the plan, the company has to recover to the planned profit rate and make up the lost ground in the remaining six months of the year. In this case, the arithmetic is fairly simple. Profits for the last half have to increase by $80 per month from the depressed level of the first half. Of that, $40 is to get back to the planned rate of $100 per month and another $40 is to make up the loss.

As is often the case, the only place to get the $80 per month profit improvement is by reducing expenses, which are budgeted and running at $300 per month. That's a 27% cut in expense spending ($80 / $300). A pretty deep slash.

But there's more bad news. In the short run, the company can't cut most of its fixed costs; it can only reduce flexible overhead items like people. Suppose, as is typical, expenses are about 50% fixed, things like depreciation on equipment and rent on buildings. Suppose the other 50% is people cost, which can be reduced through layoffs. That means in order to quickly reduce expenses by 27% the staff would have to be cut by about 52%.

But remember that all this started because sales dropped off by just 10%. Can the company handle 90% of its former volume with just under half the people? Probably not. That means planned profit performance was irretrievably lost from the beginning. Management never had a chance to hold onto its objective.

CONTINGENCY PLANNING

Good business planning management addresses the issues we've been discussing by doing things that minimize all three time lags. First, it sets up a system to monitor operations so that the discovery time for problems is made as short as possible. This involves watching market and financial results and carefully analyzing the implications of all changes. Second, it involves working out action plans in advance so that as little time as possible is spent in deciding what to do after a problem is recognized. And third, it involves having the courage to implement the action plan quickly and decisively.

Trigger Points

A system should be set up defining when the business is starting to slide into trouble. For example, management might establish an explicit policy that says if revenue is down by X% for two consecutive months, adjustments will be made to compensate for the losses created. Or if development slips more than one month behind schedule on project Y, a major rescheduling and reallocation of resources will take place within two weeks.

Trigger points are signals with respect to particular parameters that raise warning flags. It's often a good idea to have two sets of warnings: a yellow flag and a red flag. A certain drop-off in revenue says be careful, start looking for trouble and thinking about what to do about it. A specified, larger drop in subsequent

months says implement the contingency plans you've developed.

Trigger points should be developed for all of the ways a business can get into trouble: revenues, cost/expense, development, customer satisfaction, etc. Each area should have a measured level that signals alarm. Then, the parameters should be monitored regularly to see if they have slipped into their respective danger zones. Financial measures should be considered with each set of financial statements produced, preferably monthly. Other things should be looked at periodically.

When things start to go downhill, people often fall into something of a desperation syndrome in which emotion clouds and obscures reason. Waiting to see another month or two's results in the face of clear signals of trouble is a common way of burying one's head in the sand. People also tend to try fixes that obviously won't work because they're less painful than what really has to be done. For example, if a business downturn calls for a layoff, it's easier to try to pump up revenues by hiring a few new salespeople. Unfortunately, that usually just postpones the inevitable layoff and makes things worse in the long run. Eventually management comes to a realization that it has to shoot or be shot, but by that time the business can be in a deep hole.

ACTION PLANS

The second part of contingency planning involves working out action plans to respond to various problems ahead of time. Viable responses to downturns include reorganizing, reducing force, refocusing sales efforts, and changing product direction. These and other actions take time to think through and work out. It's important to do your agonizing in advance when you're not under a great deal of time pressure. Better decisions tend to emerge that way.

When people face business problems reactively rather than proactively, they tend to make fairly predictable mistakes. One of the most common is reducing the force in several small steps rather than in one large move. An extended period of repeated layoffs has a devastating effect on morale and productivity. It's much better to make one clean move that's over quickly than to drag it out.

Another common problem involves short-run thinking. Downturns generally involve profit shortfalls. Quick spending cuts that limit deterioration in profitability can hurt the company's long-term prospects. It's hard to make a proper evaluation if there's no time to do it carefully.

How Deep Is the Miss?

An important aspect of contingency planning involves evaluating the severity of a deviation from plan. Missing the plan can mean anything from revenue being a little less than expected to sales dropping by more than half or a major development proving unworkable.

Clearly, smaller misses call for adjustments to the existing plan. Changes in emphasis, reductions in the work force, or reduced hiring plans are appropriate.

Larger misses mean rethinking the entire business. Whole functions can change or be eliminated, while a smaller size can mean an entirely different approach to the market. Ultimately, a big-enough miss means the business isn't viable, and management has

to consider an exit strategy that focuses on saving as much as possible rather than continuing in business.

Addressing a major miss with an action plan for a minor issue can be worse than not having a contingency plan at all. Unfortunately, this is a common mistake. People are reluctant to admit that their whole world has changed, and that their businesses aren't what they dreamed. As a result, there's a tendency to try superficial fixes on major problems. That just postpones the inevitable.

Separate action plans should be formulated for small problems and major disasters, since the two require different thinking.

PROMPT IMPLEMENTATION

Contingency plans don't do any good if they aren't implemented in a timely manner. Procrastination is the enemy of effective crisis management. The discussion of time lags presented earlier illustrated how quickly a business can sink into fiscal quicksand. The way to avoid that is to have a series of contingency plans available with which to confront adverse conditions, and to have the conviction to implement them quickly when the appropriate trigger points are encountered.

The problem is that you're never one hundred percent sure when it's time to implement an action plan. When you're sure beyond a doubt that you need to do something, it's usually too late for that level of action. Moving decisively at the right time takes courage and an almost instinctive insight into the workings of your business and the market in which it operates.

THE PRESENTATION OF CONTINGENCY THINKING

Contingency planning in formal business plans is a delicate issue. Entrepreneurs want their audiences to know they've thought through all the things that can go wrong and have plans to deal with them. On the other hand, a plan with too much emphasis on potential catastrophe is likely to detract from the enthusiasm of readers and worry them unnecessarily. This can jeopardize the success of securing funding.

As a result, contingency thinking is best kept as a backup issue. That is, planners should have one or two complete contingency plans worked out and ready to present with appropriate visual aids if the audience asks about them. It's also important to be able to intelligently discuss the kinds of things that can go wrong and what you'll do about them.

Contingencies are very much a credibility issue, especially in new businesses. Someone who makes only one plan and depends on everything going right is viewed as immature and unsophisticated. A competent businessperson knows things can and probably will go awry and prepares for it.

Contingencies in the Plan Document

Most business plans don't include a section explicitly dealing with contingency plans. Instead, the issue is dealt with in the financial section. The most common practice is to include two or more financial projections. The base case projection is the one the entrepreneur considers most likely, and builds the plan on. Then you can include best and worst case scenarios. The worst case is, of course, one of the possibilities we've been talking about here.

The alternative scenarios are supported by written assumptions that show how the entrepreneur expects to deal with adversity or good fortune. However, the written detail is not extensive in the plan itself.

In addition to alternative financial projections, brief discussions of risk are appropriate in the marketing and operations sections.

The main purpose of these presentations is to show that the planner has thought about problems. It is *not to present* solutions in great detail as that might prove counterproductive by worrying the audience excessively.

PART

3

FINANCIAL PROJECTIONS

A SHORT COURSE IN FINANCE FOR NONFINANCIAL PLANNERS

The financial management of a firm deals with more than handling the company's money. In modern businesses, everything the firm does is recorded in a series of monetary transactions. The record of what the firm makes, sells, and acquires is primarily financial, backed up with verbal explanations of what's going on. Managements also use financial accounting systems to control most businesses.

Accounting systems produce several reports that are fairly standard for all companies. These basic tools of management are called *financial statements*.

Financial statements can reflect the past performance of a company or can be projections of future performance. Projected statements are sometimes called *pro-forma statements* or simply financial projections.

WHAT ARE FINANCIAL STATEMENTS?

A business's financial statements are numerical representations of what the business is physically doing. Keep that concept firmly in mind as we go forward. The idea behind these statements is to portray a picture of what's happening within the company and between the company and the rest of the world. The language used is dollars and cents, because almost every transaction is denominated in terms of money.

Financial statements paint a picture of a business organization's performance for two audiences, outsiders and the company's own management. Outsiders use statements to make judgments about the financial health and viability of the concern. They want to make such judgments because they're interested in either buying into the firm, lending it money, or doing business with it. Managers use financial statements to give themselves insights into how to run the company more effectively both physically and financially.

The idea that financial statements are designed to portray a picture of physical as well as monetary operations is important, because sometimes the idea produces counterintuitive results. That is, financial statements don't necessarily say what a person who is untrained in accounting might logically think they're saying. Here's an example:

Is Income "Income"?

Most people think of income as the money they're paid, and except for payroll withholding, what they take home. In other words, income means cash in your pocket or cash paid to Uncle Sam for your taxes.

One of the standard financial statements is the income statement. It starts off with the dollar amount the company has sold, deducts costs, expenses, and taxes, and winds up with a figure called net income. Most people would expect that figure to represent cash in the pocket of the business or its owner just like a paycheck. However, it doesn't mean that at all. Several accounting concepts get in the way and give net income a character of its own. We'll describe two major differences between net income and cash flowing into or out of the company. These differences are related to accounts receivable and depreciation.

Accounts Receivable. It's customary for businesses to sell on credit. When a firm does, it doesn't get money for product, but it receives a promise of payment at a later date.

Nevertheless, accounting theory says that the firm has done everything it has to do to earn the income from the sale. It's built the product, sold it, and delivered the merchandise to the customer. Since the work has been done and the customer has the product, theory says that the sale should be recognized in the financial statements. Therefore, the sale dollars are counted into the sales (revenue) line of the income statement, while the cost of the product sold is added to the cost line. Hence the difference between revenue and cost becomes part of net income even though the firm as yet has no cash to show for its efforts.

In fact, the firm probably has less cash than it would have had if it never made the sale at all. That's because, while it hasn't collected from the customer, it did supply product, and to do that it had to pay for labor and materials. Uncollected payments for sold product are called accounts receivable.

Depreciation. Another idea that seems strange to the uninitiated is the way fixed assets are handled financially. Suppose a company buys a machine for $10,000, paying cash at the time of purchase. Assume the machine is expected to last five years. How is the cost of the machine recognized as a cost of doing business?

Someone unfamiliar with finance might think the cost would be recognized along with the outflow of the money that pays for the machine. That is, that the company would have a $10,000 cost in the year it purchases the item. However, accounting theory says that to properly reflect the workings of the business, we have to match the cost of the machine with the period over which it gives service. Therefore, we *prorate* the $10,000 cost over the five-year life of the machine. That's done with a financial device called *depreciation*. If the *proration* is even over the life of the machine or asset, depreciation would allocate $2,000 to cost in the income statement in each of the asset's five years of life. (Evenly prorated depreciation is called straight-line depreciation.)

That convention creates a strange situation in terms of the relation between cash in the company's pocket and cost recognized in the financial statements. In the first year the firm spends $10,000 but can declare only $2,000 as a cost of doing business. In other words, it uses a lot more cash than the income statement indicates. In each of the subsequent four years the business doesn't spend anything on the asset but still gets to declare $2,000 in cost. So, in those years the income statement seems to say that the company spent more money than it actually does.

Clearly, these practices indicate that accounting income is conceptually different from paycheck income. Financial statements are concerned with more than just the flow of money in and out of the business. They also try to tell us something about what's physically going on. A depreciated machine, for example, can be assumed to be worn out. You might or might not be able to figure that out by looking at it.

Financial Statements in Business Planning

Financial statements are an indispensable part of business planning. All business plans should display projected statements for a minimum of three years. The first year is forecast in monthly detail, and later years are projected by quarter. If the business being planned already exists, the plan document should also contain actual statements for the last three years.

In a very real sense, financial projections are the heart of a business plan. The financial information tells investors how they can expect to get their money back. It's one of the first things financial backers look at. Potential investors also ask detailed questions about the assumptions that are behind the projections.

Entrepreneurs who present business plans to investors must be thoroughly conversant with what their financial projections are saying. A plan with inadequate financial projections isn't likely to succeed. Further, an entrepreneur who doesn't understand his or her own financials is in trouble.

In order to understand what financial statements are saying, a person has to know at least a little of their language and how they're put together. That can create big problems, because people who start businesses frequently have little or no training in finance or accounting. Financially unsophisticated entrepreneurs have traditionally done one of three things with respect to the financial portion of business planning. They've either done the job themselves, often with major errors; hired someone else to do the job but failed to really

understand the result; or used a spreadsheet computer program generally without understanding the mass of numbers produced.

Each of these approaches leaves the business plan vulnerable. A businessperson who doesn't understand exactly what his or her proposal is saying is likely to lose credibility when his or her ignorance is discovered, as it probably will be.

In the pages that follow, we'll present enough information about financial statements and how to project them into the future to enable an entrepreneur to do a credible job of constructing his or her own. Spreadsheet computer programs are recommended for doing the actual calculations, but they're only as good as your understanding of the information you input to them and the meaning of the numbers they crank out.

The Three Financial Statements

The three statements that are of interest to business planners are the income statement, the balance sheet, and the cash flow statement. There is a fourth, which deals with changes in owner's equity, but we won't be concerned with it here.

The income statement and the balance sheet are the basic statements that derive from the books of account. The cash flow is developed from the income statement and balance sheet.

We'll consider each statement in some detail later, but first it's important to understand the basics of accounting.

The Accounting System

An accounting system is an organized set of rules by which every transaction involving the firm is recorded in a set of records. The records are collectively known as the company's *books*. Books used to be kept in ledgers that looked like books, hence the name. Today they're more likely to be records in a computer. Smaller companies, however, sometimes still use ledger books.

The books are separated into a series of accounts. An *account* generally holds records of transactions of a particular type or those dealing with a particular part of the business. For example, a revenue account receives all transactions involving the sale of product to customers, while a fixed asset account receives records regarding the acquisition and disposal of equipment and machinery.

Transactions include things like selling product, buying inventory, paying wages, building product, borrowing money, paying taxes, and paying dividends—all of the things that firms do. A business transaction is recorded in the books by an entry. An *entry* generally means that we add or subtract a dollar figure to or from the balance in an account.

The Double-Entry System

Most accounting systems use the double-entry system of keeping records. Double entry means that each entry has two equal parts, called sides. Each side of an entry is made to a different account.

The double-entry concept is a little hard to grasp at first. You can get used to the idea by thinking of certain kinds of entries in which the two sides represent where we get money and what we do with it. For example, suppose we bought a machine on credit for $1,000.

That essentially means that we bought the machine and took out a loan for the purchase price at the same time. One side of the entry that records this transaction would involve adding $1,000 to the fixed assets account to show that the company now has the machine. The other side would involve adding $1,000 to a loans payable account to reflect an obligation to repay the money. The asset side of the transaction shows what we did with the money, the loan side shows where we got the money.

Here's another example. Suppose we take some of our cash and buy a piece of inventory, say, for $100. One side of the entry would reduce the cash account by $100, while the other side would increase the inventory account by the same amount.

The two sides of an entry are called debits and credits. In any entry, the total debit must equal the total credit.

Consider one more example, recording a sale. Suppose we sold an item to a customer for $200. One side of the entry would be to add $200 to the sales account, but what would the other side be?

The answer depends on the terms of the sale. If the customer paid cash, the other side would simply add $200 to the cash account to reflect that the firm now has that additional money. However, if the customer bought on credit, the $200 is added to accounts receivable to reflect the fact that the company is owed the money.

Every entry must have two equal or "balancing" sides. Thus it's common to say that correctly kept books are balanced.

Accounting Periods and Closing the Books

In business, time is divided into *accounting periods*, usually months, quarters, and years. Transactions are accumulated during each period. At the end of each period, all the transactions occurring in the period are totaled up, and the company's books are brought up to date as of the last day of the period. The process is called *closing the books*, and usually takes place in the weeks immediately following the last day of an accounting period.

Certain procedures are applied to the closed books, which generate the financial statements with which we began our discussion. It's important to understand that financial statements are associated with particular accounting periods. The balance sheet is associated with the point in time at the end of the period, while the income statement and cash flow are related to the entire period.

Remember that last year's financial statements don't actually say anything about this year or next year. They can, however, be used as an indication of what is likely to happen in subsequent years. Past financial statements are a little like a person's medical history. If you were sick last year, you're more likely to be sick next year than if you were healthy. However, a sick person can get well, and a healthy person can get sick and die. Similarly, a firm that was financially sound last year can fail next year if it's mismanaged or something dramatic happens to its business.

Stocks and Flows

There is a fundamental difference in the nature of the two basic financial statements. The income statement reflects *flows* of money *over a period of time*. The balance sheet represents *stocks* of money *at a point in time*.

The income statement deals with money flowing in and out of the organization. Revenues flow in while costs and expenses flow out. The difference is profit, commonly called net income. The balance sheet makes a statement at a moment in time. It says at this instant the company owns a particular list of assets and owes a particular list of creditors.

A set of statements involves an income statement for an accounting period and a balance sheet at the end of that period.

THE INCOME STATEMENT

An income statement shows how much money a company has earned during an accounting period. The most commonly presented statement is for a year. Monthly income statements can be added up to get an annual statement.

Presentation

Most income statements have a form similar to the following:

Sales (Revenue)	$1,000
Cost of Goods Sold	600
Gross Margin	$ 400
Expenses	230
Earnings Before Interest & Taxes	$ 170
Interest Expense	20
Earnings Before Tax	$ 150
Tax	50
Net Income	$100

Sales (Revenue)

Sales represents the total receipts from selling whatever it is the company is in business to sell. Revenue is another name for sales. Sales are generally receipts from normal business operations.

If the company receives some other money from activities outside of its main business dealings, that's usually recorded in another line called "Other Income." For example, a retail business might sell the store it operates out of to move to another. That sale of real estate would be included in Other Income, not in the sales line.

Cost and Expense

The Cost of Goods Sold (often abbreviated COGS or just referred to as "cost") and expenses are subtracted from sales to arrive at Earnings Before Interest and Taxes (EBIT). Both cost and expense represent monies spent to do business, but there's an important distinction between them.

Cost. Cost represents items that are closely associated with the production of the product or service being sold. In a retail business, cost is essentially the wholesale cost of product plus incoming freight.

In a manufacturing business, cost is more complex. It generally includes the cost of the labor and material directly expended in production as well as any peripheral spending in direct support of those efforts. Such peripheral spending can be substantial. It generally includes the cost of factory management and supervision, spending associated with the factory building like rent, heat, and light, and depreciation on machinery and equipment.

In a service business, cost includes the wages of those providing the services, depreciation on their tools and equipment, travel costs of getting to sites requiring service, and the cost of any facilities housing service operations.

Expense. Expenses represent monies spent on things that, although necessary, aren't closely related to production. These items include functions like marketing and sales, accounting, personnel, research, and engineering. The money spent in those areas tends to be related to the passage of time rather than the amount produced. Therefore, expenses are sometimes called period costs. Spending within expense areas includes salaries and wages, rent, and depreciation on equipment and facilities.

Depreciation. Depreciation is an important item that we will return to later. For now, notice that both cost and expense contain depreciation. However, it does not have a separate line of its own on the income statement. It is generally buried among other costs and expenses in each department. A detailed listing of spending by department would show a line for depreciation within each.

Gross Margin

Gross margin, sometimes called gross profit margin, is simply sales revenue less cost. It's a fundamental measure of profitability, getting at what it costs to make the product or service before consideration of selling, distribution, or accounting expenses. Gross margin takes into account cost but not expense.

Interest and Earnings Before Interest and Taxes

Most but not all income statement presentations show interest expense separately and calculate an earnings figure before interest has been paid.

Interest. If the firm has borrowed money, it has to pay interest on its loans. Such interest is a period expense and is included as a separate item within the expense category. It's important to realize that there's a big difference in the amount of interest that various companies have to pay. If a business is started with the entrepreneur's own money, we say it's *equity financed*. In such a case, there's no interest at all. If the entrepreneur borrows part of the money, the business is *burdened with debt*. We say burdened because of the required interest payments that come with the debt. A company financed with debt is also said to be leveraged.

Earnings Before Interest and Taxes (EBIT). Earnings before interest and taxes is an important line on the income statement because it shows the profitability of the firm's operations before consideration of how it is financed. The line is sometimes referred to as operating profit.

To understand the concept of EBIT, imagine that we wish to compare the performance of two businesses that are identical in every respect except one, the method of financing. Assume that one business is entirely equity financed while the other has a significant amount of debt. That is, suppose the entrepreneur borrowed half of the money required to start the business.

If we try to judge the two companies on the basis of the bottom line, net income, we won't be getting a true picture of the relative strengths of business operations. That's because the second firm will have its profit reduced by the interest it has to pay on its borrowed money. But the amount the entrepreneur had to borrow to get into business has nothing to do with how well the product sells, what it costs to make and market it, or how well the firm is being managed.

Interest is paid to investors who lend money to businesses. Dividends are paid to those who make equity investments. The problem arises because interest is shown on the income statement as an expense payment to an outsider. Dividends, on the other hand, come out of net income, which belongs entirely to the owners. Owners can pay themselves dividends or reinvest the money in the company. In any event the dividend isn't shown on the income statement. Therefore, a company with debt financing will look weaker than an otherwise identical firm that's equity financed regardless of how well the businesses are doing.

To get around this problem, we create the EBIT line. It shows the profitability of business operations before the results are muddied up by the method of financing.

Earnings Before Tax, and Tax

Gross margin less all expenses, including interest, yields earnings before tax. This is what the business produces before Uncle Sam and the state government take out their bite.

Tax. The tax line in the income statement means income taxes on the amount of earnings before tax. Companies pay other taxes like sales tax and property tax, but they don't show up here. They appear as cost or expense items further up on the income statement. Tax here just means income tax.

The statutory tax rate applied to earnings before tax doesn't always give the tax shown on the statement. There can be a variety of credits and adjustments behind the final number.

The tax figure also doesn't necessarily reflect the tax actually due. Some income statement items are calculated differently for tax purposes than for reporting purposes. Depreciation is a prime example. When the tax due is different from the tax shown, some of the tax is deferred. Current taxes can be deferred or previously deferred taxes can be due now. Some complicated accounting is generally involved.

The complexities of the tax system aren't usually too important in business planning, especially in forecasting. In planning, we generally just apply the statutory tax rates to earnings before tax.

Net Income

Net income is calculated by subtracting tax from earnings before tax, and is the proverbial bottom line. It is not, however, cash in your pocket. In some cases, it may be close to cash flow, but in others it's significantly different. It takes the cash flow statement to figure out how much the company is really making in the short run. We'll come to that later.

Net income is money belonging to the company's owners. Two things can be done with it. It can be paid out to the owners or retained in the company. If it's retained, it's called retained earnings and becomes an addition to the owner's equity in the company.

Inconsistent Terminology

Commonly used terminology regarding the income statement is far from consistent. The words *income*, *profit*, and *earnings* are generally synonyms, so you may see those on the various lines instead of the expressions used here. Profit before and after tax (PBT and PAT) are particularly common.

THE BALANCE SHEET

In simple terms, the *balance sheet* lists everything a company owns and everything it owes at a moment in time. Stated another way, it shows where all of the business's money has come from and what it has been used for. It is a fundamental principle that all the sources and uses of money must be equal.

The firm's money comes from people who have lent to it or extended credit in one form or another. Those actions create a *liability* on the part of the firm to pay the money back. Funds also come from owners who have invested in the company or let past earnings remain in use rather than drawing them out. Such investments of owners are called *equity*. In a loose sense, the firm "owes" its owners their equity investments. A firm uses its money to acquire assets, both tangible and intangible.

Presentation

A balance sheet has two sides. One side lists all the company's assets, while the other lists all of its liabilities and equity.

The Balance Sheet can be thought of as an equation:

$$Assets = Liabilities + Equity$$

On one side, we have assets, what the company has done with the money. On the other side we have liabilities and equity, where the firm's money has come from. If everything has been accounted for properly, the two sides must be equal. In other words, the equation must balance, hence the name balance sheet. The balance sheet is also sometimes called the statement of financial position.

A typical balance sheet looks like the following:

	ASSETS		LIABILITIES	
Cash	$1,000	Accounts		
Accounts			Payable	$1,500
Receivable	3,000	Accruals		500
Inventory	2,000	Current		
Current Assets	$6,000		Liabilities	$2,000
Fixed Assets			Long-Term Debt	$5,000
Gross	$4,000	Equity		2,000
Accumulated				
Depreciation	(1,000)	Total Capital		$7,000
Net	$3,000	Total Liabilities		
Total Assets	$9,000	and Equity		$9,000

Notice that total assets must equal total liabilities plus equity.

This illustration is somewhat simplified, but it will serve to explain the important features of a balance sheet. We'll start on the asset side and work through the entire statement.

Liquidity

Both assets and liabilities are arranged in decreasing order of liquidity. *Liquidity*, in this context, means the readiness with which the asset can be turned into cash or the liability will require cash. On the asset side, the most liquid asset is cash itself. Next, comes accounts receivable, because one expects that in the normal course of business receivables will be collected within a few days. Inventory is next because it is normally sold in short order generating cash or a receivable. Fixed assets are low on the list because they would generally have to be sold on a used equipment market to turn them into money. Similar logic applies on the liabilities side.

ASSETS

We'll consider each of the important asset items in turn, and present those financial workings that are important to a basic understanding of the ideas involved.

Cash

Cash doesn't mean just currency, although that is included in the definition. Cash mainly means money in checking accounts, that is, cash in the bank. Companies keep cash balances in bank accounts to do business and pay bills. They also hold it as a precaution against unforeseen emergencies.

Many larger companies hold a near cash item called marketable securities as well as cash itself. *Marketable securities* are generally short term government securities, which pay a modest return and are very secure. These can be sold for cash almost immediately if the need arises. Thus, they fill the precautionary need for cash, but earn a little interest at the same time.

Accounts Receivable

Accounts receivable represent sales made to customers on credit that have not yet been paid. Under normal conditions, these should be paid in cash within a matter of weeks.

Although there are significant exceptions, most companies sell on credit terms of approximately 30 days. Customers usually push those terms a little, and pay in 40 or 50 days. That means an average company will have about 45 days of credit sales in receivables at a time. That's (45 / 360 =) 12.5% of a year's revenue.

Documentation. When goods are shipped to a customer, an invoice or bill is also sent. Sending the invoice triggers an accounting entry. One side increases sales by the dollar amount of the shipment. The other side increases accounts receivable by the same amount. When a customer's payment is received, an entry is made increasing cash. The other side of that entry decreases receivables to reflect the payment.

The Bad Debt Reserve. Receivables are usually stated net of a small offsetting account called the allowance for doubtful accounts or the bad debt reserve. As the name implies, this offset accounts for the fact that most businesses experience some credit sales that are never paid. These are usually a small percentage of total sales. If such bad debts amount to more than 2% of sales, the company should seriously review its credit-granting policies.

The bad debt reserve is created and maintained by adding an amount equal to a small percentage of sales to its balance each month. This estimates credit sales that will never be collected, even though nobody knows which ones will prove bad when they are made. The amount added each month is generally based on experience. The other side of the entry that maintains the reserve is an expense, that is, a reduction to profit.

Writing Off a Receivable. When a receivable is known to be uncollectable, say, because the customer is bankrupt, it should be *written off*. Writing a receivable off means reducing the balance of the accounts receivable account by that amount. The other side of the entry normally reduces the bad debt reserve, which has been provided regularly each month for that purpose.

If the lost receivable is unusually large, it becomes necessary to take the other side of the entry writing it off directly to an expense

account, which is ultimately a reduction in profit.

Overstated Receivables. Profit reductions caused by uncollectible receivables are unquestionably distasteful to management. It is also frequently less than one hundred percent certain that a bad receivable will never be collected. Therefore, managers sometimes postpone writing off bad debts beyond the time that they should be recognized.

This results in a receivables balance that includes amounts that will never be collected. Such an account is said to be *overstated*. Anyone buying a company should look very carefully at the makeup of the receivables balance to be sure it's not overstated.

Inventory

Inventory is product held for sale in the normal course of business. In a manufacturing company, inventory can be in one of three forms: raw materials, work in process (WIP), and finished goods. A retailer only has one kind of inventory: finished goods.

Work-in-Process Inventories. The nature of raw materials and finished goods is self-explanatory, but WIP deserves a little explanation. As raw materials move through the production process, labor is expended to produce product. We think of that labor as being embodied in the inventory. For example, if in a certain production step a piece of wood costing $10 was worked on for one hour by a worker who makes $17 an hour, we would think of the wood as having a value of $27 when it emerged from that process. Thus, work-in-process inventory contains the cost of raw materials and the cost of an increasing amount of labor as it moves toward becoming finished product.

In addition to labor, most accounting systems reason that the cost of factory overhead (the cost of the building and equipment, heat, electricity, supervision, etc.) should also be embodied in product as it's produced. To effect this, overhead is usually added to the value of inventory as labor is added to the product. Thus, WIP inventory also contains dollar amounts for factory overhead as well as for labor and materials.

We'll discuss these ideas in more detail later when we get to cost accounting.

The categories of inventory may or may not be displayed on a balance sheet, but will always be available in backup detail if they are not.

The Inventory Reserve. Inventory on the balance sheet is assumed to be usable in production or salable, but it frequently isn't. A number of things can happen after it's purchased to make inventory worth less than the firm paid for it. Items can be damaged, can spoil, can be stolen (called shrinkage), and can become obsolete. Such losses diminish the value of inventory on the shelves but don't affect the value recorded on the company's books. Firms conduct periodic physical counts of inventory to discover shrinkage, but other damage often goes undetected until an attempt is made to use the product. Salability reviews to discover spoilage and obsolescence should be made regularly, but sometimes aren't. Inventory whose recorded, or "book value," exceeds its actual value due to any of these things is said to be overstated.

Balance sheet inventories are generally stated net of an inventory reserve to allow for a normal amount of problem material. The inventory reserve is conceptually similar to the bad debt reserve associated with accounts receivable. It is maintained similarly with a small addition each month whose other side is an expense.

Writing Off Bad Inventory. If inventory is discovered to be missing or otherwise damaged or obsolete, the balance sheet inventory account must be reduced to reflect the loss. The other side of the entry that reduces the recorded inventory balance normally reduces the inventory reserve. However, if the loss is large, it may be necessary to offset the reduction directly to an expense account, resulting in a reduction in current profit.

Overstated Inventory. When inventory is carried on the balance sheet at a net value that exceeds its true worth, it is said to be overstated. Writing off bad inventory or writing it down to its true value involves taking an expense in the income statement, which reduces recorded profits. Just as in the case of accounts receivable, managements usually try to avoid reducing recorded profits. That often means that they'll accept any rationalization to the effect that the inventory is holding its original value. Obsolete inventory can be a real problem in this respect. One can never guarantee that it won't sell someday, however unlikely that is.

Anyone buying a company should examine inventory carefully to be sure that everything included in the deal is current, in good shape, and entirely salable.

Current Assets

The first three assets on our balance sheet are called current assets. The term current means that in the normal course of business, these items can be expected to become cash within one year. For example, inventory is usually converted into product and sold, creating a receivable that is collected in another month or two. So we expect to see cash in less than a year. More complex businesses have a few other current items, but they are of minor importance compared with these.

The concept of current assets is important in financial analysis because it relates to a company's ability to meet its obligations in the short run. All of the money that the business receives from normal operations flows through the current assets accounts. In other words, money that isn't in current assets today may be a long time coming in. Money now in current assets can be expected to be realized as cash soon.

Fixed Assets

Longer-lived items are located below the current section of the balance sheet. Although many items can be in this category, the predominant one is usually fixed assets. Property, plant, and equipment (PPE) is another commonly used term for these items. The term *fixed* can be a little confusing. It doesn't necessarily mean fixed in place in terms of location, as a truck or railroad car can be thought of as a fixed asset. Rather, it simply implies long lived. It's important to understand the basics of fixed asset accounting and the concept of depreciation.

Depreciation. Depreciation is an artificial accounting device that spreads the cost of an asset over its estimated useful life regardless of how it is acquired or paid for. If the cost is spread evenly over the life of the asset, we say the depreciation is *straight line*. The idea behind depreciation is to match the flow of the asset's cost into the income statement with the delivery of its services over time. This matching concept is an important accounting principle.

In some cases, an argument is made that cost flows out of an asset more rapidly in the early years of its life than in the later years.

Depreciation can be structured to be heavier in the early years to reflect that idea. When the depreciation schedule is front-loaded like that, it's called accelerated depreciation.

Financial Statement Representation. Depreciation appearing on the income statement reflects an asset's cost. The same depreciation also appears on the balance sheet, where its cumulative value helps to reflect the remaining worth of the asset. Recall that every accounting entry has two sides. The entry posting depreciation expense to the income statement on one side posts the same amount to a balance sheet account called *accumulated depreciation*. Accumulated depreciation is carried as an offset to the value of an asset, so at any time the net worth of the asset is the difference between its original cost and its accumulated depreciation. An example should make the idea clear.

Suppose a firm buys a truck for $10,000 and decides to depreciate it over a useful life of four years at $2,500 each year. On the income statement, we'll see a $2,500 expense item each year, but each year's balance sheet will have three relevant numbers relating to the asset. These will be its gross value, its accumulated depreciation, and its net value. It's important to understand the pattern of the numbers over time. The accounts will appear as on page 143 at the end of each year.

Notice that each year's depreciation expense is the same. That's because the example is using straight-line depreciation. If accelerated depreciation were being used, the early years would have larger numbers and the later years smaller numbers. The total depreciation expense, however, would still be the same $10,000 cost of the asset. (We're assuming that at the end of its life the asset will have a zero salvage

INCOME STATEMENT			BALANCE SHEET	
Year 1:	Depreciation Expense	$2,500	Gross	$10,000
			Accumulated Depreciation	(2,500)
			Net	$7,500
Year 2:	Depreciation Expense	$2,500	Gross	$10,000
			Accumulated Depreciation	(5,000)
			Net	$5,000
Year 3:	Depreciation Expense	$2,500	Gross	$10,000
			Accumulated Depreciation	(7,500)
			Net	$2,500
Year 4:	Depreciation Expense	$2,500	Gross	$10,000
			Accumulated Depreciation	(10,000)
			Net	–0–

value. If a positive salvage value is assumed, we would depreciate only the difference between the original cost and that value. Otherwise, the procedure would be the same.) That's an important idea. Total depreciation can never exceed the cost of the asset. Also notice that accumulated depreciation grows each year by the amount of depreciation expense in that year, but the asset's gross value stays the same. The asset's true value at any point in time is approximated by the net line, which is known as the item's *book value* or *net book value* (NBV).

Disposing of a Used Asset. Net book value is not market value. The asset may be salable on the used truck market for an amount more or less than its NBV at any time. It's important to understand the accounting treatment if that occurs.

Suppose the truck in the example was sold after two years for $6,000. The firm would recognize revenue of $6,000 at that time. The cost associated with that revenue, however,

would be the truck's NBV at that time, $5,000. The difference would be a gain, or profit, on the disposal of the asset. That gain would not be part of operating income, because selling used trucks isn't the company's business. It would be recorded as an item of other income. Such a gain would generally be taxable.

The transaction recording the sale of the truck would remove both its gross value and accumulated depreciation from the books. The net of these, $5,000, becomes the used asset's cost.

The Life Estimate. Depreciation runs over the estimated useful life of an asset. It's quite common for things to last beyond that estimated lifetime. Assets still in use beyond their life estimates are said to be fully depreciated. Such an asset's gross value remains on the books entirely offset by accumulated depreciation. If it is sold after that time, there is zero cost.

Tax Depreciation. The government provides many incentives to business through the tax system. One of the most prominent involves depreciation. Depreciation is a tax-deductible expense. Higher depreciation in a given year means the firm pays less tax in that year because taxable profit is lower. That means that accelerated depreciation reduces taxes early in the life of an asset by claiming higher expense and lower profit in those early years. There will be lower expense and higher taxes in the later years, but the net effect is to defer taxes if accelerated depreciation is used.

Unfortunately the lower recorded profit in early years caused by accelerated depreciation isn't something management likes to see. It makes the company look less successful in the short run than if straight-line depreciation were being used.

To get around this conflict, the government allows business to use different depreciation schedules for tax purposes than for financial reporting purposes. The term *tax books* is used to mean financial records and statements generated using the tax rules. The term *financial books* or just book is used to mean the regular statements for financial reporting. Tax accounting is complex and results in an account called deferred tax on the financial books. A typical entrepreneur doesn't need to know much more about it than what we've just presented. That is, you should be aware that the issue exists and use a professional to do your taxes.

The issue tends to be relatively minor in business plans unless very substantial assets are expected to be purchased early on.

Depreciation Is a Noncash Expense. Depreciation is a financial fiction. It doesn't represent a current flow of money even though it's treated as a cost or expense. It has nothing to do with how an asset is acquired or paid for.

Consider the example of the $10,000 truck we saw before. Imagine that the company acquired the truck in one of two different ways. It could have paid cash upon purchase, or taken out a loan for the entire amount. In either case, depreciation on the asset would be exactly the same. Had cash been paid up front, there would have been a $10,000 outflow in the first year and no cash flow at all in subsequent years.

If the money had been borrowed, there would not have been an outflow in the beginning, and cash would have been required to pay off the loan and interest over some period of time. However, the loan payments would not have been related to the depreciation schedule at all, and the term of the loan is unlikely to have been the same as the estimated useful life of the asset. The loan would have been a separate item on the liability side of the balance sheet.

In short, cost recognized through depreciation has nothing to do with cost in the sense of money out of pocket. This very important idea is commonly misunderstood.

Total Assets

The things we've talked about so far constitute most of the left-hand side of the balance sheet. Their sum is total assets, collectively how the company has spent its money. Now let's turn to liabilities and equity.

LIABILITIES

Liabilities represent what the company owes to outsiders. Such obligations vary a great deal in their formality. Some liabilities are supported by detailed contracts and documentation, while others are created more casually by precedence and convention along with standard business forms.

Accounts Payable

Accounts payable arise when a firm buys something from a vendor on credit. The arrangement is usually referred to as trade credit. Payables and receivables are opposite sides of the same coin. When a credit sale is made, the seller records a receivable and the buyer records a payable. The bulk of accounts payable generally arise from the purchase of inventory.

When a purchase of inventory is made on credit, the arrival of the goods triggers an accounting entry to increase inventory by the amount of their value. The other side of that entry increases accounts payable by the same amount. When a bill is paid, an entry is made decreasing cash to reflect the disbursement. The other side of that entry reduces payables to reflect the extinguishment of the liability.

The Nature of Trade Credit. It's important to understand that trade credit isn't like buying something with a credit card. When you purchase on a credit card the seller receives its money immediately from the bank, which has loaned the money to you through a credit card company like MasterCard or Visa. You, the buyer, are then responsible for paying off the loan. The seller is out of the picture immediately. Further, the bank and the credit card company don't care if you don't pay your loan off right away as long as you make your monthly payments, including interest.

Trade credit is simply an understanding between a buyer and a seller, more commonly called a vendor, that the bill will be paid in full within a specified period.

Terms of Sale. The length of time allowed until payment is due is determined by what are called the *terms of sale*. Common terms involve payment within 30 days. Terms also commonly include a discount for prompt payment. Terms of *two, ten, net thirty* mean a 2% discount is allowed if payment is received within 10 days or the full amount is due if payment is received within 30 days. Trade credit is generally free, in that no interest is charged if the full amount is paid within the specified time.

Vendors become upset if their bills aren't paid in the times specified under the terms of sale. Delaying payment of trade payables is called *stretching payables* or *leaning on the trade*. If a customer abuses a vendor's terms, the credit privilege is likely to be revoked, and the seller will subsequently demand cash in advance before shipping goods.

Getting Trade Credit. Vendors don't grant trade credit to just anyone. Customers have to demonstrate a good credit history and financial stability. This is usually accomplished through a credit rating service, often called a credit bureau.

Unfortunately for beginning entrepreneurs, vendors are usually reluctant to grant credit to unproven start-ups. That is not, however, a universal rule, so if your money is tight it doesn't hurt to negotiate with your vendors about credit. Sometimes they're hungry enough for sales to take a chance.

Documentation. Purchases are normally initiated by the buyer's issuing a purchase order to the vendor. Goods are shipped along with an invoice (bill). These papers are the only contractual documents involved in most trade sales. The back of each form calls out the terms under which each party is willing to do business. They should match, but often don't. That causes some disputes.

Understated Payables. When we discussed accounts receivable and inventory, we were concerned that they were overstated. That is, the balance sheet purports to have more assets than the company really does. On the liabilities side, a financial statement reader is concerned about understatement; that is, that the firm has liabilities that are not reflected on the balance sheet. For example, it's possible for a firm to receive goods from a vendor, use them, and simply not recognize the transaction financially. Eventually, the vendor will demand payment, and the issue will be raised, but that may take quite a while.

Accruals

Accruals are poorly understood by most nonfinancial business people. They are an accounting construct to recognize expenses and liabilities associated with transactions that are not entirely complete.

A Payroll Accrual. The best way to understand accruals is to consider a simple example involving a payroll accrual. Suppose a company pays its employees every Friday afternoon. Assume it pays for work right up through payday. In other words, as of Friday afternoon all workers are fully paid and are owed nothing. Now suppose that the last day of a particular month falls on a Wednesday, so the books must be closed as of Wednesday afternoon. Graphically the situation looks like this:

Thurs Fri Sat Sun Mon Tues Wed Thurs Fri Sat

Payday   Payday
                        End of Month
                           Close

As of the close of business on Wednesday, the financial statements have to embody two things that aren't reflected by paper transactions. These arise from the fact that employees have worked Monday, Tuesday, and Wednesday, days that are in the first month but which will not be paid until the second month.

First, the firm owes its employees for the work done during those days, and that debt (liability) must be reflected in the financial statements. Second, the work effort that went into the month just closing should be reflected in the cost and expense of the first month regardless of the fact that employees will not actually be paid for it until Friday, which is in the next month.

If we were to recognize payroll expense when the cash is paid, the first three days' labor expense would go into the second month, and there would be no recognition of the liability at the end of the first month.

It's important to realize that this problem arises because employees don't submit a bill for their labor every day. If they did, accountants would just put Monday's, Tuesday's, and Wednesday's bills in the first month as if they were payables.

The way around the problem is to make up an accounting entry as of the close of the month called an accrual. The entry takes place in the first month. Its amount is three days' wages for everyone who worked Monday, Tuesday, and Wednesday. One side of the entry increases the accruals account on the balance sheet, and the other side increases expenses in the closing month. What we see on the balance sheet is the debt to the employees. It's important to realize, however, that the debt will be paid off in two days at the next payday.

Other Accruals. There are accruals for any number of things. For example, suppose a company is billed in arrears (after the period rather than in advance) for property tax at the end of a government fiscal year that's over in June. If the firm closes its books at the end of December, it owes the local government for six months of property tax even though it has received no bill and won't until June. A property tax accrual correctly recognizes that expense.

Planning for Accruals. Planners don't generally work in enough detail to estimate a company's accruals precisely. They usually make an estimate of a total average amount for a multitude of small accruals and work out the large ones, usually payroll, by looking at a calendar.

For plans for start-ups, it's generally acceptable to assume that everything is paid in the month it's incurred, so there is no need for accruals.

Current Liabilities

The two items we've talked about so far are said to be current liabilities, and are subtotaled as such on the balance sheet. Current liabilities are those that will need to be paid within one year. The concept is similar to current assets. Most of the money that flows out of the company in the normal course of business goes through current liabilities.

Notes Payable. There are often other items included in this category. *Notes payable* is a common addition to what we've shown here. A note is a short-term financial obligation supported by a written agreement, called the note. Conceptually, a note is the same as a loan supported by a written loan agreement. The difference is the term, which in the case of a note is less than a year. Sometimes vendors are reluctant to grant trade credit to a business without additional legal documentation in support of the obligation. In such cases, they may demand a note, making what would ordinarily be an account payable into a note payable.

Short-Term Loans. Banks often extend short-term credit to businesses under a variety of conditions. The most common arrangements are *loans, revolving credit agreements*, and *lines of credit*. These are virtually always expected to be repaid within a year.

The Current Portion of Long-Term Debt. A long-term loan is clearly not a current liability when it is first taken out. However, as time passes, there is a period during which the loan's due date is less than a year away. During that period the loan must be reclassified as a current liability. This is done under the heading Current Portion of Long-Term Debt to distinguish it from other liabilities that are short term all of their lives.

WORKING CAPITAL

Working capital is an important financial concept, especially for small businesses. It must be distinguished from the term capital used by itself.

The term *capital* refers to both the things that are bought with money and the money that buys them. The word capital used by itself generally refers to the sum of long-term debt and equity. This is the money that finances getting the firm into business and acquiring its long-lived assets. *Working capital* is completely different; it is the money that supports day-to-day, short-term operating activities.

Long-Term vs. Short-Term Activities and Money. A business can be thought of as doing two different kinds of things. On a daily basis, it buys inventory, builds product, pays wages, sells product, and collects receivables. Then, it takes the collected money and starts over again buying inventory, building product, and so on. These things can be thought of as a cycle that the business continually goes through to operate.

However, every once in a while, a company has to acquire the big items it needs on a long-term basis. These include buildings, machinery, computers, and other such equipment.

The later activity deals with long-term assets sometimes called *capital assets*. They are acquired and supported with long-term money known as capital. The former activities, the ones that are repeated virtually every day, deal with short-term assets like cash, receivables, and inventories. These are supported with money that is called *working capital*.

Supporting the Short-Term Activities. In order to do business, a company has to have enough money on hand to support an adequate level of its current assets: cash, receivables, and inventory. The larger the company is and the more it sells, the more money it needs for this purpose. In effect, it must open a bank account, buy the receivables balance, and buy a stock of inventory.

However, the amount required to buy these things is reduced somewhat by the fact that they all don't have to be paid for immediately. Specifically, some inventory may be available without immediate payment, because vendors are willing to sell on credit. That credit is reflected in the company's accounts payable.

Similarly, employees aren't paid every day—some of their wages are accrued. In effect, they lend the company their labor until payday. These offsets to the working capital required are essentially the normal current liabilities accounts.

Hence, the amount of money the company must provide to support short-term activities is the difference between current assets and current liabilities. This amount is known as *net working capital*, the word net reflecting the netting of the two amounts. However, common usage more frequently refers to this net amount as simply working capital. It is wise to remember this important definition:

$$\text{Working Capital} = \text{Current Assets} - \text{Current Liabilities}$$

Working Capital in Business Planning. For development of funding requirements for new businesses it's important to include a provision for working capital. *This provision is frequently omitted by financially unsophisticated entrepreneurs!*

People tend to list all the hardware they will need, and all the payments they expect to make to get started, but imagine that daily operations will fund themselves from sales. **They won't!** A new business must provide money to get current operations off the ground. Inventory has to be purchased and a bank account established. Further, money for wages has to be set aside until sales receipts start to come in. If the business is going to sell on credit, enough money has to be provided to keep going until customers begin to pay their bills. That can be a month or two (or longer) after the first sales are made.

CAPITAL: LONG-TERM DEBT AND EQUITY

The money spent on getting started, major expansions, and acquiring long-lived assets is called capital. Capital generally consists of long-term debt and equity, the owners' investment.

Long-Term Debt

A company's most significant noncurrent liability is long-term debt. It's common practice to refer to long-term debt simply as debt, especially if there isn't much short-term debt.

The nature and characteristics of debt were discussed at length in Chapter 4. It's a good idea to review that chapter now.

Debt is conceptually simple, but a lender may put serious restrictions on how a business is run.

Leverage. A business that is financed with debt is said to be *leveraged*. The word implies that when things are going well, using borrowed money can enhance the return on an entrepreneur's own investment. It works like this:

Suppose a business is started with a total investment of $100,000 and earns an after-tax profit of $15,000 in the first year. First, imagine that the invested money is entirely from the entrepreneur's own pocket. The return on his or her investment is 15% ($15,000 / $100,000).

Now, suppose the entrepreneur had borrowed half the money, $50,000, at an interest rate that nets to 10% after tax. In that case, profit would be reduced to $10,000 by the $5,000 interest paid (10% of $50,000) on the loan, but the entrepreneur's investment would be

only half as much, $50,000. Hence, the return on his or her investment would be 20% ($10,000 / $50,000). Borrowing money would have *levered* the return up from 15% to 20%.

In general, a business is able to produce a higher return to the entrepreneur's invested funds by using borrowed money *if* the return on the total amount of invested money exceeds the interest rate being paid on the loan. Otherwise, the effect is in the opposite direction and the return is worse using borrowed money.

Fixed Charges. The most significant concern about borrowed money is the interest charge. It's important to keep in mind that interest charges are fixed. That means they must be paid regardless of how the business is doing. You can't go to the bank and say, "Sales are down a little this month, do you mind if I skip the interest payment?" That can be a real problem in tough times. Many businesses have gone bankrupt due to fixed financial obligations.

Equity

Equity represents funds supplied to businesses by their owners. These funds are in two forms, *direct investment* and *retained earnings*. Direct investment by owners usually occurs at the beginning of a company's life, when the entrepreneur puts in money to get started. However, it can also happen later on. When businesses are in need of funds, owners often kick in more of their own cash.

The Representation of Direct Investment by Owners. If a business is incorporated, its direct equity investments are reflected in two stock accounts. One is entitled Common Stock and represents an arbitrary amount called the *par value* of each share times the number of shares outstanding. The other account is usually called *Paid in Excess* and represents the amount paid for the stock over its par value. The two together represent the total direct equity investment, that is, the money paid for the stock. It's important to understand that the par value is an arbitrary and largely meaningless number. If the business isn't incorporated, the two separate accounts aren't necessary.

Retained Earnings. When a business earns an after-tax profit, that money belongs to the owners. They can do one of two things, pay it out to themselves or leave it in the business. Earnings paid out are said to be distributed; those kept in the business are said to be retained. If a business is incorporated, the balance sheet will show retained earnings separately from the directly invested money shown in the stock accounts. This may or may not be so in an unincorporated business. Money retained or "reinvested" in a business is just as much the contribution of its owners as is money directly invested by them. That's because they could have taken it out and used it elsewhere if they wanted.

The *retained earnings account* is often misunderstood. Probably due to the name, people often think retained earnings represent a reserve of cash upon which the firm can draw in time of need. That isn't so. Just like any other invested funds, retained earnings are generally spent on assets shortly after they become available. The retained earnings account shows all earnings ever retained by the company, just as the stock accounts show all the money ever invested directly by owners. Neither is generally available as cash at any point in time, but tend to have been spent to build the business.

The Relationship Between Net Income and Retained Earnings. It is very important to understand the interaction between net income and retained earnings in the financial statements.

Net income (or profit after tax) becomes part of retained earnings and therefore part of equity at the end of the accounting period *if* it is not distributed to the owners. That means if no new equity investments are made and nothing is paid out to the owners during an accounting period:

$$\text{Beginning Equity} + \text{Net Income} = \text{Ending Equity}$$

If something is paid out to owners, generally as a dividend, the relation is:

$$\text{Beginning Equity} + \text{Net Income} - \text{Dividends} = \text{Ending Equity}$$

Beginning balance sheet figures including equity are those of the balance sheet dated at the end of the prior accounting period. For example, the beginning balance sheet for 2007 is the ending balance sheet for 2006. Therefore, 2007's beginning equity is 2006's ending equity.

Total Capital

The sum of long-term debt and equity is total capital. As we have already said, these funds are generally used to support long-term assets.

Total Liabilities and Equity

The sum of the right-hand side of the balance sheet reflects where all of the company's funds have come from and the obligations it has to outsiders and owners as a result of those advances. Total liabilities and equity must always equal total assets.

THE CASH FLOW STATEMENT

In the preceding discussion, we've made the point several times that income as reported in the income statement does not equal cash in the pocket of the business or its owner. Income includes things like depreciation, which is an artificial device designed to make the income statement a representation of the long-run health and condition of the enterprise. Businesses, however, are run with cold, hard cash on a day-to-day basis. Therefore, another statement is required, which supplies users with information detailing the actual movement of cash. That document is the cash flow statement.

The cash flow statement is often misunderstood. It shows a reader where the firm's money came from and what it was spent on during the period covered.

The formal name for the cash flow statement is the *statement of changes in financial position*, but people rarely use that awkward title. It comes from the fact that the balance sheet can be called the statement of financial position, and, technically, the cash statement analyzes changes in the balance sheet. Common usage involves the words *cash flow* or *funds flow*. Sources and uses or sources and applications of cash or funds are typical ways of referring to what we will call the *cash flow statement*.

Cash flow statements involve inflows and outflows of money. Inflows are usually represented by positive numbers while outflows are negative. It is common practice in finance and accounting to use parentheses ( ) to indicate negativity rather than a minus sign.

The income statement and balance sheet emerge directly from closing the books. The cash flow statement is constructed from the former two statements after they're produced.

How the Cash Flow Statement Works

The best way to gain an understanding of the role of cash in financial statements is to appreciate how the cash flow statement is put together from the balance sheet and income statement.

It takes two balance sheets and an income statement to build a cash flow statement for an accounting period. The income statement is from the period and the two balance sheets are as of its beginning and end. (A beginning balance sheet is the ending balance sheet of the previous period.)

The cash flow statement analyzes where money has come from and gone to by doing two things. First, it takes net income for the period and adjusts it for the items that make it different from the everyday concept of income as cash in one's pocket. Second, it takes the two consecutive balance sheets and analyzes the *changes* in everything the company has and everything it owes to determine how those changes have affected the cash balance.

Applying these ideas can be a little difficult if we jump right into a business example. It helps to first consider personal examples involving familiar assets and liabilities.

Example #1. Suppose Joe Jones has, after tax, income of $50,000 and spends $40,000 on normal living expenses during a year. Also assume that at the beginning of the year he had a bank balance of $10,000 and no other assets or liabilities. Further, assume that during the year, he buys a new car costing $30,000, financing $25,000 at the bank with a car loan. At the end of the year, there's $15,000 in the bank.

The cash flow statement lays out these transactions in a way that highlights where the cash comes from and goes to. The "where from" and "where to" are commonly called *sources* and uses of cash. The statement goes on to demonstrate that the beginning balance in the bank plus the net cash flow equals the ending balance in the bank.

The idea is conceptually illustrated by the following:

Cash Income	$50,000	
Cash Used on Living Expenses	(40,000)	
Net Available Cash from Income		$10,000
Use of Cash to Buy Auto		($30,000)
Source of Cash from Loan		$25,000
Net Inflow/(Outflow) of Cash		$ 5,000

RECONCILIATION

Beginning Cash Balance	$10,000
Net Cash Flow	5,000
Ending Cash Balance	$15,000

In this example, the net available cash from income is analogous to a business's net income adjusted for noncash items. This item is an important source of cash for Joe.

The next paragraphs are very important. It's a good idea to read them several times, making sure you understand what each line is saying.

Joe *used* $30,000 to buy an automobile. In other words, he *increased* his assets by $30,000.

In general, any time assets are increased, cash is used. He also *received* $25,000 from the bank when he took out the loan, which is a liability. In other words, he realized a source of cash of $25,000 by *increasing his liabilities*. In general, any increase in liabilities results in a source or inflow of cash.

It's important to keep the car and the loan separate in your mind. In our personal lives we tend to think of going into a car dealer with a down payment and coming out with a car and loan payments all in one transaction. To understand the cash flow statement, you have to keep the asset (the car) and the liability (the loan) separate. When he bought the car, Joe didn't just spend $5,000. He spent $30,000 and borrowed $25,000 at the same time.

Adding Joe's sources (income and loan) and uses (car purchase) together, we get his net cash flow. Next, we reconcile our cash flow calculations with Joe's bank account. Assuming all his money is in the bank, the beginning balance plus the net cash flow have to equal the ending balance. If it doesn't, something is wrong with the record keeping or accounting.

Example #2. Suppose at the beginning of a year, Sally Smith has an expensive car with a current market value of $20,000 and a $14,000 loan outstanding on it. At the same time, her bank balance is $6,000. During the year she has after-tax income of $60,000, but spends $62,000 on living expenses. In an effort to economize, she sells her big car for $20,000 and buys a small economy model for $9,000 in cash (no loan). When she sells the old car, she pays off the loan. Sally's cash flows look something like this:

Cash Income	$60,000
Cash Used on Living Expenses	(62,000)
Net Available Cash from Income	($2,000)
Source of Cash from Selling Old Car	$20,000
Use of Cash to Buy New Car	(9,000)
Net Source of Cash from Cars	$11,000
Use of Cash to Pay Off Loan	($14,000)
Net Inflow/(Outflow) of Cash	($5,000)

RECONCILIATION

Beginning Cash Balance	$6,000
Net Cash Flow	(5,000)
Ending Cash Balance	$1,000

In this case, Sally *reduced her assets* by selling the old car for $20,000. That sale was a *source* of cash. In general, when assets are reduced, the reduction is a source of cash. She also bought a new car, which was a use of cash. Notice that we've netted these asset-related transactions together to produce a net source of cash of $11,000 related to cars.

Sally also paid off her car loan using cash. In doing so she *reduced a liability*. In general, a liability reduction is a use of cash.

Notice that Sally's net available cash from income was negative simply because she spent more than she made this year. That added to the fact that she spent more than she gained on the cars and loan together means she has a net negative cash flow for the year. She accomplished that by pulling down her bank balance. If she didn't have any money in the bank, she could still have done it by borrowing.

These examples help to illustrate the ideas involved in cash flow because we're all familiar with automobiles as assets and loans as liabilities. In the context of business financial statements, things get a little confusing when assets include things like accounts receivable and liabilities that include items like accounts payable and accruals. In other words, it's not as easy to see that an increase in receivables is a use of cash as it is to understand that you need cash to buy a car. A decrease in accruals is also more difficult to fathom as a use of cash than is paying off a loan.

Cash Flow Rules

In practice, we don't have to worry about thinking through how cash flows in and out of every account. Four simple rules were illustrated in the preceding examples, which can be applied to any business's financial statements. All we need to do to analyze cash is to keep those rules in mind. The rules are that *changes in balance sheet accounts result in sources and uses of cash as follows*:

Asset Increase = Use

Asset Decrease = Source

Liability Increase = Source

Liability Decrease = Use

A BUSINESS CASH FLOW

Now, we can look at putting together a cash flow statement for a business. As we said before, to construct a cash flow statement we need balance sheets at the beginning and end of the period in question and an income statement for the same period. Consider the following example in which the sides of the balance sheets are arranged vertically instead of side by side.

ASSETS

	Beginning	Ending
Cash	$1,000	$1,400
Accounts Receivable	3,000	2,900
Inventory	2,000	3,200
Current Assets	$6,000	$7,500
Fixed Assets		
Gross	$4,000	$6,000
Accumulated Depreciation	(1,000)	(1,500)
Net	$3,000	$4,500
Total Assets	$9,000	$12,000

LIABILITIES

	Beginning	Ending
Accounts Payable	$1,500	$2,100
Accruals	500	400
Current Liabilities	$2,000	$2,500
Long-Term Debt	$5,000	$6,500
Equity	2,000	3,000
Total Capital	$7,000	$9,500
Total Liabilities and Equity	$9,000	$12,000

INCOME STATEMENT

Sales	$10,000
COGS	6,000
Gross Margin	$4,000
Expense	$1,600
Depreciation	500
EBIT	$1,900
Interest	400
Earnings Before Tax	$1,500
Tax	500
Net Income	$1,000

A business's cash flow statement shows cash flows from three different kinds of activities: operating, investing, and financing. *Operating activities* have to do with running the business on a day-to-day basis. *Investing activities* occur when the firm buys (invests in) or sells things such as fixed assets that enable it to do business. *Financing activities* occur when the company borrows money, pays off loans, receives more equity from its owners, or pays earnings out to owners.

Operating Activities. Cash flow from operating activities is reflected by net income adjusted for noncash charges and credits plus the changes in all current balance sheet accounts other than cash.

In the present example, the only adjustment necessary to net income is for depreciation, which has been shown separately on the income statement for convenience. Depreciation has been subtracted in the calculation of net income but does not represent a cash outlay. Therefore, it must be added back to arrive at a figure representing cash flow. Net income plus depreciation is sometimes known as operating income:

Net Income	$1,000
Depreciation	500
Operating Income	$1,500

Next, we analyze the current balance sheet accounts other than cash and classify the changes between the beginning and end of the period as sources or uses of cash according to the cash flow rules. Accounts receivable decreased from $3,000 to $2,900, providing a $100 source of cash because, according to the second rule, an asset decrease is a source. Similarly, inventory increased from $2,000 to $3,200 for a use of $1,200 according to the first rule. Apply the third and fourth rules to the changes in accounts payable and accruals to get the source and use shown:

Account	Source/(Use)
Receivables	$100
Inventory	(1,200)
Payables	600
Accruals	(100)
	$(600)

Hence, cash from operating activities is:

Net Income	$1,000
Depreciation	500
Net Changes in Current Accounts	(600)
Cash from Operating Activities	$900

Investing Activities. Cash from investing activities is simple in this example. The company increased its fixed assets by $2,000 during the time period, and that appears to

be all. This is reflected by the increase in gross fixed assets from $4,000 to $6,000, which is a use of cash according to the first rule.

Notice that we use the gross fixed assets account for this calculation rather than the net. The change in accumulated depreciation is the other side of the entry that put depreciation on the income statement. That depreciation is already included in the cash flow in the operating activities section so we don't want to repeat it here. Therefore, we ignore the change in accumulated depreciation and the change in the net fixed assets account.

Hence, cash from investing activities is:

Purchase of Fixed Assets	($2,000)

Financing Activities. The only financing activity present is the increase in long-term debt, a source according to the third rule. The company appears to have taken out another loan. Notice that there is an increase in equity, but that isn't a result of financing in this case. Rather, it represents the period's undistributed net income passing into retained earnings. Net income is included in the cash statement in the operating activities section and needn't be included here.

Cash from financing activities is:

Increase in Long-term Debt	$1,500

If new stock had been sold, it would have shown up as an additional increase in equity, and be reflected as a source of cash in this section. If a dividend had been paid, it would have diminished the amount by which net income adds to equity and would have appeared as a use of cash in this section.

The entire cash flow statement would look as follows:

Cash from Operating Activities

Net Income	$1,000
Depreciation	500
Net Changes in Current Accounts	(600)
Cash from Operating Activities	$900

Cash from Investing Activities

Purchase of Fixed Assets	($2,000)

Cash from Financing Activities

Increase in Long-term Debt	$1,500
Net Cash Flow	$400

RECONCILIATION

Beginning Cash Balance	$1,000
Net Cash Flow	400
Ending Cash Balance	$1,400

Conclusions. In this case, examination of the cash flow statement leads to some concern. The firm is quite profitable, earning 10% on sales, but still had to borrow substantially during the year. Clearly the fixed assets purchase had something to do with the additional funds required. One must ask if that expenditure was entirely necessary. Another real concern is the sudden increase in inventory. Does this mean that some of the existing inventory isn't good? If so, this could portend a big loss.

To summarize, the cash flow statement takes information from the income statement and balance sheet and displays it in a manner that highlights the movement of cash. There is no new information created. What is already there is simply arranged in a way that's more usable in the day-to-day running of the business.

You should always keep in mind the fact that it's cash that really counts in business, not net income.

In order to drive that point home, let's take another look at the business in the example we've just put together. Notice that during the year, it had to borrow an additional $1,500 from the bank (long-term debt). Is the bank likely to have extended that additional credit?

A bank might easily have been reluctant to advance any more money to this company. Notice that the firm's capital is in the neighborhood of 70% debt. That's far beyond the comfort level of most lenders to small businesses. The bank could have refused further advances, putting the company in a cash bind. If that caused it to fail to make its payroll, it could have been out of business overnight.

Yet the company is earning great profits in terms of net income—10% of sales. Take the lesson to heart: You can go broke profitably. Small businesses do it all the time.

RATIO ANALYSIS

People who make judgments about businesses by reading financial statements, including those in business plans, have developed some relatively standard methods to analyze information. The general technique is known as *ratio analysis*, and its use is virtually universal among financial professionals. Every entrepreneur can expect to have the financial history and projections of his or her business examined under the microscope of ratio analysis during the search for funding. It is therefore important that entrepreneurs seeking acceptance be familiar with the basic technique and a few of the more commonly used ratios.

Ratio analysis involves taking sets of numbers out of the financial statements and forming ratios with them. The numbers are chosen so that each ratio has a particular meaning to the operation of the business.

An example will make the idea clear. The *current ratio* is formed by dividing current assets by current liabilities. The ratio is significant in terms of the firm's liquidity, which reflects its ability to pay its bills in the short run. That is, how likely is it that the firm will run out of cash in the next year. Recall that most of the incoming money generated by normal operations passes through current assets. Similarly, most outgoing money normally passes through current liabilities. Further, the definition of current is that cash is generated or required within a year.

It's clear then that expected short-term inflows had better exceed expected short-term outflows if the firm is to remain solvent. Thus the current ratio, the ratio of current assets to current liabilities, had better exceed 1.0 or the firm will be in trouble. In fact, the ratio generally needs to be quite a bit bigger than 1.0, because if inflows and outflows are just equal, timing problems can be expected if the outflows come before the inflows.

There are numerous ratios that like the current ratio have special significance. We'll discuss nine of the most common shortly.

Comparisons

Ratios by themselves have some value, but not as much as they have when they're compared with other, similar figures. For example, a current ratio of 1.8 in a particular business might seem all right by itself but could be of concern if competing firms all have current ratios in excess of 3.0. In such a case, we would suspect that some characteristic of the business required great liquidity and that the firm we were analyzing doesn't have it.

Ratio analysis is usually conducted in the context of one or more of three comparisons. These are made with respect to history, the competition, and budget.

History. Comparison with history means looking at a ratio next to the same figure calculated for the same organization in prior periods. The idea is to look for trends. If a firm's current ratio is decreasing steadily the analyst asks why. Clearly, a comparison with history can't be done for a proposed new business.

The Competition. The performance of competitors and industry averages are good yardsticks for evaluating one's own performance. Analysts try to find similar businesses with which to compare proposals. Industry average data is often available through trade associations or investment analysts.

Budget. When actual financial performance is being evaluated, people always want to compare the organization's actual performance with that projected in the plan (budget). If your plan does get funded, you can expect your backers to analyze your business plan projections against actual results as soon as the latter are available.

COMMON SIZE STATEMENTS

The construction of *common size statements* is usually the first step in ratio analysis. We'll deal only with a common size income statement. The idea also can be applied to the other statements, but that's done less frequently.

A common size income statement is formed by stating each line item as a percent of revenue. The percentages are usually stated to the first decimal place and displayed next to the dollar figures. Here's an example:

INCOME STATEMENT

	$	%
Sales	$1,000	100.0
Cost of Goods Sold	600	60.0
Gross Margin	$400	40.0
Expenses	230	23.0
Earnings Before Interest & Taxes	$170	17.0
Interest Expense	20	20.0
Earnings Before Tax	$150	15.0
Tax	50	5.0
Net Income	$100	10.0

Each percentage figure below Sales is a ratio of that line's dollars to revenue dollars. The cost of goods sold ratio is generally called the cost ratio, while expenses as a percentage of revenue can be called the expense ratio. Net income as a percent of sales has a name of its own, return on sales, and is included as one of the ratios we'll look at below.

The first thing many analysts do is calculate the common size income statement and study the resulting figures. Each percent figure is a ratio that can be compared to similar ratios for history, the competition, or budget. In common size analysis, however, the most frequent comparison is historical. We look for trends in the ratio. For example, if marketing expense is increasing as a percent of revenues each year, we want to know why.

RATIOS

An explanation of a few of the most commonly used ratios follows.

The Current Ratio

$$\frac{\text{Current Assets}}{\text{Current Liabilities}}$$

The current ratio is the primary measure of a company's liquidity. We've already discussed its implications.

The Quick Ratio or Acid Test

$$\frac{\text{Current Assets} - \text{Inventory}}{\text{Current Liabilities}}$$

The liquidity measure provided by the current ratio depends upon the conversion of inventory to cash in a reasonable time. Inventory is particularly subject to valuation problems and overstatement. It also takes more time to convert to cash than other current items. Therefore, people look for a liquidity measure that doesn't depend on inventory. The quick ratio simply takes inventory out of current assets in the numerator of the calculation.

The Average Collection Period (ACP)

The *average collection period* represents the average number of days it takes the firm to collect its receivables, that is, how long it takes to get the money when it sells on credit. The ACP is also known as the DSO for days sales outstanding and the receivables cycle. The ACP is stated in *days* and is calculated as follows:

$$\frac{\text{Accounts Receivable} \times 360}{\text{Sales}}$$

Clearly, the longer it takes a firm to collect its money the worse off it is. If the ACP exceeds the company's terms of sale by more than 30%, there may be a serious problem with the firm's credit policies.

Collection problems have several important implications. The most apparent is that the firm may be granting credit to customers who lack either the ability or intent to pay. Another possibility, however, is that customers are finding something wrong with the company's product. Customer dissatisfaction frequently results in a reluctance to pay the bill.

The ACP represents an average collection period. A high average may imply that while most receivables are being collected promptly, a few are very old and are unlikely to ever be realized in cash. Such old receivables should be written off without delay or at least reserved through an addition to the Allowance for Doubtful Accounts.

The Inventory Turnover

$$\frac{\text{Cost of Goods Sold}}{\text{Inventory}}$$

Holding inventory costs money. Inventory costs include interest, storage, insurance, and taxes. In addition, the more inventory a company holds the more it has at risk of spoiling, becoming obsolete, or being stolen. Inventory turnover measures how many times a year the firm uses up an average stock of goods. A higher turnover is better in that it implies doing business with less inventory and lower inventory cost.

A low turnover figure can mean there's old inventory on hand that isn't being used. Such old stock should be disposed of quickly.

However, operating with too little inventory can create problems, too. Excessively low inventory causes stock outs, running out of raw material in the factory or not having the product a customer wants on hand. That results in work stoppages and lost sales. There's definitely a right amount of inventory somewhere in between too much and too little. The inventory turnover ratio helps to find that level.

The Debt-to-Equity Ratio

The *debt-to-equity ratio* measures the relationship between debt and equity within the firm's capital. It's generally stated as a proportion rather than as a decimal. For example, a firm with $25 in debt and $75 in equity (capital = $100) could be said to have a 25:75 debt-to-equity ratio.

A high debt-to-equity ratio is viewed as risky by investors, especially lenders. They want to see a substantial amount of the entrepreneur's own money in the business.

Times Interest Earned (TIE)

Times interest earned (TIE) measures the number of times interest can be paid out of earnings before interest and taxes (EBIT).

$$\frac{\text{EBIT}}{\text{Interest}}$$

Clearly, the more times earnings cover existing interest, the safer it is to lend the firm more money.

Return on Sales

$$\frac{\text{Net Income}}{\text{Sales}}$$

The return on sales (ROS) ratio is a fundamental indication of the overall profitability of the business. It gives insight into management's ability to control cost and expense.

Return on Assets (ROA)

$$\frac{\text{Net Income}}{\text{Total Assets}}$$

Return on assets (ROA) measures the overall ability of the firm to utilize the assets in which it has invested to make a profit.

Return on Equity (ROE)

$$\frac{\text{Net Income}}{\text{Equity}}$$

Return on equity (ROE) measures the firm's ability to earn a return on the owners' invested equity.

Categories

Ratios can be categorized according to the kinds of issues they address. The current and quick ratios are *liquidity ratios*. ACP and Inventory Turnover are two of many *asset management ratios*. The debt-to-equity ratio and TIE are *debt management ratios*. And ROS, ROA, and ROE are *profitability ratios*.

COST ACCOUNTING

Cost accounting deals with the financial records of complex manufacturing operations. It is one of the most complicated areas in finance and is the source of innumerable problems and misunderstandings between financial and nonfinancial management.

Standard Cost

Most cost accounting systems work around the idea of the *standard cost* of a product. The standard cost is what it is expected to take to produce the product under the conditions expected to prevail at the time the cost is developed. It contains three components: direct material, direct labor, and overhead. In other words, the total cost of the factory spread over all of its production results in standard cost.

This seemingly simple concept becomes vastly complicated because factories don't produce just one product. Most produce several, each with different amounts of labor and material. The question that complicates things is how much overhead is applicable to each product.

Direct Costs. Direct labor and direct material are straightforward concepts. They are the hands-on labor actually used to produce product and the material that physically goes into it.

Overhead. Overhead is more complex. It includes things like the cost of owning and operating the factory building, supervisory labor, and consumable supplies that are used up but don't become part of the product. It also includes indirect labor, things that people have to do to support the direct production process.

A good example of indirect labor is receiving and incoming inspection. Materials have to be brought into the factory and inspected for compliance with quality standards, but that activity isn't part of the fabrication process.

Planning Standard Cost. When a plan is put together for factory operations, a certain amount of production is anticipated. The amount of direct labor and direct material in each unit is generally known fairly accurately from the engineering makeup of the product. Therefore, the total direct labor and direct material costs for the planning period are found by multiplying the number of units planned by the "standard" direct labor and material in each unit.

Factory overhead is estimated for the period based on the planned production level. Some overhead items are fixed and some are variable with activity. The total factory overhead is then divided among the planned number of units to be produced.

Standard cost is the sum of the three cost components, materials, labor, and overhead, on a per unit basis. Total factory cost for the planned period is all of these rolled up at the planned production level.

Actual Production—Absorption

Overhead is usually applied to actual production along with one of the direct inputs, most commonly labor. Suppose total planned direct labor for the production period is 1,000 labor hours at $20 per hour for a cost of $20,000. At the same time, suppose factory overhead is planned at $60,000. Then, there is $3 of overhead for every $1 of direct labor. It is common to establish an *overhead rate* of 300% in such a case.

Then, during actual production, every dollar of direct labor that is spent on a unit is accompanied by applying $3 of overhead to the same unit. The overhead is said to be *absorbed* into the product in this way.

If everything goes as planned, all of the overhead spending is absorbed into product, which emerges at the anticipated standard cost.

Variances

Unfortunately things just about never go entirely as planned. The direct labor and material usage per unit can turn out to be more or less than anticipated, as can the rates paid for those inputs. Overhead spending, like spending in any area, can be more or less than planned. And perhaps, most significantly, the number of units produced can turn out to be more or less than expected because sales are up or down from plan.

When these things happen, standard cost no longer reflects the true cost of product. But it's important to know where the change in cost is. Is it due to excessive spending in overhead departments or just the fact that lower production levels require spreading the same overhead over fewer units? Perhaps labor was more efficient than planned, costing less per unit. But if that happens, all the overhead won't be absorbed and some will be left not included in product cost. What happens to those dollars?

These questions are answered by a complex set of variance reports that analyze production operations and pin down where actual cost is different from the planned standard. The variance reporting system can explain how much of the variation in cost that actually happens is due to differences in input prices, efficiency rates, overspending, and the volume of production.

Further treatment is beyond the scope of what we're trying to do here—to introduce the ideas and give a general understanding of what's behind them.

Cost Accounting in the Business Plan

Fortunately, cost accounting doesn't get too complicated in the planning mode. Trying to figure out how actual results differ from the planned results often gets messy.

In developing a plan, we lay out factory operations and select a level of production. Then, we forecast direct labor and material requirements and overhead spending based on that level. Next, we determine the basis for overhead absorption, very often direct labor, and allocate overhead to product types according to their use of that input. The result is a planned, or standard, cost per unit.

HOW TO MAKE FINANCIAL PROJECTIONS FOR YOUR BUSINESS

THE ROLE OF FINANCIAL FORECASTS IN THE BUSINESS PLAN

It's worthwhile at this point to step back and recall what business planning is all about. In most cases, entrepreneurs put together business plans to raise money. That is, plans are aimed at financial backers, usually lenders (banks) or venture capitalists. It's important to remember that there's a big difference in viewpoint between entrepreneurs and financial backers.

Money isn't the number one motivator for the best entrepreneurs. Financial success is important, but the excitement and independence of running your own businesses in your own field is the real driving force. In your eyes, the heart of a business plan probably lies in the concepts surrounding your firm's mission, its market, and its operations. Financial projections are necessary but not very exciting.

To a financial backer, however, your business is strictly an investment. The backer is not interested in glory or personal fulfillment or a new life as your own boss. You're interested in those things, that's why you're the entrepreneur. Your backer just wants the best possible return on his or her money with the least possible risk. *To your financial backer the heart of your plan is in its financial projections.* The rest of the plan is material that makes him or her believe the financial projections will come true.

This difference in focus often leads entrepreneurs to shortchange the financial section in the eyes of investors. If that happens, you'll be lucky if the reader sends your plan back for revision and amplification. If you're not lucky, he or she will just reject it, and you'll have missed the boat with that funding source forever.

Because lenders and financial backers focus on the dollars and cents, it's important to prepare competent, professional financial projections for your business. It's equally important to be able to discuss your financial projections intelligently when you make your personal presentation. You must be able to demonstrate a total understanding of the numbers. You will lose credibility and hurt your chances of success if you can't explain how your physical assumptions are reflected in your numbers and how one period's numbers flow into those of the next.

But I Don't Know Anything About Accounting

The importance of the financials to plan audiences may seem daunting if you have no previous background in finance or accounting. After all, people spend their entire lives studying finance and accounting; how can you be expected to learn enough to plan the finances for a whole business in a short time?

The answer is that accounting for the future is a lot simpler than accounting for the past.

In the planning mode, a great many simplifying assumptions are made that reduce the technical financial knowledge necessary to a minimum. If you understand what's in the last chapter and this one, you will be well prepared.

However, you do have to master this basic set of ideas. Your chances of success will be doubled if you have the contents of these two chapters firmly in your bag of tricks!

THE FINANCIAL PLANNING PROCESS

We'll outline the procedures necessary to construct a credible financial plan in the next few pages. We'll start with several principles and then move into a straightforward example.

Projecting Physical Activity First

It is a fundamental truth of financial planning that *dollar projections should follow projections of physical activity.*

This point is misunderstood or ignored too often. It's dangerous to forecast dollars without first thinking about the underlying physical activity. In the revenue area, that means beginning with a forecast of how many units of what products you're going to sell and at what prices. In the cost and expense area, it means deciding how many people you're going to hire and what materials, equipment, and services you will buy. In terms of the balance sheet, it means thinking through exactly what you'll want on hand and where you'll get the money to acquire it. In other words, the *financial* planning process starts with laying out a complete *physical* plan of what you expect to happen in the future.

It's possible to shortcut this principle somewhat when forecasting for an existing business, but the idea of forecasting things before dollars is crucial when planning for a new business.

An Existing Business. A planner forecasting the next year for a business that had revenues of $10 million last year can sometimes get away with just assuming a growth rate. If the business is to grow at 10%, next year's revenue will be $11 million, and a credible plan can often be made by just assuming that most variable resources will have to increase by about 10% too.

Doing that makes the physical activity assumptions implicitly. The planner is assuming that the mix of products and services sold last year will remain the same, and that the company can deal with the world of the future as it's presently organized. That can be a little risky if the things that may be changing in the environment haven't been thought through carefully. However, if conditions are relatively stable a decent plan can usually be produced that way.

A New Business. Using an approach like that for a start-up can lead to real trouble. For example, suppose an entrepreneur wants to start a manufacturing operation and builds a dollar-based plan on the following reasoning:

Gross margins are 50% of sales in similar types of manufacturing businesses, and expenses run about 35%. That leaves a reasonable 15% pre-tax profit on which he or her decides to plan. It is also known that factory overhead usually runs about 50% of cost and that a minimum-sized factory will have overhead of about $250,000 a year.

If these things are true, total cost is about ($250,000 × 2 =) $500,000 and sales have to be twice that or about $1,000,000 a year. So the business person builds a plan to sell a million dollars of "product." The plan may be a beautiful piece of work detailing everything that has to happen to make the business succeed.

The problem with the approach is that it puts the cart before the horse. Factory size is dictating what the business has to do in the marketplace, and there's no reason to believe the market will go along. A plan based on what has to be done to make the numbers work is a house of cards that will collapse in the first strong wind that comes along. Countless businesses fail because people think they can make the financials work once they get established. They can't, if the market basics aren't there in the first place, and a good-looking business plan won't make them appear.

In order to build a successful business, the entrepreneur has to think the other way around. The business planner must first decide what can be sold in the market and whether the demand will support a volume and price combination that makes a factory feasible.

The General Approach

A financial forecast is simply a projected set of financial statements. It's built up by addressing the statements one line at a time, starting with revenue. It's important to start with unit sales and dollar revenues, because that sets the level of activity for the whole organization. Once sales and the production required to meet those sales are established, the various statement line items can be developed one at a time.

The forecasting procedure works down the income statement through the cost and expense lines, stopping just before interest. It also projects the line items of the balance sheet, working through the left side until a figure for total assets is reached and liabilities are projected down to long-term debt.

The Interest/Debt Planning Problem

At that point, the planner is at an impasse. The next items required are interest on the income statement and debt on the balance sheet. Unfortunately, each depends on the other.

Calculating interest requires a forecast of the debt on which the interest is paid. Forecasting debt requires an estimate of equity at the end of the period. However, forecasting equity requires a projection of the period's profit. And that can't be done without a forecast of interest. It's a classic "chicken or egg" situation, and every financial forecast runs into it.

The problem is solved with a numerical approach. A guess is made at interest, which enables the planner to complete the income statement. Net income is then added to beginning equity to get ending equity. Since total assets are known, so are total liabilities and equity. That allows the calculation of ending debt, which completes the forecast financial statements. However, this is generally incorrect because it's based on a guess of interest.

The guess of interest is checked by multiplying *average* debt by the interest rate. If the calculated interest is different from the guess (it usually is), replace the guess with that figure and work through the procedure again. Keep going until the interest is consistent with the calculated debt. These instructions undoubtedly seem confusing. Bear with us. The procedure will be made clear in an illustrative example later in this chapter.

Getting Started: Projecting Physical Things—Then Dollars

When approaching a financial forecast, the first thing a planner must do is to pull together all the information already available.

Write down a list of everything you expect to sell. Next, write down a list of every functional department that will be required to do business. Finally, write down a list of all the equipment and inventory that will have to be purchased, including the facility to be occupied. Be sure the equipment is identified to the department, which will use it if you want to keep track of depreciation by department.

Now, take a spreadsheet and forecast all the physical activity you've listed, turning it into monetary projections as you go along. Let's look at a simple example:

EXAMPLE: A SMALL MANUFACTURING START-UP

Suppose a new company plans to sell a manufactured product. We'll lay out a number of assumptions about the operation to illustrate the forecasting techniques involved.

Assumptions

Pricing. The product will sell for $2,500 per unit.

Direct Cost. The direct cost to build a unit will be $500 in material and $1,000 in labor.

Inventory and Payment for Material Inputs. Assume the materials arrive one month before the product is completed and sold, and must be paid for two months after they arrive. Also assume finished product is sold immediately, that is, there's no finished goods inventory.

Labor. For simplicity, we'll assume all labor is paid at the end of the month in which it is done, that is, there are no accruals. We'll also assume labor isn't inventoried into work-in-process but is simply expensed as paid.

Cost and Expense Departments. There are just two departments, production (cost) and sales (expenses). General administration is done in the latter department.

In the cost department, the firm will hire enough direct labor personnel to supply the total labor requirement for production at a cost of $1,000 per unit if each person makes $2,000 a month. In other words, one person can build one or two units, but to build a third takes another entire person even though he or she will only be half-utilized. We'll also assume one manager making $3,000 a month in the production area.

In sales, we'll assume a single salesperson in the first half year and an additional one in the second half. Each makes $3,000 a month. There will also be a clerical person making $1,500 a month in the second half year and a general manager who gets $4,000 a month.

Each department will have a few representative expenses, including depreciation. (A real venture would have many more categories of expense.)

Cost Accounting. For simplicity in illustration, we won't assume that the company develops a standard cost of product. The production department's labor and other expenses will just be recognized in the months in which they're expended. The material cost of product will be recognized in the month in which the product is sold and the inventory is relieved. It will be charged to the production department at that time.

Fixed Assets and Depreciation. Assume that right after start-up, $60,000 of fixed assets are purchased. These are to be depreciated over a five-year life using straight-line depreciation. This yields a total depreciation cost/expense of $1,000 per month. Assume that 60% of the assets are in the production area and 40% are in sales so that depreciation expenses in those departments are $600 and $400 per month, respectively.

The Owner's Contribution and the Opening Balance Sheet. We'll assume that the entrepreneur wants to contribute $100,000 of his own cash to this venture and borrow the rest. We'll also assume that he has enough collateral to borrow several hundred thousand additional dollars.

He therefore proposes to open a business bank account with his $100,000 before doing anything else. That means the opening balance sheet will have only two entries: Cash and Equity, both of $100,000.

The Bank Loan. If the proposal is approved, the business will draw cash out of the bank, increasing its long-term debt as the year goes by. It will pay interest on the outstanding amount of the loan each month at an annual rate of 10%.

Calculation Procedures

In the following illustration we'll forecast the business's financial statements for its first twelve months. The procedure details exactly how to lay out a financial forecast from the assumptions that have been made above. Keep in mind that the financial forecast follows the physical forecast.

Notice that when *flow* items from the income statement (such as revenue) are forecast, a full year column is added. That's just the sum of the twelve months. For the *stock* items of the balance sheet that isn't done because the forecast at the end of the twelfth month is simply the forecast for year end.

Revenue, Collections, and Accounts Receivable

We begin by laying out product sales in units by month along a spreadsheet line. Then multiply by price to get monthly revenues on the next line. We lag revenues two months for collections. Then *accumulate* sales less collections for accounts receivable (A/R).

Accumulate means start with the first column in which there is activity; add the amount in sales and subtract the amount in collections. The result is the amount in receivables. Then carry that amount forward, adding the next period's sales and subtracting its collections. For example, in the fourth column, start with the A/R balance in period three, $10,000. Add sales of $7,500 and subtract collections of $2,500 to get the fourth month's receivables of $15,000. Carry this balance into the fifth column. Keep working to the right.

Work through the following figures and be sure you can calculate every number.

MONTHS

ITEM	1	2	3	4	5	6	7
Units sold	1	3	3	4	4	5	
Sales $ @ $2,500	$2,500	$ 7,500	$ 7,500	$10,000	$10,000	$12,500	
Collections			$ 2,500	$ 7,500	$ 7,500	10,000	
Accounts Receivable	$2,500	$10,000	$15,000	$17,500	$20,000	$22,500	

ITEM	8	9	10	11	12	Total Year
Units sold	5	7	9	10	11	62
Sales $ @ $2,500	$12,500	$17,500	$22,500	$25,000	$27,500	$155,000
Collections	$10,000	$12,500	$12,500	$17,500	$22,500	$102,500
Accounts Receivable	$25,000	$30,000	$40,000	$47,500	$52,500	

This procedure has given us the revenue line in the income statement and the accounts receivable line in the balance sheet as well as an estimate of when collections will occur.

Cash

Our assumption about cash on hand will be very simple. We'll assume the business keeps $5,000 in its checking account on which to operate.

Inventory and Accounts Payable

Additions to raw material inventory are $500 per unit sold in the month prior to the sale. Removals from inventory are the same amounts in the month of sale. Figure the inventory balance in each month by accumulating the additions less the removals from left to right across the page.

Accounts payable increases with the other side of the entry that adds to inventory, but

ITEM	1	2	3	4	5	6	7
Units sold		1	3	3	4	4	5
Inventory							
Adds	$500	$1,500	$1,500	$2,000	$2,000	$2,500	$2,500
Removals		$500	$1,500	$1,500	$2,000	$2,000	$2,500
Balance	$500	$1,500	$1,500	$2,000	$2,000	$2,500	$2,500
Accounts Payable							
Adds	$500	$1,500	$1,500	$2,000	$2,000	$2,500	$2,500
Removals			$500	$1,500	$1,500	$2,000	$2,000
Balance	$500	$1,500	$2,500	$3,000	$3,500	$4,000	$4,500

ITEM	8	9	10	11	12	13
Units sold	5	7	9	10	11	11
Inventory						
Adds	$3,500	$4,500	$5,000	$5,500	$5,500	
Removals	$2,500	$3,500	$4,500	$5,000	$5,500	
Balance	$3,500	$4,500	$5,000	$5,500	$5,500	
Accounts Payable						
Adds	$3,500	$4,500	$5,000	$5,500	$5,500	
Removals	$2,500	$2,500	$3,500	$4,500	$5,000	
Balance	$5,500	$7,500	$9,000	$10,000	$10,500	

it doesn't get relieved until the bill is paid. We've assumed that's two months later. Accumulate from left to right for the payables balance as shown on page 168.

Fixed Assets and Depreciation

The entire equipment list amounts to $60,000. For simplicity, we're assuming the assets all have five-year (60-month) lives. Then, depreciation will be $1,000 per month as an expense and as an addition to accumulated depreciation. The fixed assets accounts will appear as shown below.

Costs and Expenses

Costs and expenses are incurred and projected by department. The most effective way to project expenses is to lay out a spreadsheet with time periods across the top and expense categories down the left side.

Step one is to project headcount across the first few rows and then develop wage costs by applying estimated salaries to the headcount figures. In this example, we'll ignore complications like fringe benefits and overtime. They're handled by adding additional lines.

Next, project individual expense line items by thinking about what goes on in the department. Travel is a good example. Assume a short trip costs about $300. We wouldn't expect too many in Production, maybe two in a year for the manager to visit suppliers. In sales, on the other hand, calling on customers is the name of the game, so travel costs will be a lot higher. Estimate how many trips each salesperson will make each month and multiply by the number of salespeople on board. Then, multiply by the cost per trip, remembering that a sales trip is probably more expensive than the production manager's trip, because salespeople may be expected to entertain customers. We'll estimate $400 each for sales trip and assume each salesperson makes two a month.

Other expenses are straightforward. Rent is allocated to departments based on the space they occupy. The phone bill is based on usage. Here again, Sales is going to be a lot higher than Production. Think through each item and decide how spending patterns can be expected to run for that department.

We'll show the cost of direct materials in the production department by charging a cost line when inventory is relieved as product is sold.

ITEM	1	2	3	4	5	6	7
Fixed Assets							
Gross	$60,000	$60,000	$60,000	$60,000	$60,000	$60,000	$60,000
Accumulated Depreciation	$ 1,000	$ 2,000	$ 3,000	$4,000	$5,000	$6,000	$7,000
Net	$59,000	$58,000	$57,000	$56,000	$55,000	$54,000	$53,000

ITEM	8	9	10	11	12
Gross	$60,000	$60,000	$60,000	$60,000	$60,000
Accumulated Depreciation	$ 8,000	$ 9,000	$10,000	$11,000	$12,000
Net	$52,000	$51,000	$50,000	$49,000	$48,000

In other words, the other side of the entry that removes materials from inventory goes into production cost.

This kind of thinking yields the following expense projections for the production and sales departments.

PRODUCTION DEPARTMENT

ITEM	1	2	3	4	5	6	7
People							
Labor	1	1	2	2	2	2	3
Manager	1	1	1	1	1	1	1
People $							
Labor	$2,000	$2,000	$4,000	$4,000	$4,000	$4,000	$6,000
Manager	$3,000	$3,000	$3,000	$3,000	$3,000	$3,000	$3,000
Total Wages	$5,000	$5,000	$7,000	$7,000	$7,000	$7,000	$9,000
Other Expenses							
Rent	$2,000	$2,000	$2,000	$2,000	$2,000	$2,000	$2,000
Travel		300					
Depreciation	600	600	600	600	600	600	600
Supplies	100	100	100	100	100	100	100
Phone	50	50	50	50	50	50	50
Labor and Overhead Cost	$7,750	$8,050	$9,750	$9,750	$9,750	$9,750	$11,750
Materials		$500	$1,500	$1,500	$2,000	$2,000	$2,500
Total Cost	$7,750	$8,550	$11,250	$11,250	$11,750	$11,750	$14,250

ITEM	8	9	10	11	12	Year
Labor	3	4	5	5	6	
Manager	1	1	1	1	1	1
People $						
Labor	$6,000	$8,000	$10,000	$10,000	$12,000	$72,000
Manager	$3,000	$3,000	$3,000	$3,000	$3,000	$36,000
Total Wages	$9,000	$11,000	$13,000	$13,000	$15,000	$108,000
Other Expenses						
Rent	$2,000	$2,000	$2,000	$2,000	$2,000	$24,000
Travel				300		600
Depreciation	600	600	600	600	600	7,200
Supplies	100	100	100	100	100	1,200
Phone	50	50	50	50	50	600
Labor and Overhead Cost	$11,750	$13,750	$15,750	$16,050	$17,750	$141,600
Material	$2,500	$3,500	$4,500	$5,000	$5,500	$31,000
Total Cost	$14,250	$17,250	$20,250	$21,050	$23,250	$172,600

SALES DEPARTMENT

ITEM	1	2	3	4	5	6	7
People							
Sales	1	1	1	1	1	1	2
Manager	1	1	1	1	1	1	1
Clerical							1
People $							
Sales	$3,000	$3,000	$3,000	$3,000	$3,000	$3,000	$6,000
Manager	$4,000	$4,000	$4,000	$4,000	$4,000	$4,000	$4,000
Clerical							$1,500
Total Wages	$7,000	$7,000	$7,000	$7,000	$7,000	$7,000	$11,500
Other Expenses							
Rent	$1,000	$1,000	$1,000	$1,000	$1,000	$1,000	$1,000
Travel	800	800	800	800	800	800	1,600
Depreciation	400	400	400	400	400	400	400
Supplies	100			100			
Phone	50	50	50	50	50	50	100
Total Expenses	$9,350	$9,250	$9,250	$9,350	$9,250	$9,250	$14,600

ITEM	8	9	10	11	12	Year
People						
Sales	2	2	2	2	2	
Manager	1	1	1	1	1	
Clerical	1	1	1	1	1	
People $						
Sales	$6,000	$6,000	$6,000	$6,000	$6,000	$54,000
Manager	$4,000	$4,000	$4,000	$4,000	$4,000	$48,000
Clerical	$1,500	$1,500	$1,500	$1,500	$1,500	$9,000
Total Wages	$11,500	$11,500	$11,500	$11,500	$11,500	$111,000
Other Expenses						
Rent	$1,000	$1,000	$1,000	$1,000	$1,000	$12,000
Travel	1,600	1,600	1,600	1,600	1,600	14,400
Depreciation	400	400	400	400	400	4,800
Supplies		100				300
Phone	100	100	100	100	100	900
Total Expenses	$14,600	$14,700	$14,600	$14,600	$14,600	$143,400

The Income Statement and Balance Sheet

Now that we have monthly detail for all of our financial statement line items before interest on the income statement and before debt on the balance sheet, we can construct a projected set of incomplete monthly statements. In an actual business plan, you would indeed do that for the first projected year, switching to quarterly projections in the second and third years.

For purposes of illustration, however, we will go to an annual format at this point, using the year totals developed above for income statement items and the year end figures for balance sheet items. Let's write out the information that we have at this point in statement format, showing balance sheets for the beginning and end of the year.

Notice that we're projecting a loss at EBIT in the first year. This isn't unusual. We'll discuss it more later.

Also notice that we don't have a value for interest because we don't know how much debt to base it on. Therefore we don't have anything below interest on the income statement.

We also don't have a number for ending debt and equity on the balance sheet. We do, however, know the value of total liabilities and equity because it must be equal to total assets at the end of the year.

FORECASTED FINANCIAL STATEMENTS

Balance Sheet

Assets	Beginning	Ending
Cash	$100,000	$5,000
Accounts Receivable		52,500
Inventory		5,500
Current Assets	$100,000	$63,000
Fixed Assets		
Gross		$60,000
Accumulated Depreciation		(12,000)
Net		$48,000
Total Assets	$100,000	$111,000
Liabilities		
Accounts Payable		$10,500
Debt	0	?
Equity	$100,000	?
Total Liabilities and Equity	$100,000	$111,000

Income Statement

Sales	$155,000
Cost	172,600
Gross Margin	($17,600)
Expense	$143,400
EBIT	($161,000)
Interest	?
Earnings Before Tax	?
Tax	?
Earnings After Tax (Net Income)	?

If we knew earnings after tax (EAT), we could add it to beginning equity to get ending equity. With that we could compute debt. But we don't have EAT because we don't know interest. We need interest to get debt and debt to get interest!

We solve this dilemma by taking a guess at interest, completing the financial statements, and then checking to see if our guess was right. If not, we guess again, using the result of the first calculation.

In this illustration, we'll begin by guessing at an interest expense of $15,000. First, complete the income statement using that figure:

EBIT	($161,000)
Interest	15,000
EBT	($176,000)
Tax	0
EAT	($176,000)

Now, complete the balance sheet using this loss figure. The loss is subtracted from beginning equity, reducing it to a deficit amount. That is, $100,000 minus $176,000 equals ($76,000), the ending equity. Then, the total liabilities and equity of $111,000 plus the deficit in equity of $76,000 less the accounts payable of $10,500 gives an ending debt of $176,500.

LIABILITIES

	Beginning	Ending
Accounts Payable		$10,500
Debt		176,500
Equity	$100,000	($76,000)
Total Liabilities and Equity	$100,000	$111,000

Check the Guess. Assume that this debt was drawn more or less evenly during the year. Then, the interest charge would be based on an average balance between zero debt in the beginning and $176,500 at the end. Recall that the interest rate was 10%.

$$\frac{(0 + \$176,500)}{2} \times .10 = \$8,825$$

It's apparent that this interest figure does not equal the guess of $15,000.

Recalculate. Guess at interest again using the $8,825 just calculated and go through the procedure again. First, the income statement:

EBIT	($161,000)
Interest	8,825
EBT	($169,825)
Tax	0
EAT	($169,825)

Then, the Balance Sheet:

LIABILITIES

	Beginning	Ending
Accounts Payable		$10,500
Debt		170,325
Equity	$100,000	($69,825)
Total Liabilities and Equity	$100,000	$111,000

Check the Second Guess. Average debt and the interest charge are:

$$\frac{(0 + \$170,325)}{2} \times .10 = \$8,516$$

This is close enough for planning purposes. To get even closer, you can guess again with $8,516, but it isn't necessary.

The Final Statements. The complete forecasted statements are as follows:

FORECASTED FINANCIAL STATEMENT

Balance Sheet

Assets	Beginning	Ending
Cash	$100,000	$5,000
Accounts Receivable		52,500
Inventory		5,500
Current Assets	$100,000	$63,000
Fixed Assets		
Gross		$60,000
Accumulated Depreciation		(12,000)
Net		$48,000
Total Assets	$100,000	$111,000
Liabilities		
Accounts Payable		$10,500
Debt	0	$170,325
Equity	$100,000	($69,825)
Total Liabilities and Equity	$100,000	$111,000

Income Statement

Sales	$155,000
Cost	172,600
Gross Margin	($17,600)
Expense	$143,400
EBIT	($161,000)
Interest	$8,825
Earnings Before Tax	($169,825)
Tax	0
Earnings After Tax	($169,825)

The Forecasted Cash Flow Statement

The cash flow statement can be developed from these statements using the method developed in Chapter 14. The procedure is straightforward. The resulting statement is as follows:

FORECASTED CASH FLOW STATEMENT

Cash from Operating Activities	
Net Income	($169,825)
Depreciation	12,000
Increase in A/R	(52,500)
Increase in Inventory	(5,500)
Increase in Payables	10,500
	($205,325)
Cash from Investing Activities	
Increase in Fixed Assets	($60,000)
Cash from Financing Activities	
Increase in Debt	$170,325
Net Cash Flow	($95,000)

RECONCILIATION

Beginning Cash	$100,000
Net Cash Flow	(95,000)
Ending Cash	$5,000

A Few Words About the Example

The business in the example seems to be doing very poorly in its first forecasted year. However, that may be what is expected. Manufacturing ventures often take a while to turn a profit. In the meantime, equipment and facilities have to be acquired and an investment in marketing has to be made to contact customers and win them over. These things lead to a big cash drain before profitability is achieved.

Remember that the entrepreneur or equity investor is ultimately at risk for all this money. That's why it's hard to get venture capital funding.

PART

4

APPENDICES

A SELF-TEST TO SEE IF YOU'RE CUT OUT TO BE IN SMALL BUSINESS

This appendix deals with self-evaluation. Read it carefully and take its message to heart; it may save you a lot of money and heartache. At a minimum, it will help to prepare you for the problems ahead as you launch your business.

CHARACTERISTICS OF AN ENTREPRENEUR

Would you rather be an entrepreneur or an employee? If asked that question, most people respond that they'd rather own their own business. In fact, the majority don't even think about it. They respond immediately as if being on their own was a lifelong dream. The result is troubling, because only a small fraction of the population ever try it on their own. If so many would like to be entrepreneurs, why do so few ever try?

The reason lies in people's perceptions of the life of a business owner. The mental image entrepreneurship conjures up in most minds isn't consistent with reality.

People imagine being business owners who relax behind oversized desks at the top of successful organizations and enjoy independence, prestige, flexible hours, and wealth. They compare that with their humdrum jobs and it looks pretty good. Reality is that the picture just described is the end result of entrepreneurship only when it's extraordinarily successful. And even then the road along the way is arduous.

Entrepreneurship generally means at least several years of long hours, incredibly hard work, financial sacrifice, and STRESS. And after all that, there's no guarantee of success.

People who go into their own businesses focused on the trappings or results of success are likely to fail. They usually don't have the personal characteristics it takes to weather the years of struggle necessary to get to that end. This appendix is intended to help you make sure you haven't fallen into the trap of projecting yourself to a successful conclusion without considering what you'll have to go through to get there.

Don't go into small business just because you want that end result. Go into it because you're fascinated and excited by the work and challenge you'll encounter along the way, because the lifestyle appeals to you, and because you're obsessed with the operation of the business you're going to run.

QUESTIONS FOR SELF-EXAMINATION

Over the years researchers have identified a number of characteristics that indicate the type of person who will be better suited to entrepreneurship. In what follows, the findings are presented in the form of a series of multiple-choice questions. Your responses to these questions will tend to indicate whether you have a background and personality consistent with a high probability of success in running your own business.

The questions are designed to stimulate introspection. Think carefully about each issue. Choose an answer before looking at the explanation. Record that answer and then read the question's explanation. Mark those questions in which your answer indicates that you wouldn't make a good entrepreneur, and come back and think about them again after considering all the questions.

If you come up with a preponderance of negative responses, you probably shouldn't go into your own business. If you're like most people, you'll fall in the middle of the road on most issues. In that case, you may want to go ahead, but be careful that you really understand what you're getting into.

A Self-Test for the Prospective Entrepreneur

1. Are You a Self-Starter?

(a) I generate work for myself and others.

(b) I am adept at solving well-defined problems.

(c) I complete any assignment in an outstanding way and look to my boss for the next one.

A small business owner must have drive and initiative. He or she has to be the prime mover for getting things done day in and day out. Some people say that this is the single most important characteristic of an entrepreneur. Unfortunately, it's sometimes hard to tell if you have this characteristic if you've spent most of your career in a corporate job in which your work is initiated by someone else. If you chose answer (a), and consistently generate your own ideas (even in a corporate setting) you have an advantage over those who wait for others to set their goals.

2. Do You Like and Get Along with People?

(a) I have rarely met anyone I didn't like and respect.

(b) I have a few good friends that I enjoy, but have little interest in knowing a great many people.

(c) I'm not antisocial, but the great majority of people are jerks.

Nearly all small businesses succeed through people, primarily customers and employees. People who don't genuinely enjoy interpersonal contact on a regular basis are at a distinct disadvantage. Many start-up opportunities are in service businesses where personal contact is especially important. If you can honestly choose answer (a), you are better equipped to function in a small business environment than if not.

3. Has Your Career So Far Been Primarily in:

(a) Small business (less than 200 employees)?

(b) Medium-sized business (200 to 1,000 employees)?

(c) Large business (more than 1,000 employees)?

(d) Government or nonprofit organizations?

The most valuable experience for your own small business is answer (a), working in someone else's small business, especially in the same field. Big business and government experience can actually be a detriment, because the characteristics for success in those areas are often negatives in an entrepreneur. Further, the small business environment is something that must be experienced to be fully understood. If you've never been there, it's hard to know just what you're getting into.

4. Did You Engage in Business Activity as a Child/Teenager?

(a) I started one or more businesses of my own.

(b) I worked all the time in a series of part-time and summer jobs.

(c) I worked when I had to.

The work ethic and entrepreneurial drive show up early; answer (a) is the most encouraging answer. If you didn't have it when you were young, you're less likely to develop it later on.

5. How Old Are You Now?

(a) 20s.

(b) 30s.

(c) 40s.

(d) Over 50.

For what it's worth, more successful entrepreneurs seem to start in their 30s than at other ages. This age seems to combine enough experience to be sensible with enough youth to be enthusiastic.

6. Have You Ever Been Fired (Not Laid Off) Because You Just Didn't Get Along with Your Boss or the Environment?

(a) More than once.

(b) Once.

(c) Never.

Within reason, it's better to have been fired. Entrepreneurs don't like working in someone else's structured organization, and they often make waves about it. They often have trouble with authority and are vocal if they don't agree with the way things are done. Be careful, though, a continuous history of firings can mean you have a serious personality problem.

7. What Is Your Main Reason for Considering Your Own Business?

(a) To be my own boss.

(b) For prestige and recognition.

(c) To get rich.

Answers (a) or (b) put you in the entrepreneur's profile. The most pervasive characteristic of entrepreneurs is that they don't like working for someone else. They like to call the shots themselves. They also tend to be extroverts who crave recognition. Money is nice but of secondary importance.

8. How Would You React If You Started a Business and It Failed, Losing Most or All of Your Savings in the Process?

(a) I'd learn from my mistakes and start over.

(b) I'd be very shaken but would eventually recover.

(c) That would be a disaster; I'd be devastated; I don't know what I'd do.

Many if not most successful entrepreneurs have started more than once. Failure is a very real part of small business. It is essential that an entrepreneur be resilient and able to bounce back. If you chose answer (c), think hard about this whole idea.

9. What Kind of Gamble Interests You the Most?

(a) A long shot with odds of 100 to 1 or more in which you can make a real killing (a payoff of 100 to 1 or more).

(b) A game in which the odds are against you (say 3 to 1) but in which you can improve your chances of winning by developing your skill at the game.

Contrary to popular belief, entrepreneurs are not big risk takers. They don't like to gamble, but are willing to take calculated risks as in (b).

10. How Much Management Experience Have You Had?

(a) Several years supervising a variety of people and projects.

(b) A little.

(c) None.

A small business owner has to manage people to be successful. It's better to have made your managerial mistakes on someone else's payroll. Answer (a) is the preferred background.

11. Do You Become Totally Involved in Your Work, Tending to Talk About It over Meals with Your Family, to Friends, at Parties, etc.?

(a) Yes, definitely.

(b) Mildly, but I'm not compulsive about it.

(c) No, I keep my business and personal lives separate.

The best entrepreneurs devote their entire energy to their businesses. They live, eat, drink, and sleep their business. If you don't do that and your competitor does, who do you think is likely to win?

Some people don't have that kind of dedication regardless of how hard they try. Some have it for whatever job they're doing. Some have it only for a certain field in which they're particularly interested. If you never experience an all-consuming affinity for work, think twice about small business. If you can only generate this kind of enthusiasm for a particular field that fascinates you, be sure that's the field your business is in.

12. Are You Prepared to Work 80 or More Hours a Week for an Indefinite Number of Years?

(a) Yes, and I'm excited about the prospect.

(b) Yes, if I have to, but I will look forward to the time when the business is secure enough for me to take it a little easier.

(c) No, that shouldn't be necessary except in the beginning. I'll work smart enough to put in reasonable hours.

Small business has been described as working 16 hours a day to get away from an 8-hour-a-day job. Experience indicates that successful entrepreneurs work terribly long hours for many years before they get to relax. If you can't honestly choose answer (a) or at least (b), you may want to rethink your plans.

13. When You Engage in Competitive Activities (Sports, Games, etc.) What Is Most Important to You?

(a) Winning.

(b) Playing with style, grace, and good sportsmanship.

(c) Enjoying myself and getting a good workout.

Small business is an extremely competitive world. The best entrepreneurs fixate on winning, on being better than the other guy.

14. Do You Belong to and Actively Participate in Church Groups, Civic Organizations, Social and Fraternal Clubs, Political Organizations?

(a) Yes, I'm a real joiner. I belong to five or more organizations. I go to meetings regularly, participate actively, and run for offices often.

(b) I belong to a few organizations but am not too active in most of them.

(c) No, I try to stay away from such activities as they take energy away from my work.

Answer (a) is best. Successful entrepreneurs tend to be outgoing people who love social contact and genuinely enjoy meetings and groups. The contacts that they make in these groups are very helpful to their businesses. If you aren't already the joiner type, don't expect to change and become one when you start your own business.

15. Do You Like to Solve Problems Yourself, or Are You Okay with Getting Help and Advice from an Expert?

(a) I don't like reinventing the wheel. The first thing I do when faced with a problem is to look around for someone who has already solved the same dilemma.

(b) I work on things myself for a while, and look for outside help if I get stuck.

(c) I take pride in working out my own solutions to my own problems.

Effective businesspeople get the best answer as quickly as possible. That usually means looking to an expert—answer (a)—even if you have to pay them.

16. How Do You Handle Getting Several Tasks Done at the Same Time?

(a) I'm able to get a number of things underway at once, dividing my time between them. I'm able to switch my attention to the hottest item and then return to the others without losing much momentum. In fact, I enjoy the variety of working this way.

(b) I find tasks yield to concentrated effort. I like to work hard on one thing until it's completed, then move on to the next item.

Small business ownership is like a juggling act. You have to keep at least a dozen balls in the air all the time. If you can't divide your attention among several concurrent activities, you're almost certain to fail. Answer (a) is best, but this is a skill that can be learned.

17. How Do You Rate Your Organizational Abilities?

(a) Great, I always know where I am and where I'm going. I force the people under me to function in the same way.

(b) Fair to good. I generally know what's going on, but occasionally get lost.

(c) I'm a mess.

The ability to organize people and tasks is an extremely important entrepreneurial task. A disorganized business is generally losing customers and money. If you're not an organized person now, the type who would honestly answer (a) or (b), you probably won't become one by going into business.

18. How Is Your Health and Energy?

(a) I'm in excellent health. I have a great deal of energy and almost never get sick.

(b) I have an average level of health and energy.

(c) I have a significant health problem and am tired a lot.

If you haven't gotten the idea by now, your own small business is going to be a tough, stressful grind. If you didn't answer (a), and don't have a great deal of physical and emotional strength and stamina, you'd better think twice.

19. Are You Unemployed?

(a) No, I'm considering leaving my current job to start my own business.

(b) Yes, but I've been considering my own business for some time and would have quit pretty soon anyway.

(c) Yes, I was recently laid off and I thought I'd look into starting my own business while I'm also looking for another job.

Answer (a) is the most promising answer; (c) can be a disaster. It's rarely a good idea to try to buy a job by starting a business. If you weren't motivated to do it before you lost your job, you're probably not going to be a good entrepreneur now. Getting fired can be a lot like getting divorced. You're very vulnerable for quite some time afterward. Be doubly careful before making any major commitments. (Don't confuse this with question 6—we're driving at a different issue here. It's okay to have been fired in the past because you were independent, but it's not a great idea to think of small business as a way to create a job if you've just been let go.)

20. How Do You Handle Conflict (as in Dissatisfied Customers or Firing Employees)?

(a) I don't like it, but I get through it as quickly as possible and put it behind me.

(b) I rather enjoy conflict and winning by dominating others.

(c) I can't stand fights. I get through them, but it takes me days to recover emotionally.

Conflicts are a way of life in business. In small business, the buck stops at the owner. There are conflicts with customers, suppliers, and employees all the time. In franchising, there's an added element, conflicts with the franchisor. An entrepreneur has to be able to deal with conflict without letting it get him or her down. Answers (a) and (b) are okay. Answer (c) may be a real problem. If you find conflict devastating, small business may be your route to a nervous breakdown!

21. How Do You Feel About Authority?

(a) I like running my own show but can accept authority that I feel is legitimate.

(b) I have to be able to do things my own way.

(c) I'm most comfortable when I have an authority figure to look up to.

The desire for independence is one of the primary motivators among successful entrepreneurs. Answer (b) indicates that you fit the profile. However, an obsession with independence can spell trouble. No one can be completely independent, especially of customers. Too independent an attitude can be a real problem if your business is a franchise. A franchisee has to be willing to accept the franchisor's model of the business. If you sign the franchise agreement and can't do it its way, you risk losing your investment. In that case, answer (a) is best. It reflects an independent personality but not one so fiercely freedom-loving that it cannot survive within a structure of rules.

22. Can You Make Decisions?

(a) I can weigh the pros and cons and make a decision quickly. The outcome is usually pretty good.

(b) I make good decisions, but it takes me a long time. I will not be rushed in important matters.

(c) I'm uncomfortable making important decisions.

Decision-making is what entrepreneurs do for a living. The ability to make reasonably quick choices and live with the outcome is an absolutely essential characteristic. Answer (a) is the best answer, (b) is a poor second, while (c) should raise a warning flag.

What's Your Bottom Line—Are You Cut Out to Be an Entrepreneur?

Think hard about the answers to these questions. Don't kid yourself! Answer honestly. No one is going to see the results but you.

Do you have the right stuff to start a small business? If so, it may be the beginning of the most exciting time in your life. If not, it's certainly better to come to that realization before investing thousands of dollars and a great deal of time.

THE PROS AND CONS OF BUYING AN EXISTING BUSINESS

Starting a new business is a risky proposition. One third of new ventures fail in their first year and another third are gone within five years. Only a few, probably less than one in twenty, can be considered real successes.

The frightening failure statistics have led many people to conclude that the only sensible way to get into your own business is to buy one that already exists, that is, one that has lasted for a reasonable length of time. Such an enterprise has the treacherous early days behind it and has proven itself to be a survivor.

Approximately 3 million businesses are sold every year. Businesses with a net worth of under $100,000 change hands, on the average, once every four years.

The reasoning behind buying an established business is basically sound, but implementation can be difficult and risky.

THE ADVANTAGES OF BUYING VS. STARTING

The advantages of buying an existing business are straightforward.

1. An ideal candidate has been in operation for some time so that its business concept and implementation are proven to work. That is, the high-risk early days in which every business has to prove it can reach its intended market are over, and their outcome has been successful. Important items in this regard include a proven location, competent employees, and usable, on-hand inventory and equipment.

2. An established business has an existing customer base, and long-standing relations with suppliers and a bank. It will also have worked the flaws out of its operating procedures.

3. Presumably the business has been profitable in the past and can be expected to make money in the future. Generally, profitability can be expected faster with an existing business than a new one.

4. The previous owner may be available to advise the new owner for some time.

5. Developing a business plan is easier with an existing business, because it has a history to project forward.

6. Getting financing can be easier because banks like to lend to businesses with track records of successful operation. Previous success under an old owner isn't as convincing as history under the person applying for the loan, but it's better than no history at all.

7. One can expect that the buyer won't have to work as hard to keep the enterprise going as the founder did to get it started.

In short, buying a business should be an easier and less risky proposition than starting from scratch.

THE PROBLEMS AND RISKS

When businesses are offered for sale, their owners naturally present them in the best possible light. That usually means overstating the positives and not mentioning the negatives if they can be avoided. As a result, identifying a business that has the characteristics of safety, stability, and profitability isn't easy. Getting a really good business for a reasonable price can be even harder.

Good businesses are from time to time offered for sale. By good, we mean reasonably profitable, growing, and free from overhanging conditions that threaten failure in the near future. Such enterprises rarely make it to the listings of brokers or to the Business Opportunities section of the newspaper. They're generally bought by people who knew the owners and their businesses before they thought of selling.

Entrepreneurs in search of businesses to buy have to be careful that they know what they're getting and aren't being deceived or swindled.

Here are some issues to consider.

Why Is the Business for Sale?

There has to be a reason why a business is offered for sale. A reason we'd like to hear is that the owner has had some change in his or her life and wants to cash out. Such changes include divorce, sickness, or retirement. Unfortunately, another common reason for selling businesses is that they're in trouble

and the owners want to unload before losing their shirts.

If a candidate for purchase is in the second category, you can't expect the current owner to tell you. He or she will make up a plausible personal reason that leaves the business looking good.

It's important to probe deeply and convince yourself that the business isn't being sold because it's a dog.

Past Financial Performance

Many small businesses have very shaky accounting systems. The current owner will probably show you a set of financial statements that indicate that the business has done well in the past, but it's often virtually impossible to verify if these are true.

If you get serious about a particular opportunity, hire a CPA to audit the books and get some level of assurance that what the seller says is real.

Is Something Disastrous Going On?

Businesses are sometimes on the market because disasters are in the works. For example, an owner may offer a grocery store for sale because he or she knows a supermarket is considering moving into the neighborhood. A buyer shouldn't expect to be told about that.

Inventory

A business can be on the market with thousands of dollars in useless inventory on the books. The owner may have bought stock that nobody wants or is for some reason unusable.

If the inventory records aren't organized, it's hard to tell how much dead inventory is mixed in with the stuff that does move.

Sellers generally want to value the inventory at cost in the purchase price calculation, that is, what they paid for it. If the buyer goes along with that, he or she can be paying a lot for nothing.

Saturated Market

A previously healthy business can be sick today because competition has moved in. Look in the Business Opportunities section of a major newspaper and see how many pizza restaurants and video rental stores are for sale. Many are on the market because they're not doing well due to intense competition.

Deteriorated Conditions

Owners sometimes let businesses go downhill. They can lose interest or get sick and not pay as much attention to operations as they should. When that happens, the firm's relations with customers, suppliers, and its bank can deteriorate. Then, a buyer can get a good deal of ill will for his or her money.

Facilities Problems

A business may be stuck with obsolete facilities and equipment or be about to lose its lease. Any of these can be a major problem.

PRICING A BUSINESS

Establishing a price for a business can be difficult and arbitrary. There are two basic approaches, the market value of assets less liabilities and the capitalized value of earnings. These provide starting points, but after

that it's up to the negotiating abilities of the parties.

Market Value of Assets Less Liabilities

The market value of assets is simply what the items could be sold for currently. It is not the book or depreciated value. Assets included are usually real estate, equipment, and inventory. If receivables are included, be sure the seller is liable for any that prove uncollectible.

Liabilities are whatever debts are coming with the business. Be sure there aren't any you don't know about. Make the seller sign an agreement to be responsible for any debts that show up later that are due to activity prior to the date of sale.

Capitalized Value of Earnings

The value of a profit stream that's expected to continue indefinitely into the future is determined by dividing the annual earnings figure by an appropriate interest rate. For example, if a prospective business buyer feels that an acceptable return on funds that he or she might invest in a business is 15%, and a particular business is expected to earn profits of $10,000 per year, the value of that stream is:

$$\$10,000 \, / \, .15 = \$66,666.67$$

This is called *capitalizing* the earnings at 15%. Many business buying discussions start at ten times earnings, reflecting the implicit use of a 10% interest rate.

In small business dealings, a rate of return much higher than 10% is usually in order to reflect the high risk involved. If, say, 25% is used, the capitalized value of a dollar of earnings is $4 (1 / .25).

Potential

Business owners generally want more than either of these approaches will yield for their businesses. Their argument is usually based on the "potential" of the business. It's impossible to make a general statement about the validity of such arguments, but real caution is in order. If you pay too much for a business, you'll never get that money back. Be especially careful of businesses that aren't making an acceptable return but "will turn around shortly."

Buyers sometimes rationalize a high purchase price by saying, "Well, the business lost money last year, but if I buy it and change this, this, and that, it'll make money from now on." Be careful of that logic. If you can see changes that will make money, why didn't the former owners? Be sure the profit-making changes you're thinking about are grounded in concrete knowledge or experience on your part and not just on brainstorming.

Don't let the excitement of owning your own business stampede you into paying too much.

Most sellers will come down, especially if the business has been on the market for some time.

Business Brokers

Business brokers work like real estate brokers. Sellers list businesses with brokers and pay a commission (usually 10%) when the business sells. Some business brokers are large sophisticated organizations that specialize in selling particular kinds of businesses. Others are real estate or insurance agents who have decided to try to broker businesses on the side.

The broker's primary motivation is to make the deal happen and collect a commission. Therefore, they're very optimistic about everything. Also remember that brokers work for sellers. That's who pays their commissions.

Most importantly, keep in mind that the best deals never see a broker's office!

WHAT ABOUT A FRANCHISE?

For most Americans, the word franchise conjures up an image—McDonald's Golden Arches or the smiling face of "Colonel" Sanders happily clutching a bucket of fried chicken. These are appropriate images representing some of today's most successful franchised operations.

The term franchise comes from the French verb franchir, meaning to free. It literally means a freedom from some burden or restriction. Alternatively, it is a right or privilege. In modern commerce it has come to mean the right or privilege to conduct business under someone else's proprietary name and style.

Franchising has actually been around for a long time, but most of us don't associate the older forms with what we think of as franchising today.

TYPES OF FRANCHISING

The traditional forms of franchising are called product and trade name franchising. Product franchising was started in this country in the middle of the nineteenth century. The Singer Sewing Machine Company was an early pioneer in the 1850s. Product franchising is a relationship in which a dealer signs up to sell a manufacturer's product under the manufacturer's name. The most common modern examples are automobile dealerships and gas stations. The dealer owns his or her own business but takes on a great deal of the identity of the manufacturer. The manufacturer doesn't invest its money in dealerships but participates in the arrangement in order to establish a distribution network.

Trade name franchising involves the use of an organization's name without the requirement that a particular product be involved. A retail store, for example, might be franchised under a particular name like Western Auto or Ben Franklin, but might not be required to get all of its merchandise through the franchisor.

Product and trade name franchising have been around in a big way for years, but most of us don't think of them as "franchising." When we hear that term, we think of McDonald's and Burger King, which are examples of *business format franchising*. This is the kind of franchise that interests most small business people today.

The essence of the business format arrangement is the provision of an entire business operation neatly delivered in a manageable package. The person going into business is known as the franchisee, while the organization providing the package is the franchisor. When the franchisee opens the package, he or she gets a ready-made business idea that has been successful in other places.

Definition

In today's business world, the word franchise signifies a relationship between the franchisor and franchisee. The franchisee pays the franchisor for the initial idea and for continuing assistance in running the business.

The International Franchise Association provides the following definition: "a continuing relationship in which the franchisor provides a licensed privilege to do business, plus assistance in organizing, training, merchandising, and management in return for a consideration from the franchisee."

The idea that the relationship is a continuing one is important. Payment by the franchisee and assistance from the franchisor must be long term.

Franchising in the Economy

The bulk of the sales made through franchised businesses remains in automobile retailing and gasoline. These are product and trade name franchises. The fastest growing segment of the franchise industry is the business format franchise. It is also the most realistic for average people who want a career in small business. Restaurants are the most popular form of business format franchising, followed by convenience food stores. Outside of these, the trend seems to be toward service busi-nesses, for example, travel agencies, maid services, quick lube, etc.

All forms of franchising together amount to roughly one third of the retail sales in the United States, most of which is from auto dealers and gas stations.

THE BUSINESS FORMAT FRANCHISE

Ideally, the business format arrangement provides a franchisee with a proven, prepackaged

business. The idea comes complete with a recognized name and a product or service that already has customer acceptance. It has instructions and diagrams on how to set everything up, signs, building designs, uniforms for employees, lists of required equipment, including places to buy it, lists of approved vendors from whom to buy product, and much more.

Perhaps most important, the package comes with instructions on how to run the business. Such instructions take the form of operating manuals and formal training.

In summary, we can say that the business format franchise provides the franchisee with not only the business idea, but with the system behind the business. By system, we mean all of the knowledge, procedures, and practices that it takes to make the business work successfully.

This is a tremendously important concept. Business failure is a chilling fact of life for any entrepreneur. According to the Small Business Administration, almost a third of nonfranchised start-up ventures fail in their first year of operation. Another third will fail within five years. But fewer than 4% of franchised businesses are discontinued each year.

The overwhelming majority of small business failures aren't due to bad business ideas. In most cases, small businesses fail because the entrepreneurs don't know how to manage what they start. In a business format franchise, the know-how comes with the package. This is an important reason why franchise failure rates are a fraction of those of unfranchised business.

The business format franchise enables someone with little experience or knowledge about a field to get into business in relatively short order with a minimum of hassle. And because the business is a proven idea and the operating system is provided, the probability of failure is dramatically lower than it is in an unfranchised startup.

Related Business Ideas

There are a few things around that look like franchising but aren't. A distributorship is a prime example. In a distributorship, one has the right to sell the products of a particular manufacturer and use its name in advertising and promotion. In an exclusive distributorship the manufacturer agrees not to distribute through anyone else in a geographic area. A distributorship agreement may also preclude the distributor from handling anyone else's product.

A distributorship isn't a franchise because the manufacturer doesn't help the distributor run the business. There is no guidance or training, and the manufacturer doesn't receive a fee beyond the wholesale price of the product.

There are also some business opportunities advertised in which you get a business idea and the opportunity to buy product but little else. These aren't franchises, either. A franchise is a continuing relationship in which the franchisor provides help and guidance in managing the business.

Franchising—the Pros and Cons

Many experts say that franchising is the wave of the future for small business. This is due to the fact that our economy is increasingly dominated by large, powerful companies. Franchising is seen as the only way that small operators can match the name recognition, advertising clout, and operating efficiency of the big guys.

Most franchisors demand hefty fees before setting up a franchisee and a continuing stream of royalty payments after opening. The total commitment from a small business operator can be hundreds of thousands of dollars before he or she opens the doors for business.

It is also important to realize that not all franchisors are reputable. The woods are full of smooth-talking operators who sell naïve investors packages that don't exist. Guaranteeing success, they collect the franchise fee and provide only a fraction of the promised support.

Even reputable franchises don't always work out. There are numerous sources of conflict between franchisee and franchisor, not the least of which is the loss of independence that goes with the arrangement. At the end of the day, a franchise owner doesn't get the satisfaction of saying, "I did it my way!" You either do it the franchisor's way or not at all. There are also territorial disputes, advertising charges, and a host of other issues.

Let's look at the advantages and disadvantages in more detail.

Advantages

Franchisors essentially sell their method of doing business. The system is what makes the franchise successful, because it provides comprehensive guidance to each and every facet of the business as well as the advantages inherent in being part of a franchise network.

Let's assume, for example, that Joe Jones is a genuine expert on hardware; he knows the nuts and bolts not only of nuts and bolts, but also of paint, building materials, plumbing, and every product sold in hardware stores.

Why, one might ask, should such a person pay a hefty fee and continuing royalties to become part of a nationwide chain? There are a number of possible reasons.

Know-How

Joe may be an expert on hardware, but is he equally well versed in inventory control, advertising strategies, and employee benefits? Does he know how to set up a cash register system and keep the books?

Each of these operations can be as important to the success of a hardware store as the knowledge of product. A major franchisor will help Joe put his business systems into place and provide him with training and continued support on using them.

Discounts

As part of a national chain, Joe may be eligible to receive volume discounts obtained because the franchisor can buy for all of its outlets at once. Wholesale prices are apt to be much lower than those available to the sole proprietor of one small store.

Name Recognition

Joe's franchised store will have instant name recognition. People tend to prefer recognized goods and services. It is likely that consumers would feel more confident buying expensive tools at True Value or Ace outlets than at Mom and Pop's World of Hardware.

Advertising

Joe's business may also benefit from the franchisor's national advertising campaign. While individual franchise owners do, in the long run, pay for this advertising, they are buying into an advertising system that has proven its effectiveness.

Territory

If Joe buys into a well-known franchise, he is generally assured that the franchisor will not open a directly competing outlet in his territory. While there's nothing to prevent another chain or an independent operator from starting up a hardware store across the street, Joe's status as a franchisee of a well-known firm will probably discourage competitors from locating in his immediate area.

Start-Up

Finally, Joe will be in for a much easier start-up if he signs on with a national franchise. His questions will not only be answered but anticipated. The franchisor will know he needs help in setting up an accounting system, selecting a site, outfitting the building, and hiring help. He'll receive training and assistance in all these matters.

This list of advantages was applicable to a person who already knew the hardware business pretty well. A franchise relationship is even more valuable to someone who doesn't have that knowledge. In that case, the entrepreneur will rely on the franchisor for virtually everything.

Disadvantages

There's no such thing as a free lunch. The franchisee has to pay real dollars for the franchisor's name, methods, and expertise. Let's look at some of the realities involved in making that purchase, including the capital investment in facilities, franchise fees, other start-up costs, advertising fees, and royalties.

Investment in Facilities

An independent businessperson can choose to get by with the cheapest facility available. That may not be so with a franchise. Franchisors generally have strict requirements with respect to physical plant. Generally they are concerned with image and will not allow franchisees to compromise that image with substandard facilities.

Franchise Fees

The initial payment for joining the franchisor's organization is called the franchise fee; it can be a considerable sum of money. The franchise fee is designed to cover the franchisor's costs of recruitment and training among other things. Franchise fees alone can be over $50,000.

Other Start-Up Costs

The franchise fee is only a portion of the up-front investment needed. A multitude of other expenses are usually required before opening the doors. These include investments in facilities, equipment, inventory, licenses, hiring, training, advertising, and a grand opening. An independent can scrimp and cut corners on many of these, but a franchisee has to do it by the book, which is usually first-class and expensive.

Advertising Fees

Franchisees are often expected to contribute to the national advertising effort. This may cost 2% or 3% of revenues. In addition, they are expected to advertise locally.

Royalties

Franchisors demand an ongoing royalty fee based on revenue, usually from 5% to as much as 12%. It's important to understand that the royalty is based on revenues, not profit. That means that the royalty is due even if a franchisee's business is losing money.

Restrictions

Let's assume that someone opened a franchised hamburger restaurant in an ethnic neighborhood in which tacos would be a profitable menu item.

In spite of their probable profitability, it's unlikely that this entrepreneur would be able to offer his or her own tacos. It's typical of franchisors to tightly control the goods and services offered by franchisees. This generally makes sense, because standardization is part of what makes the franchise appealing in the first place. Customers know what they're getting, and the national advertising campaign is geared toward selling exactly those items.

The uniformity expected of many franchisees goes beyond the nature of the inventory. They are expected to maintain a certain level of service and can be subject to surprise inspections to ensure that they do.

Independence

To some people, the most significant disadvantage of franchising is the loss of independence involved. A franchisee is simply not in business for him or herself in the same way a traditional entrepreneur is. In extreme cases, running a franchise can feel more like working as an employee than being on one's own.

Franchises and Business Planning

Franchised start-ups require business plans just like independents, but they are generally easier to put together. Some franchisors have business plan formats already developed that have been successful in the past. The franchisor is usually able to provide a wealth of information and documentation on the nature of the business that helps in writing the bulk of the plan. Franchisors also sometimes offer financial assistance. That generally means an introduction to a bank that is familiar with the business and has lent to other franchisees before.

THE SMALL BUSINESS ADMINISTRATION (SBA)

The Small Business Administration was created by Congress in 1953 to help America's entrepreneurs form successful small enterprises. Its mission is to help people get into business and stay in business.

A business is determined to be small according to standards established by the government based on number of employees or revenue. The standards vary by industry and the nature of the business. A manufacturing enterprise can be small with as many as 1,500 employees, although the limit may be as low as 500 in some fields. A wholesaler may not have more than 100 employees. Service providers must have total receipts that are less than a figure between $4 million and $29 million depending on the industry. In retailing, the range is between $6 million and $24.5 million. In construction businesses, small means revenues of less than $12 to $28.5 million depending on the industry.

Most of the businesses existing today qualify as small according to the SBA's definition.

The SBA helps entrepreneurs in essentially three ways. It provides education and counseling, it serves as a small business advocate, and it assists in obtaining financing. We'll consider each of these in turn.

EDUCATION AND COUNSELING

The SBA uses workshops, individual counseling, publications, and CDs/videotapes to help entrepreneurs understand and meet the challenges of operating a business. Help is offered in areas like financing, marketing, and management.

Technical assistance, training, and counseling are also offered by two partner organizations:

- The Service Corps of Retired Executives (SCORE) provides training and one-on-one counseling at no charge.

- Small Business Development Centers (SBDCs) provide training, counseling, research, and other specialized assistance at more than 1,000 locations nationwide, primarily at colleges and universities.

ADVOCACY

The SBA's Office of Advocacy serves as an advocate for small business interests with the rest of the government. It researches important issues, develops policy, and suggests legislation. It also monitors the effect of laws related to small business.

The Office of Advocacy also produces a number of publications, including economic and statistical reports, an annual report to Congress, and a report to the President.

The office also monitors compliance with several laws that are designed to keep government regulation from smothering small businesses.

Special Programs

The SBA has special programs to assist small businesses in exporting, research, and in doing business with the federal government. Through the Procurement Marketing and Access Network (PRO-Net), the SBA electronically brings the résumés of qualified small businesses to the desks of thousands of government procurement officials and large government prime contractors throughout the United States. There are also special programs to assist economically disadvantaged individuals, women, veterans, disaster victims, and exporters in business.

FINANCING—SBA LOANS

SBA Loans have helped thousands of small companies get started, expand, and prosper. The following will explain eligibility and business loan application procedures.

Conventional Sources First

The rules require that loan applicants first seek conventional financing from banks or other lending institutions and be turned down before they can be considered for SBA loans. The reasoning behind this is clear: the SBA is designed to help those who couldn't get started or continue in business without such help. If you're strong enough to go it on your own the government would rather you did that.

The Nature of an SBA Loan

People often misunderstand exactly what the SBA does with respect to loans. It rarely actually makes loans with government money. What it generally does is *guarantee* loans made by conventional lending institutions. That is, if you take out an SBA loan and fail to pay it back, the government will pay off the bank after your resources are exhausted. It's important to understand that the government's guarantee doesn't replace your own. It is in addition to yours.

For example, suppose you borrow money and collateralize the loan with your house but don't have quite enough equity to cover the loan request. With an SBA guarantee, the bank may be able to make the loan because the government guarantees the part you can't collateralize. However, if you default, you still lose the house.

The SBA can guarantee up to 85% of the loan amount up to $150,000. Over that the guarantee is at most 15% of the loan amount. The maximum guarantee is $1 million.

The Basic Procedure

There are three principal parties to an SBA-guaranteed loan: the SBA, the small business borrower, and the private lender. The lender plays the central role. The small business person submits a loan application to the lender for initial review. If the lender finds the application acceptable, it forwards the application and its credit analysis to the nearest SBA Office. After SBA approval, the lender closes the loan and disburses the funds. The borrower then makes loan payments to the lender.

Terms of Loans

The length of time for repayment of an SBA loan depends on the use of the proceeds and the ability of the business to repay. Working capital loans generally have maturities of five to seven years. The maximum maturity is 25 years. Longer maturities are used to finance fixed assets, such as the purchase or major renovation of business premises.

Interest rates on guaranteed loans are negotiated between the borrower and lender subject to SBA maximums.

Collateral Requirements

You must pledge sufficient assets, to the extent they are available, to adequately secure an SBA-backed loan. Personal guarantees are required from the principal business owners and from the chief executive officer of the business. Liens on personal assets of the principals also may be required.

Credit Requirements

A loan applicant must:

- Be of good character.

- Demonstrate sufficient management expertise and the commitment necessary for a successful operation.

- Have enough funds, including the SBA-guaranteed loan plus personal cash, to operate the business on a sound financial basis. For new businesses, this includes sufficient resources to withstand start-up expenses and the initial operating phase when losses are likely to occur. The SBA may require that you provide, from personal resources, up to one third or even one half of the total assets needed to launch your new business.

- Show that the past earnings record and probable future earnings will be sufficient to repay the loan in a timely manner.

More Information

For more information on how the SBA can be of help to you, contact your nearest SBA office. It is listed in the phone book under U.S. Government. You can also visit the SBA's web site at www.sba.gov.

Two sample business plans are presented in this appendix. The first proposes a retail business and is intended as an illustration of planning for a relatively simple operation. The second case represents a more complex business, the on-site service of sophisticated electronic and computing equipment. It is intended to illustrate relatively complicated planning and computational procedures.

CASE I—RETAILING

THE DECORATOR'S ART GALLERY

Case Background

Tom and Carol Eberly are interested in starting a business of their own. They both currently have jobs but aren't happy working for someone else. Tom is a middle manager in accounting at an electronics firm and makes about $60,000 a year. Carol is a buyer for a local department store and also makes about $60,000. They have a suburban home with a modest mortgage, one child, and inexpensive tastes. They feel that they could live adequately on Tom's salary alone. Their plan is for Carol to quit her job and to open their own business. If the business is successful, Tom will eventually join her; if not, he'll stay with the company he's currently with.

The Eberlys share an interest in beautiful homes and decorations. They recently met a wholesale distributor of art and interior decorating items and are interested in opening their own art gallery.

The Eberlys understand the difference between "fine" art and "decorator" art. Fine art is collectible for its own sake and may have an investment value. Decorator art comes in a variety of quality levels, is relatively inexpensive, and simply looks good on the wall. Decorator art includes prints, sculptures, and original paintings that, while handmade, are virtually mass-produced. Carol has had some experience in the furniture department of the store she used to work for. That department carried a limited number of decorator art items.

Tom and Carol are excited about their business idea but don't have the funds to put it into operation. They currently have available cash savings of $25,000, but estimate that getting started and through the first year will take almost $90,000. This is for initial inventory, leasehold improvements, a store in a shopping mall, and expenses through an initial period of slow sales.

They've thought about approaching friends and relatives for funds but have decided against the idea. First, they don't want to share ownership with anyone else and, second, they'd rather not strain personal relationships with business. Therefore, the Eberlys plan to approach a bank for a $62,000 business loan. They understand that banks do not generally make unsecured loans to new businesses regardless of how good the idea seems. However, they feel that there is over $90,000 in equity in their home, and are willing to collateralize the loan with that.

The Eberlys have put together the following business plan for their business idea.

THE DECORATOR'S ART GALLERY

BUSINESS PLAN

Presented to First Bank of Anytown, Anystate

by Carol C. and Thomas B. Eberly

CONTENTS

I
EXECUTIVE SUMMARY

MARKET

A niche market opportunity exists in the retail art/decorating business serving consumers who are affluent but not wealthy. Households in the $75,000–$150,000 income range purchase high-quality wall hangings but aren't interested in "fine" art, which is priced substantially beyond the level of items that are essentially used as decorations. It is difficult for consumers in this market segment to find a broad selection of higher-quality paintings and prints. Better furniture stores carry a few items, but their selections are limited. Interior decorators can obtain anything, but their services are expensive.

PROPOSED BUSINESS

The Decorator's Art Gallery proposes to fill this niche in the Anytown area by establishing a retail operation dealing in framed, commercially produced artwork selling from $100 to $1,000. The establishment's competitive advantage will lie in the breadth of the selection it offers customers. The gallery will also wholesale to professional decorators, who will find it more convenient in terms of location and selection than traditional wholesale outlets.

In addition to dealing in commercially produced merchandise, the business will establish itself as a traditional art gallery for the work of promising local artists.

LOCATION

The Decorator's Art Gallery will be located in a premium space within the Anytown Mall.

MANAGEMENT

The business will be operated full-time by Carol Eberly, who will leave her current job. Ms. Eberly has more than fifteen years' experience in retailing. She will be assisted on a part-time basis by her husband, Thomas, who will maintain his current employment.

LOAN REQUEST

The owners are requesting a $62,000 loan to fund inventory and start-up costs. They will contribute $25,000 of their own cash to begin the venture. Less than $25,000 will be required from the bank at opening. The full amount will be needed in seven months, after which time a steady repayment will take place out of operating cash flows. The loan will be entirely repaid two and one half years after opening.

COLLATERAL

The loan will be fully collateralized by the equity in the Eberlys' house, which is estimated to be in excess of $90,000.

II
MISSION AND STRATEGY

The Decorator's Art Gallery will establish a sophisticated setting from which it will retail traditional wall hangings and accessories designed for upper-middle-class homes. It will wholesale the same merchandise to professional interior decorators. Additionally, the gallery will act as agent for and carry the work of selected local artists.

Within three years, the gallery will become widely known as the leading source of wall hangings for households and the decorating trade in the Anytown area.

Within five years, the gallery will be recognized as a central clearinghouse for the work of the most talented artists in the area.

The Decorator's Art Gallery will base its appeal on providing traditional decorating items and expertise in a wider variety than is available at any other single location in the area. The upscale format will lend a sense of the quality of fine art to the store's offerings, as will the perceived expertise of the staff.

Comparable merchandise is currently available in furniture stores and framing studios in small quantities and limited variety. There is also little or no expert advice available in such establishments, so customers are entirely on their own. The Decorator's Art Gallery will provide a breadth of product sufficient to guarantee that consumers and professional decorators will be able to find everything they need in one or two visits. People unsure of their requirements will be assisted in their selections by an expert staff. Customers so assisted will have a sense of competence and sophistication associated with their selections.

III
MARKET

BACKGROUND

Decorative wall hangings are sold in furniture stores and art galleries. The nature of the latter varies from traditional galleries carrying "fine" art to retail establishments stocked with cheap prints. Fine art is valued for its own sake and may have an investment value. Galleries that sell it generally have an exclusive arrangement with the artists, and earn 30% to 50% of the sale price in commission.

Shops selling prints and mass-produced "original" art are a special kind of furniture store. Their product is distributed through wholesalers and is generally marked up about 100%. Such galleries often posture as being more artistic than they really are, trying to appear to be fine art galleries. Most furniture stores, however, handle only a few paintings and prints, which they classify as accessories.

Professional interior decorators often purchase paintings and prints for their clients. These products are supplied by wholesalers who specialize in the accessory end of the furniture business. Wholesalers are located in trade centers in large cities, so getting to them tends to be difficult for people who don't live nearby.

THE CUSTOMER NEED AND THE TARGET CUSTOMER

It is difficult to find a wide selection of traditional wall decorations consistent with an upper-middle-class lifestyle. Households that are affluent but not wealthy, with incomes between $75,000 and $150,000, generally don't want to employ a decorator but want something better than can be found in a print shop. Better furniture stores carry appropriate merchandise but generally have only a few pieces in stock at any time. That means that consumers in this class are hard put to find a wide selection from which to choose.

Census information indicates that within a 30-mile radius of the Anytown Mall, there are 35,000 households in this income category. These households will constitute our primary customer base.

Professional decorators generally choose color schemes, drapes, and major furniture items first and fill in the accessory items later. They too need a single, convenient place from which they can decorate the walls of an entire house without traveling to the regional trade center.

The trade association of interior decorators lists forty-six practicing interior decorators in the area.

PRODUCT DESCRIPTION

The Decorator's Art Gallery will carry a wide variety of upscale wall hangings to complement any color scheme. Offerings will include framed paintings, framed and matted prints covered in glass, and the work of a select number of local artists. A limited amount of sculpture and three-dimensional artwork will also be offered.

Decorator's will offer limited decorating advice without charge. This is intended more as a marketing device than as an actual decorating service.

Comment

A supporting attachment to the plan would show color pictures of a sampling of product.

COMPETITIVE ANALYSIS

Within the 30-mile radius of Anytown there are two major shopping malls, a downtown shopping area, and one outdoor shopping center. In addition, there are eight stand-alone furniture stores, mostly in small strip centers. The anchor stores in the shopping malls have furniture departments. There are three art galleries, which deal mostly in inexpensive prints, in the shopping malls. There are also six combination art gallery/frame shops located in various spots around the area.

The availability, price, and quality characteristics of these businesses are summarized in the following chart:

Type	Number	Average Number in Stock	Price Range	Quality
Furniture Stores	8	17	$50–$350	Good–Excellent
Furniture Departments	5	12	$40–$200	Fair
Art Galleries	3	500+	$35–$150	Poor
Frame Shops	6	75	$60–$300	Poor–Good

Our analysis indicates that none of these establishments provides substantial competition for what we are intending to do. Only the furniture stores carry comparable product, but each has a small selection. Furniture departments of department stores carry somewhat lower-quality merchandise on a smaller scale. The art galleries deal in lower-end merchandise, generally with a contemporary theme. Their market is the younger household, usually in a first home or an apartment. The frame shops have an occasional piece in our market, but most of the merchandise is of a lower quality.

None of these establishments offers any meaningful help or advice to clients.

Comment

Notice how the competitive analysis presented in chart form using numbers gives the impression of great thoroughness and understanding of the marketplace.

Competitive Advantage

A market niche exists for an establishment that carries a large selection of upscale but not exorbitantly priced decorating merchandise. The Decorator's Art Gallery's competitive advantage is that it provides that selection in one convenient location at reasonable prices. Without Decorator's Art Gallery a customer has to shop several locations to see a reasonable sampling of product. Furthermore, customers have no idea before making the trip if a particular outlet will have anything of interest at all.

BUSINESS CATEGORIES NOW AND IN THE FUTURE

The gallery will essentially operate three lines of business as follows:

Retail Trade

The bulk of Decorator's business will be selling product purchased through wholesalers to the general public. This business is expected to start off grossing approximately $10,000 per month and grow to about $30,000 per month over three years, after which it will level off.

Interior Decorators

The shop will also sell to interior decorators at a professional discount of 35% off list. The decorators price the goods at list or a little below for their customers and keep the difference. Our advantage to interior decorators is convenience. They can bring local customers to our gallery more easily than to the regional trade center.

Early expectations for the decorator business are modest. Sales are planned to increase from nothing to about $3,000 per month over three years. The average unit sold here is expected to be somewhat more expensive than that sold to the consumer directly. The lower margin means the profit contribution in this segment will be small for some time. Eventually, however, the shop will become a recognized source of quality items in the decorating trade, and this segment of the business will become substantial.

Through word-of-mouth advertising, the business with professional decorators will assist marketing to the retail business.

Local Artists

Customers like to purchase the work of local artists if their prices aren't too high. People are fond of displaying pictures and being able to say that the artist lives nearby or that they have met him or her.

Three promising artists have contracted to exhibit their work for sale through the gallery. Initial sales of approximately $1,000 a month are planned at a 33% commission rate. This segment of the business is expected to expand to $4,000 a month over a three-year period. An average price of $500 is anticipated in this line. More artists can be added in the future if it proves profitable.

Periodic "shows" of original work are planned to promote the line and to expose interested people to the rest of the gallery's offerings.

STRATEGY AND APPROACH TO THE MARKET

The Decorator's Art Gallery will pursue a niche strategy. The niche is defined by the income level of the target customer and the nature of the merchandise. Customers will be affluent but not wealthy, with household incomes of $75,000 to $150,000. The merchandise will consist of traditional, rather ornate, framed paintings and prints. The niche can be thought of as existing within either the art business or the furniture business.

Customers in this niche are currently served only by more expensive furniture stores and professional interior decorators. The market is poorly served because stores carry a scant selection and interior decorators are too expensive.

Advertising

The retail customer primarily will be reached by direct mail advertising and localized insertions in the area's major newspaper. General advertising will be limited because of the small segment of the population represented by the target market.

The professional decorator market will be approached exclusively by direct mail. A wine and cheese event for the decorating trade will be sponsored shortly after opening to acquaint them with what the gallery offers. Attendance will be encouraged by offering special one-time discounts to those who come.

The business in the work of local artists will be supported through "showings" every four to six weeks. These will be advertised in local newspapers during the week before the events.

Anytown Mall and Its Traffic

Retail malls fall into distinct categories catering to different types of customers. Some have a younger clientele and are dominated by women's clothing stores carrying teen and youthful styles. Others have a working-class orientation. Those are usually anchored by Sears and one or more discount stores. Still others cater to an upscale, affluent customer.

Malls in the latter category are anchored by expensive department stores and contain a number of fashionable boutiques. They tend to be located in the more expensive suburbs around major cities.

Anytown Mall falls into this last category, which, of course, makes sense for the kind of merchandise Decorator's will carry. Anytown is an affluent suburb of Anycity, and the mall is surrounded by upscale residential neighborhoods. Traffic has been counted at 3,500 shoppers per day, fully half of whom represent qualified customers.

The Store as a Destination Shop and as a Walk-In

The nature of Decorator's product line will support both destination shopping and a walk-in trade. People in the market for decorative artwork are likely to make a single-purpose trip to such a specialty store. At the same time, the product lends itself to impulse buying by affluent shoppers.

Once customers are aware of the gallery's presence, they will recall it and seek us out when decorating. That awareness will develop over several months due to advertising, word of mouth, and simply being observed by shoppers in the mall.

IV
PRICING, PROFITABILITY, AND BREAK EVEN

The following pricing and break-even analysis is based on the core retail business alone. The businesses with professional decorators and local artists are considered higher-risk sidelines. The following shows that the core business is viable.

PRICING

The price of artwork depends on its quality and its size. Sizes are quoted, excluding the width of the frame. A 24" x 36" over-the-sofa piece provides a benchmark for pricing. Decorator's will carry such articles ranging in price (list) from $250 to $800. Smaller pieces will be commensurately less expensive. The largest selling sizes and their list price ranges are as follows:

24" × 36"	$250–$800
20" × 24"	$125–$275
18" × 20"	$100–$225
9" × 12"	$50–$125

More of the smaller articles will be sold. The mix of sales by size is expected to be as follows:

24" × 36"	15%
20" × 24"	25%
18" × 20"	20%
9" × 12"	40%
	100%

This size mix is developed from industry averages reported in a study made by *Decorating World*,* a widely read trade publication. The large percentage of small pieces is due to the fact that customers purchase them individually and in groupings. Overall, the average sale is expected to be in the neighborhood of $175 at list.

* A hypothetical publication.

MARK-UP AND PROFIT MARGIN

The mark-up in the retail furniture business is generally 100%. That is, product is priced at twice its wholesale cost. However, as much as 30% of a typical retailer's business is done at discounted "sale" prices. An average discount is 20%. Therefore, the average discount on all sales is calculated as follows:

70% at list	$100 \times .70 = 70$
30% at 20% off list	$80 \times .30 = \underline{24}$
	94

In other words, the average sale is made at 94% of list or at a 6% discount. If cost is 50% of list, the cost ratio (cost as a percentage of revenue) is:

$$50 / 94 = 53.2\%$$

The gross margin percent is then 46.8%.

BREAK-EVEN ANALYSIS

The only significant variable cost is expected to be the wholesale cost of product, so the contribution margin is also 46.8%.

Fixed costs are estimated on a monthly basis as follows:

Rent	$ 3,947
Utilities	350
Depreciation	364
Insurance	150
Advertising	1,500
Interest	750
Salaries	<u>6,402</u>
	$13,463

Hence, break-even volume is:

$$\$13,463 / .468 = \$28,767$$

Assuming the average sale will be in the neighborhood of $175 list or $165 discounted, the break-even volume requires about 175 sales per month ($28,767 / $165). That's a little under six per day, a figure that is eminently reasonable for a busy mall location.

Comment

An air of precision and competence is given to the work and its author by the numerical treatment in this section. The writer seems familiar with the business and what he or she expects out of it. Reference to hard statistics from trade publications adds credibility.

V
OPERATIONS

MERCHANDISING

Merchandise is purchased from one of several wholesale distributors and shipped into the store. Display items are unwrapped and hung in the showroom. Typically, a backroom inventory will be maintained of about twice the size of what is on display.

Suppliers

Preliminary agreements have been reached with three wholesale distributors. These are:

IJK Limited
RSV and Company
MNO, Inc.

All are well known in the art/furniture field.

The initial agreements involve paying cash in advance and at full wholesale prices. Credit will become available after approximately six months of successful business. Discounts may also become available if volume levels warrant. However, none is included in the financial projections to add an element of conservatism to the forecast.

COSTS

A variety of initial and ongoing costs are anticipated. Each is discussed below.

Rent

Rents in enclosed malls are in the neighborhood of $25–$40 per square foot per year. This total includes a variety of service charges and a contribution to an advertising fund. In addition, the mall gets a percentage of annual revenues in excess of some specified amount. A requirement of 10% of amounts over $500,000 a year isn't uncommon. Rents vary somewhat with location within the mall.

To adequately display its merchandise, the gallery will need approximately 1,500 square feet of space. Anytown Mall has two viable spaces available in that size range. Preliminary negotiations suggest a prime location of 1,480 square feet can be rented on a three-year lease at $32 per foot plus 8% of revenues over $500,000. The base rent is then $3,947 per month (1480 × $32 / 12). The mall has agreed to give the month before opening free as a get-ready period and will require a deposit of only $2,500. Rents, however, must be paid in advance.

Leasehold Improvements

The only significant leasehold improvements necessary in the proposed space are lighting and signage. The cost of rewiring and hanging display lights has been bid at $1,800 by HIJ Electrical Contractors.

Signage has been quoted at $2,300 by UVW Signs, Inc. A variety of additional minor touch-ups and improvements are necessary, including a fresh coat of paint. The cost of these is estimated at $2,500.

Fixtures and Equipment

The display of wall hangings requires that the space be broken up into a number of bays to increase the available wall area. This can be done with movable partitioning. A preliminary floor plan is provided in the supporting backup to this plan. Partitioning in accordance with this floor plan has been priced at $3,500. Counters will cost an additional $1,500 and a cash register system has been priced at $1,500. Due to the nature of the product, sophisticated anti-theft devices and bar coded inventory systems are not believed to be necessary.

Depreciable Total

The depreciable costs listed above are summarized as follows:

Leasehold Improvements	$ 6,600
Fixtures and Equipment	6,500
	$13,100

These will be depreciated over the life of the three-year lease anticipated. The monthly depreciation charge will therefore be $364 ($13,100 / 36).

Other Start-Up Costs

Other start-up costs are anticipated as follows:

Incorporation	$ 700
Banking Fees	300
Deposits	1,000
Permits, Licenses	300
Grand Opening	2,000
Misc. Unanticipated	1,000
	$5,300

All start-up costs are expensed in the financial projections except deposits, which are carried as a balance sheet item.

Utilities

Utilities are limited to electricity and phone. These are estimated at $250 and $100 per month, respectively, based on the experience of similar businesses in the mall.

Insurance

A business insurance policy including general insurance liability coverage has been quoted at $150 per month by the QRS Insurance Company.

Terms of Sale

Sales will generally be paid with cash, check, or credit card. The professional decorating trade will be offered sixty days in which to pay upon credit approval. This is expected to be the only way to get their business, as they are cash short until payment by their customers.

Inventory Levels

Since broad selection is key to the gallery's success, a substantial inventory is an absolute necessity. A $40,000 stock is anticipated, which will represent approximately 450 pieces. About one third of these will be displayed in the showroom and the remainder kept readily available in the back room. The plan involves opening with $25,000 and building to $40,000 within three months.

Business Organization

The business will be organized as a limited liability corporation (LLC). The only members of the LLC will be the Eberlys who will own the enterprise jointly with the right of survivorship. Therefore, no stockholder or buy/sell agreements are necessary for the time being.

VI
MANAGEMENT AND STAFFING

The gallery will require a staff of four, three full-time and one part-time. Carol Eberly and two employees will work full-time, while Thomas Eberly will keep the books on a part-time basis and help out in the store when necessary.

CAROL EBERLY

The Decorator's Art Gallery will primarily be run by Carol Eberly. Carol is a mature woman of thirty-eight who has worked all of her adult life. She has a Bachelor of Science degree in Business Administration with a specialty in Marketing. Within marketing she has always concentrated in retailing.

After graduating from DEF College, Carol spent eight years with ABC stores in Boston, Massachusetts. She began as a stock clerk in the firm's management internship program and was subsequently exposed to virtually all facets of retail operations. After completing the two-year internship program, she was an assistant department manager in ladies' apparel and then a department manager in furniture.

Carol joined XYZ stores in Anycity eight years ago and has successfully worked as an assistant buyer, a buyer, and again as a department manager.

Altogether, Ms. Eberly has fifteen years' experience in the retail business, including four years in furniture. She will draw a salary of $25,000 a year from the gallery after the first six months. She will draw no salary during the first six months.

TOM EBERLY

Tom Eberly will assist Carol in operating the store on a part-time basis. Tom is a professional accountant and will be primarily responsible for the company's books and finances.

Tom graduated from LMN College sixteen years ago with a degree in Accounting and joined PQR Electronics shortly thereafter. He's been with the firm ever since and has risen to the department manager level. He's currently in charge of financial reporting and has a staff of fifteen people working under him. He will not draw any compensation from the operation.

EMPLOYEES

The gallery will employ two additional staff members in inside sales. One person can be a relatively unskilled clerk, but the second will be someone with some background in decorating. The latter individual will be called a sales consultant. Compensation for these individuals will be $8 and $12 per hour, respectively. Both will be required from the beginning.

SALARY EXPENSES

Total monthly compensation expenses are estimated as follows.

Manager	$2,100
Consultant	2,080
Clerk	1,387
	$5,567
Benefits @ 15%	835
	$6,402

Since there will be no salary for the manager in the first six months, the expense will be reduced by $2,415 ($2,100 × 1.15) per month to $3,987 during that period.

VII
CONTINGENCY PLANS

In the event that the gallery's acceptance is slower than anticipated, expenses can be reduced as follows:

Ms. Eberly can work without salary indefinitely, as the family can live on Mr. Eberly's income. This reduces planned monthly expenditures by $2,415.

The sales consultant position can be eliminated, saving $2,392 per month.

Inventory can be reduced by $20,000, which will save approximately $300 per month in interest.

These savings reduce operating expenses by a total of $5,107 per month, and reduce the monthly break-even volume in the core business by $10,912, from $28,767 to $17,855.

VIII
FINANCIAL PROJECTIONS

BACKGROUND AND ASSUMPTIONS

The following financial projections are based on sales forecasts in the three distinct areas of activity. The core business is the retail sale of commercially produced artwork to consumers. In addition, sales to decorators are separately forecast, as are sales of original work by local artists.

Each forecast is stated in terms of an equivalent "average" unit, that is, a hypothetical unit that represents a weighted average of the sizes and qualities sold. Implicit in the use of an average unit is the assumption that the size mix of product within each line will remain constant over time. It is a simple matter to change that assumption or to forecast each size individually. However, the use of an average unit makes the buildup of revenue and cost considerably easier to follow.

The following averages are being used:

	Price	Cost	Margin %
Retail	$165	$ 88	46.8%
Decorator	$195	$150	23.1%
Originals	$500	$333	33.3%

The retail price reflects an average discount of 6% from list, while the decorator figure represents a 35% discount.

All projections are presented by month for the first year and by quarter for the following two. The projected financial statements are in standard form.

Revenues and Profits

First-year sales are anticipated at approximately $250,000. These will grow to $422,000 in the second year and $500,000 in the third. At the half-million-dollar sales level, the business will generate profits of approximately $58,000 for a return on sales of 11.6%.

The gallery is expected to lose money at a decreasing rate during the first year of operation while it builds a customer base. Profitability will improve until the end of the third year, when it will level off along with sales volume.

Opening Capital Structure

The business can open with less than $22,000 in borrowed funds. At that point the debt-to-equity ratio will be 48% debt to 52% equity.

APPLICATION AND REPAYMENT OF THE LOAN

The loan requested will be used to set up the business and enable it to operate during the first year. Profits will be negative for the entire first year, while cash flows will turn positive after nine months. Bank borrowings will peak in the ninth month at just under $62,000. Subsequent to that time the loan will be steadily reduced by operating cash flows until it is entirely repaid during the second quarter of the third year. In other words, borrowed monies will be outstanding for approximately two years and four months.

PROJECTED REVENUE BUILDUP AND FINANCIAL STATEMENTS

Decorator's Art Gallery
Unit Sales and Revenue
First Year by Month

		1	2	3	4	5	6	7	8	9	10	11	12	TOTAL
								MONTHS						
Retail Trade Units		100	60	70	80	90	100	110	120	130	140	150	150	1,300
Average Price	$165 (Discounted)													
Revenue		$16,500	9,900	11,550	13,200	14,850	16,500	18,150	19,800	21,450	23,100	24,750	24,750	$214,500
Cost	0.532	$8,778	5,267	6,145	7,022	7,900	8,778	9,656	10,534	11,411	12,289	13,167	13,167	$114,114
Gross Margin		$7,722	4,633	5,405	6,178	6,950	7,722	8,494	9,266	10,039	10,811	11,583	11,583	$100,386
Decorator Trade Units		0	1	2	2	3	4	5	5	7	9	10	11	59
Average Price	$195 (Discounted)													
Revenue		0	$195	390	390	585	780	975	975	1,365	1,755	1,950	2,145	$11,505
Cost	0.769	0	$150	300	300	450	600	750	750	1,050	1,350	1,500	1,650	$8,847
Gross Margin		0	$45	90	90	135	180	225	225	315	405	450	495	$2,658
Local Artists Units		2	3	4	4	4	5	5	5	6	6	6	6	56
Average Price	$500 (Discounted)													
Revenue		$1,000	1,500	2,000	2,000	2,000	2,500	2,500	2,500	3,000	3,000	3,000	3,000	$28,000
Cost	0.667	$667	1,001	1,334	1,334	1,334	1,668	1,668	1,668	2,001	2,001	2,001	2,001	$18,676
Gross Margin		$333	499	666	666	666	833	833	833	999	999	999	999	$9,324

Decorator's Art Gallery
Income Statement
First Year by Month

MONTHS

	1	2	3	4	5	6	7	8	9	10	11	12	TOTAL
Revenue	$17,500	$11,595	$13,940	$15,590	$17,435	$19,780	$21,625	$23,275	$25,815	$27,855	$29,700	$29,895	$254,005
Cost	$9,445	$6,417	$7,779	$8,656	$9,684	$11,045	$12,073	$12,951	$14,462	$15,640	$16,668	$16,818	$141,637
Gross Margin	$8,055	$5,178	$6,161	$6,934	$7,751	$8,735	$9,552	$10,324	$11,353	$12,215	$13,032	$13,077	$112,368
Expenses													
Rent	$3,947	$3,947	$3,947	$3,947	$3,947	$3,947	$3,947	$3,947	$3,947	$3,947	$3,947	$3,947	$47,364
Salaries	$3,987	$3,987	$3,987	$3,987	$3,987	$3,987	$6,402	$6,402	$6,402	$6,402	$6,402	$6,402	$62,334
Advertising	$1,500	$1,500	$1,500	$1,500	$1,500	$1,500	$1,500	$1,500	$1,500	$1,500	$1,500	$1,500	$18,000
Util/Insur	$500	$500	$500	$500	$500	$500	$500	$500	$500	$500	$500	$500	$6,000
Depreciation	$364	$364	$364	$364	$364	$364	$364	$364	$364	$364	$364	$364	$4,368
Start-Up Expense	$4,300												$4,300
Total	$14,598	$10,298	$10,298	$10,298	$10,298	$10,298	$12,713	$12,713	$12,713	$12,713	$12,713	$12,713	$142,366
EBIT	($6,543)	($5,120)	($4,137)	($3,364)	($2,547)	($1,563)	($3,161)	($2,389)	($1,360)	($498)	$319	$364	($29,998)
Interest	$410	$575	$725	$800	$835	$850	$880	$910	$920	$890	$850	$850	$9,495
EBT	($6,953)	($5,695)	($4,862)	($4,164)	($3,382)	($2,413)	($4,041)	($3,299)	($2,280)	($1,388)	($531)	($486)	($39,493)
Tax	$0	$0	$0	$0	$0	$0	$0	$0	$0	$0	$0	$0	$0
EAT	($6,953)	($5,695)	($4,862)	($4,164)	($3,382)	($2,413)	($4,041)	($3,299)	($2,280)	($1,388)	($531)	($486)	($39,493)
Dividends													$0

Decorator's Art Gallery
Balance Sheet
First Year by Month

MONTHS

	Opening	1	2	3	4	5	6	7	8	9	10	11	12
Assets													
Cash	$5,000	$5,000	$5,000	$5,000	$5,000	$5,000	$5,000	$5,000	$5,000	$5,000	$5,000	$5,000	$5,000
Accounts Receivable	$0	$0	$0	$195	$390	$390	$585	$780	$975	$975	$1,365	$1,755	$1,950
Inventory	$25,000	$30,000	$35,000	$40,000	$40,000	$40,000	$40,000	$40,000	$40,000	$40,000	$40,000	$40,000	$40,000
Current Assets	$30,000	$35,000	$40,000	$45,195	$45,390	$45,390	$45,585	$45,780	$45,975	$45,975	$46,365	$46,755	$46,950
Deposits	$3,500	$3,500	$3,500	$3,500	$3,500	$3,500	$3,500	$3,500	$3,500	$3,500	$3,500	$3,500	$3,500
Fixed Assets													
Gross	$13,100	$13,100	$13,100	$13,100	$13,100	$13,100	$13,100	$13,100	$13,100	$13,100	$13,100	$13,100	$13,100
Accumulated Depreciation	$0	($364)	($728)	($1,092)	($1,456)	($1,820)	($2,184)	($2,548)	($2,912)	($3,276)	($3,640)	($4,004)	($4,368)
Net	$13,100	$12,736	$12,372	$12,008	$11,644	$11,280	$10,916	$10,552	$10,188	$9,824	$9,460	$9,096	$8,732
Total Assets	$46,600	$51,236	$55,872	$60,703	$60,534	$60,170	$60,001	$59,832	$59,663	$59,299	$59,325	$59,351	$59,182
Liabilities													
Accts Payable	$0	$0	$0	$0	$2,885	$3,228	$5,523	$6,037	$8,634	$9,641	$15,640	$16,668	$16,818
Current Liabilities	$0	$0	$0	$0	$2,885	$3,228	$5,523	$6,037	$8,634	$9,641	$15,640	$16,668	$16,818
Debt	$21,600	$33,189	$43,520	$53,213	$54,323	$56,998	$56,948	$60,306	$60,838	$61,747	$57,162	$56,691	$56,858
Equity	$25,000	$18,047	$12,352	$7,490	$3,326	($56)	($2,469)	($6,511)	($9,809)	($12,089)	($13,477)	($14,008)	($14,493)
Total Liabilities & Equity	$46,600	$51,236	$55,872	$60,703	$60,534	$60,170	$60,001	$59,832	$59,663	$59,299	$59,325	$59,351	$59,182

Decorator's Art Gallery
Cash Flow Statement
First Year by Month

MONTHS

	1	2	3	4	5	6	7	8	9	10	11	12	TOTAL
Cash from Operating Activities													
Net Income	($6,953)	($5,695)	($4,862)	($4,164)	($3,382)	($2,413)	($4,041)	($3,299)	($2,280)	($1,388)	($531)	($486)	($39,493)
Depreciation	$364	$364	$364	$364	$364	$364	$364	$364	$364	$364	$364	$364	$4,368
Decr/(Incr) in A/R	$0	$0	($195)	($195)	$0	($195)	($195)	($195)	$0	($390)	($390)	($195)	($1,950)
Decr/(Incr) in Inventory	($5,000)	($5,000)	($5,000)	$0	$0	$0	$0	$0	$0	$0	$0	$0	($15,000)
Incr/(Decr) in A/P	$0	$0	$0	$2,885	$343	$2,295	$514	$2,597	$1,007	$5,998	$1,028	$150	$16,818
Cash from Operations	($11,589)	($10,331)	($9,693)	($1,110)	($2,675)	$50	($3,358)	($532)	($909)	$4,585	$471	($167)	($35,258)
Cash from Investing Activities													
Decr/(Incr) in Fixed Assets	$0	$0	$0	$0	$0	$0	$0	$0	$0	$0	$0	$0	$0
Cash from Financing Activities													
Incr/(Decr) in Debt	$11,589	$10,331	$9,693	$1,110	$2,675	($50)	$3,358	$532	$909	($4,585)	($471)	$167	$35,258
Dividends	$0	$0	$0	$0	$0	$0	$0	$0	$0	$0	$0	$0	$0
Cash from Financing Activities	$11,589	$10,331	$9,693	$1,110	$2,675	($50)	$3,358	$532	$909	($4,585)	($471)	$167	$35,258
Net Cash Flow	$0	($0)	$0	$0	($0)	$0	$0	$0	($0)	($0)	($0)	$0	$0
Beginning Cash Balance	$5,000	$5,000	$5,000	$5,000	$5,000	$5,000	$5,000	$5,000	$5,000	$5,000	$5,000	$5,000	
Net Cash Flow	$0	($0)	$0	$0	($0)	$0	$0	$0	($0)	($0)	($0)	$0	
Ending Cash Balance	$5,000	$5,000	$5,000	$5,000	$5,000	$5,000	$5,000	$5,000	$5,000	$5,000	$5,000	$5,000	

Decorator's Art Gallery
Unit Sales and Revenue
Second Year by Quarter

		QUARTERS				
		1	2	3	4	TOTAL
Retail Trade Units		475	500	550	600	2,125
Average Price	165 (discounted)					
Revenue		78,375	82,500	90,750	99,000	$350,625
Cost	0.532	41,695.5	43,890	48,279	52,668	$186,533
Gross Margin		36,679.5	38,610	42,471	46,332	$164,093
Decorator Trade Units		33	35	38	40	146
Average Price	195 (discounted)					
Revenue		6,435	6,825	7,410	7,800	$28,470
Cost	0.769	4,948.515	5,248.425	5,698.29	5,998.2	$21,893
Gross Margin		1,486.485	1,576.575	1,711.71	1,801.8	$6,577
Local Artists Units		20	21	22	23	86
Average Price	500 (discounted)					
Revenue		10,000	10,500	11,000	11,500	$43,000
Cost	0.667	6,670	7,003.5	7,337	7,670.5	$28,681
Gross Margin		3,330	3,496.5	3,663	3,829.5	$14,319

Decorator's Art Gallery
Income Statement
Second Year by Quarter

	QUARTERS				
	1	2	3	4	TOTAL
Revenue	$94,810	$99,825	$109,160	$118,300	$422,095
Cost	$53,314	$56,142	$61,314	$66,337	$237,107
Gross Margin	$41,496	43,683	$47,846	$51,963	$184,988
Expenses					
Rent	$11,841	$11,841	$11,841	$11,841	$47,364
Salaries	$19,206	$19,206	$19,206	$19,206	$76,824
Advertising	$4,500	$4,500	$4,500	$4,500	$18,000
Util/Insur	$1,500	$1,500	$1,500	$1,500	$6,000
Depreciation	$1,092	$1,092	$1,092	$1,092	$4,368
Total	$38,139	$38,139	$38,139	$38,139	$152,556
EBIT	$3,357	$5,544	$9,707	$13,824	$32,432
Interest	$2,500	$2,300	$1,950	$1,390	$8,140
EBT	$857	$3,244	$7,757	$12,434	$24,292
Tax	$0	$0	$0	$0	$0
EAT	$857	$3,244	$7,757	$12,434	$24,292
Dividends					$0

Decorator's Art Gallery
Balance Sheet
Second Year by Quarter

	QUARTERS			
	1	2	3	4
Assets				
Cash	$5,000	$5,000	$5,000	$5,000
Accts Receivable	$2,145	$2,145	$2,275	$2,470
Inventory	$40,000	$40,000	$40,000	$40,000
Current Assets	$47,145	$47,145	$47,275	$47,470
Deposits	$3,500	$3,500	$3,500	$3,500
Fixed Assets				
Gross	$13,100	$13,100	$13,100	$13,100
Accumulated Depreciation	($5,460)	($6,552)	($7,644)	($8,736)
Net	$7,640	$6,548	$5,456	$4,364
Total Assets	$58,285	$57,193	$56,231	$55,334
Liabilities				
Accounts Payable	$17,771	$18,714	$20,438	$22,112
Current Liabilities	$17,771	$18,714	$20,438	$22,112
Debt	$54,150	$48,871	$38,428	$23,423
Equity	($13,636)	($10,392)	($2,636)	$9,799
Total Liabilities & Equity	$58,285	$57,193	$56,231	$55,334

Decorator's Art Gallery
Cash Flow Statement
Second Year by Quarter

	QUARTERS				
	1	2	3	4	TOTAL
Cash from Operating Activities					
EAT	$857	$3,244	$7,757	$12,434	$24,292
Depreciation	$1,092	$1,092	$1,092	$1,092	$4,368
Decr/(Incr) in A/R	($195)	$0	($130)	($195)	($520)
Decr/(Incr) in Inventory	$0	$0	$0	$0	$0
Incr/(Decr) in A/P	$954	$943	$1,724	$1,674	$5,295
Cash from Operations	$2,708	$5,279	$10,443	$15,005	$33,435
Cash from Investing Activities					
Decr/(Incr) in Fixed Assets	$0	$0	$0	$0	$0
Cash from Financing Activities					
Incr/(Decr) in Debt	($2,708)	($5,279)	($10,443)	($15,005)	($33,435)
Dividends	$0	$0	$0	$0	$0
Cash From Financing Activities	($2,708)	($5,279)	($10,443)	($15,005)	($33,435)
Net Cash Flow	($0)	$0	$0	$0	$0
Beginning Cash Balance	$5,000	$5,000	$5,000	$5,000	$20,000
Net Cash Flow	($0)	$0	$0	$0	$0
Ending Cash Balance	$5,000	$5,000	$5,000	$5,000	$20,000

Decorator's Art Gallery
Unit Sales and Revenue
Third Year by Quarter

		QUARTERS				
		1	2	3	4	TOTAL
Retail Trade Units		610	625	640	650	2,525
Average Price	165 (discounted)					
Revenue		100,650	103,125	105,600	107,250	$416,625
Cost	0.532	53,545.8	54,862.5	56,179.2	57,057	$221,645
Gross Margin		47,104.2	48,262.5	49,420.8	50,193	$194,981
Decorator Trade Units		42	45	50	55	192
Average Price	195 (discounted)					
Revenue		8,190	8,775	9,750	10,725	$37,440
Cost	0.769	6,298.11	6,747.975	7,497.75	8,247.525	$28,791
Gross Margin		1,891.89	2,027.025	2,252.25	2,477.475	$8,649
Local Artists Units		24	25	25	26	100
Average Price	500 (discounted)					
Revenue		12,000	12,500	12,500	13,000	$50,000
Cost	0.667	8,004	8,337.5	8,337.5	8,671	$33,350
Gross Margin		3,996	4,162.5	4,162.5	4,329	$16,650

Decorator's Art Gallery
Income Statement
Third Year by Quarter

	QUARTERS				
	1	2	3	4	TOTAL
Revenue	$120,840	$124,400	$127,850	$130,975	$504,065
Cost	$67,848	$69,948	$72,014	$73,976	$283,786
Gross Margin	$52,992	$54,452	$55,836	$56,999	$220,279
Expenses					
Rent	$11,841	$11,841	$11,841	$11,841	$47,364
Salaries	$19,206	$19,206	$19,206	$19,206	$76,824
Advertising	$4,500	$4,500	$4,500	$4,500	$18,000
Util/Insur	$1,500	$1,500	$1,500	$1,500	$6,000
Depreciation	$1,092	$1,092	$1,092	$1,088	$4,364
Total	$38,139	$38,139	$38,139	$38,135	$152,552
EBIT	$14,853	$16,313	$17,697	$18,864	$67,727
Interest	$700	$175	$0	$0	$875
EBT	$14,153	$16,138	$17,697	$18,864	$66,852
Tax	$0	$293	$4,955	$5,282	$10,530
EAT	$14,153	$15,845	$12,742	$13,582	$56,322
Dividends		$9,703	$14,327	$14,999	$39,029

Decorator's Art Gallery
Balance Sheet
Third Year by Quarter

	QUARTERS			
	1	2	3	4
Assets				
Cash	$5,000	$5,000	$5,000	$5,000
Accts Receivable	$2,600	$2,730	$2,925	$3,250
Inventory	$40,000	$40,000	$40,000	$40,000
Current Assets	$47,600	$47,730	$47,925	$48,250
Deposits	$3,500	$3,500	$3,500	$3,500
Fixed Assets				
Gross	$13,100	$13,100	$13,100	$13,100
Accumulated Depreciation	($9,828)	($10,920)	($12,012)	($13,100)
Net	$3,272	$2,180	$1,088	$0
Total Assets	$54,372	$53,410	$52,513	$51,750
Liabilities				
Accts Payable	$22,616	$23,316	$24,005	$24,659
Current Liabilities	$22,616	$23,316	$24,005	$24,659
Debt	$7,804	$0	($0)	($0)
Equity	$23,952	$30,094	$28,508	$27,092
Total Liabilities & Equity	$54,372	$53,410	$52,513	$51,750

Decorator's Art Gallery
Cash Flow Statement
Third Year by Quarter

	QUARTERS				
	1	2	3	4	TOTAL
Cash from Operating Activities					
EAT	$14,153	$15,845	$12,742	$13,582	$56,322
Depreciation	$1,092	$1,092	$1,092	$1,088	$4,364
Decr/(Incr) in A/R	($130)	($130)	($195)	($325)	($780)
Decr/(Incr) in Inv	$0	$0	$0	$0	$0
Incr/(Decr) in A/P	$504	$700	$689	$654	$2,546
Cash from Operations	$15,619	$17,507	$14,327	$14,999	$62,452
Cash from Investing Activities					
Decr/(Incr) in Fixed Assets	$0	$0	$0	$0	$0
Cash from Financing Activities					
Incr/(Decr) in Debt	($15,619)	($7,804)	($0)	($0)	($23,423)
Dividends	$0	($9,703)	($14,327)	($14,999)	($39,029)
Cash from Financing Activities	($15,619)	($17,507)	($14,327)	($14,999)	($62,452)
Net Cash Flow	($0)	$0	$0	$0	($0)
Beginning Cash Balance	$5,000	$5,000	$5,000	$5,000	
Net Cash Flow	($0)	$0	$0	$0	
Ending Cash Balance	$5,000	$5,000	$5,000	$5,000	

APPENDICES

Appendices should be included as required and appropriate for the plan. They might include résumés, equipment lists, illustrative material from suppliers, price quotes from vendors, a floor plan of the facility, and anything else that might be relevant.

All appendices need not be attached to every copy of the plan but should be available to readers upon request.

Business plan appendices are not included here, as their illustrative value is minimal.

CASE II—MAX UPTIME, INC.

The following business plan for Max Uptime is designed to illustrate presentation techniques for a relatively complicated business. The plan proposes building an organization that services computer equipment for business customers. The plan's complexity stems from two sources. First, the business isn't something that is commonly understood. That is, readers aren't likely to know anything about how it's run or what factors are important for success. As a result, the plan has to educate readers about the business before it has a chance of selling them on the idea.

Second, planning for this particular business involves a complicated set of numerical assumptions and relationships. The physical world here involves a system of equipment characteristics, manpower requirements, and travel expenses. These translate into financial projections through a rather complex model and an involved set of arithmetic calculations. Those relationships must be made clear to an uninformed but interested reader. That can be relatively hard to do.

CASE BACKGROUND

Joe Updyke and Charlie Conners are field technicians for BigTech, a large company that manufactures and sells sophisticated computer and networking equipment. Field technicians are highly skilled individuals who repair and maintain equipment on customers' premises, that is, in the field. They are hourly employees at most companies. Few field technicians are college educated; most receive their training at a trade school or in the military.

Joe and Charlie are typical in this respect. Joe has a high school education and learned his technical skills during a four-year enlistment in the Navy. Charlie is also a high school graduate, and got his technical education at a one-year trade school. He has, however, been continuing his education at night.

Both men are in their early thirties. Charlie is a senior technician and makes about $45,000 per year. His total earnings can be as high as $55,000 with overtime. Joe is a district man-ager and makes about $65,000 but doesn't get overtime, even though he often puts in 55 hours a week. Neither sees much room for advancement beyond their current level. They're both approaching the top of their pay scales and higher-level management jobs are hard to get.

Joe and Charlie are interested in quitting their jobs and starting their own service company, which they will call Max Uptime, Inc. The name is meant to convey the idea that customers will maximize the uptime of their equipment by using the firm, because the service will be quick and efficient. (Up and down are vernacular terms applied to machinery meaning it is working or not working due to technical problems.)

There is some precedent for small, independent service companies, but they must generally price substantially below the service offerings of manufacturers or distributors. It's possible to do that because of the lower overhead carried by the smaller firms.

Joe and Charlie know the IT directors of the accounts they currently service for BigTech.

(IT stands for Information Technology, the most common title for computer departments in American companies. The IT director is the executive in charge of operating and maintaining computer and communications equipment.) They have cautiously felt these individuals out and believe that several would switch to their firm if they were on their own and offered a hefty price advantage. In addition, they believe many others would sign up if a cost savings were offered.

A service business doesn't require a lot of capital, but some equipment is necessary to get started. The men also need working capital to set up shop, get into business, and support operations until the business can manage on the cash it generates itself. They estimate their total requirements at $175,000. Between them, they can contribute $25,000 from savings, so they need about $150,000 more. Unfortunately, neither has much to offer in the way of collateral. Therefore, they hope to secure a loan guaranteed by the SBA. They have prepared the following business plan for presentation to the First National Bank of BigCity.

MAX UPTIME, INC.

BUSINESS PLAN

Presented to the First National Bank of BigCity

by Joseph P. Updyke and Charles F. Conners

CONTENTS

I
EXECUTIVE SUMMARY

MARKET

Business owners of computer and network equipment must contract with service specialists to maintain that equipment. They generally have three choices: manufacturer's service, large service companies, and local independent firms. The appeal of local firms is based largely on price, which is in the neighborhood of 30% below that of the manufacturers and 15% to 20% below the large service companies.

Existing local firms have about 10% of the market but show little growth because they have not marketed themselves aggressively or presented their service offerings innovatively.

From a customer's viewpoint, the key factors in service are price and the speed with which the provider responds to emergency calls when essential equipment is down. Rapid-response arrangements are available, but at a considerable price premium. Customers feel that rapid response is generally over-priced for what they get.

PROPOSED BUSINESS

Max Uptime, Inc. proposes to enter the independent market for service. It will distinguish itself from other independents in two major ways. First, it will aggressively market itself to the computer community, something the other independents have not done. Second, it will provide an innovatively packaged rapid response option that will be perceived by customers as being considerably cheaper than options offered by the competition. The offering will be called RRAN for Rapid Response As Needed. It will cost less to provide than the additional revenue it generates.

MANAGEMENT

Max Uptime will be operated by Joseph P. Updyke and Charles F. Conners, each of whom has many years of experience in technical service. The entrepreneurs are dedicated, enthusiastic experts in their field. They have researched the market and the venture thoroughly and are confident of its success.

LOAN REQUEST

The owners are requesting a loan to support working capital until the business grows to a point at which it can fund itself internally. Borrowed funds will increase over the first two years to a maximum of $150,000. Subsequently, internally generated cash will pay off the loan by the middle of the fourth year. The owners will invest $25,000 of their own at the outset. However, they do not have the personal resources to collateralize a debt of this magnitude, so an SBA-backed loan is requested.

II
MISSION AND STRATEGY

MISSION

Max Uptime, Inc. will serve the business computing community of BigCity by providing quality on-site maintenance and repair services on selected equipment at a substantial cost savings to customers. The firm will grow from the two founders and two employees to employ approximately thirteen people, including nine Field Technicians over a four-year time span. Its annual revenues in the fourth year will be in the neighborhood of one million dollars with profitability at close to 15% of sales. This will rank the firm third among local, independent service firms.

STRATEGY

The firm will succeed in the marketplace through aggressive pricing and innovative contracting. It will offer its customers more for their money than the competition. The emphasis will be on packaging a rapid response service in a way that makes customers perceive that they're getting a very substantial price advantage. Profits will be achievable at these lower prices due to the efficiencies inherent in limiting the geographic scope of operations and the variety of equipment serviced.

III
MARKET

BACKGROUND

In today's business world, computers are a vital part of the daily operation of companies. When a computer goes down, some or all of the user's organization stops functioning. Such interruptions can cost large sums of money and result in damaged relations with customers and suppliers. Because the operation of computers is so critical, customers purchasing or leasing equipment consider service an important and integral part of the package they're buying. Fast, remedial service is as important as product quality and reliability, because even the best machines break occasionally. How long they're down is a function of the organization providing service. Clearly, regular preventive maintenance is also important in minimizing the disruptions caused by inoperative equipment.

The Cost of Service as a Part of Acquiring Equipment

The cost of service is an important element in the buyer's purchase decision. A customer buying equipment today must pay for service during its entire life. This has led to the use of a lifetime cost in evaluating computer and networking equipment. That is, the total cost of acquisition is the purchase price plus the present value of five or more years of maintenance. When viewed like this, maintenance is often a larger component of computer and networking cost than is the equipment itself!

The Service Function of Manufacturers

Equipment manufacturers generally offer to service what they sell. They often have large technical departments serving the entire country.

The maintenance function for smaller manufacturers is generally a money-losing operation because of geography and equipment density. Limiting the geographic scope of service hurts sales, so large areas have to be covered. Overhead costs are therefore substantial relative to the revenue produced, and it's next to impossible to run the service business profitably.

However, after a manufacturing firm has been in business for a while and the number of installed units grows fairly large, the service business usually turns profitable. As the density of equipment installations increases, field technicians can be used more effectively with less time wasted traveling and waiting for calls. In fact, in larger, more mature companies, service can become a mainstay of the organization's earnings. That's because service revenues tend to be fairly stable and independent of the economic ups and downs that play havoc with product sales. A well-run service department can consistently earn after tax profits of 10% or more of sales on a relatively low investment.

Independent Providers and the Cost of Service

Manufacturer's service, much like dealer service on automobiles, tends to be expensive, and customers are often open to cheaper ways to get the job done. An option is available through firms that provide service directly to equipment owners. Such providers are not affiliated with the manufacturers. When equipment is leased, customers usually have no choice except to use the manufacturer's service, but purchased equipment can be maintained by anyone the owner chooses.

Independent providers can be broken into two categories. These are large organizations that provide service on virtually anything anywhere, and small privately owned firms that generally limit what they do to specific areas and selected types of equipment.

Independent service providers can be as much as 30% cheaper than manufacturers. The advantage is due to the lower overhead of the independents and the fact that they don't have to take customers where it doesn't make economic sense. Smaller independents usually limit their operations to densely populated areas in which there are heavy concentrations of equipment.

THE CUSTOMER NEED

Many medium-sized companies purchase their own equipment and must select an organization to provide service. To IT directors, two important criteria exist in that selection. These are cost and the expected amount of downtime that must be endured with a particular provider.

An important element of the expected level of downtime is the *response time* guaranteed by the provider. Response time is the number of hours that elapse from the time the customer reports an equipment failure until a technician arrives on site.

The time required to fix a problem once the technician is there is about the same for any provider given the standard diagnostic procedures that are built into most modern equipment. Further, once the fault is isolated, fixing it is a matter of installing a new part, usually a circuit board. The old board is either scrapped or repaired later.

The response time offered by standard service contracts in the industry is eight business hours. That essentially means next-day response, which can be a real problem for customers. If equipment fails in the afternoon, it can be more than twenty-four hours before service arrives. If the company being serviced is running second or third shifts, they can be entirely lost under a normal service contract. To make matters worse, some service providers consider a response to be a telephone contact with the customer to ascertain the nature of the problem. An on-site repair person comes only after that.

Service providers offer faster response at premium prices under special contracts. The premium can be as much as 100% of normal charges.

Customers need an approach to service that provides rapid response on critical equipment but costs less overall than the standard contracts provided by manufacturers.

THE TARGET CUSTOMER

Max Uptime will target small and medium-sized businesses with modest equipment installations. These will generally be operations with revenues between $3 million and $30 million annually. A typical customer will have an IT budget ranging from $.5 million to $1 million and will spend $50,000 to $100,000 per year on maintenance.

We will begin by approaching the forty-five companies listed in Appendix A. All of these are firms for which the authors have done maintenance in the past and whose IT managements are known to us.

We will not target larger companies, as they are unlikely to go with a new and untried provider regardless of the appeal of the deal.

MAX UPTIME'S SERVICE OFFERING

Max Uptime will offer maintenance and repair services for selected pieces of computer and network equipment. The equipment serviced will generally not be state of the art, but will be two or more years old. Spare parts and maintenance procedures are difficult and expensive to obtain for the newest equipment but are readily available for older machines. The specific pieces of equipment to be serviced are listed in Appendix B. It is anticipated that this list will expand as time passes and Max Uptime is successful.

Service will be offered under the following contractual arrangements:

Standard Contract. A standard service contract provides for periodic preventive maintenance of equipment where necessary, and repair service whenever required at a flat rate per month. A standard contract provides next-day response. It is expected that this contract will be chosen on equipment that's rarely critical to company operations. This is generally the case when firms have many copies of the same thing, such as PCs, and it's possible to run a critical application on another machine until the broken one is fixed.

Rapid Response Contract. The standard contract, with response times guaranteed down to as little as two hours from the receipt of a call, involves a substantial price premium.

Rapid Response As Needed (RRAN) Contract. This is our innovative offering. It consists of a standard contract with a variable response time. Customers pay a modest premium for the rapid response capability plus a variable fee per call. The fee depends on how fast they need someone to arrive on site. In other words, customers assess the criticality of their needs at the time failures are called in. They then choose a response time based on their own assessment and are billed an additional fee accordingly.

Time and Materials (T&M) Contract. Periodic preventive maintenance and repair services are provided only as requested. Response time is within two days. No rapid response option is provided, as we wish to discourage this arrangement.

STRATEGY AND APPROACH TO THE MARKET

Max Uptime will appeal to customers because of a combination of low price and the availability of rapid response, also at a price advantage. In general, pricing will be 30% to 35% below the manufacturers' offering for any level of service, and 15% to 20% below the major independents.

We will be able to accomplish this due to our very low overhead and the limited area in which we will operate. It is estimated that there are more than 100,000 pieces of equipment of the type we will maintain (Appendix B) within a 10-mile radius of the center of BigCity. By restricting ourselves to this area, we will enhance our flexibility and the speed with which we can respond to emergency calls. In fact, two- or three-hour response time should be little more than a minor dispatch problem under normal circumstances.

A key element is expected to be the innovative Rapid Response As Needed (RRAN) offering. Customers will perceive this as a way to achieve the insurance of a rapid response contract without paying much for it unless they actually need it. From our perspective, we will probably respond to most emergency calls nearly as fast anyway, so the extra money is a costless bonus.

Larger competitors don't offer a service product structured like RRAN, because they want to move customers into standard quick response contracts, which tend to be very profitable. Max Uptime is essentially offering a cut-rate quick response contract with this option.

The usual rapid response contract is somewhat self-defeating. Because customers pay a flat rate for rapid response, they demand it for almost any problem. In other words, problems are escalated to an emergency status whether or not they're really critical. Under the RRAN concept, customers aren't motivated to do that. Because they only pay for rapid service when they use it, they'll use it sparingly. That will reduce our cost of providing RRAN significantly below that of providing a regular rapid response contract.

Comment

Notice that Max Uptime is using a differentiation strategy based on the Rapid Response as Needed idea. An astute observer might well question whether or not that approach will work. The plan anticipates the question, and tells why others don't use the idea, but the argument isn't entirely convincing. Perhaps the reason is that it's not as easy to do as Max Uptime thinks, even for them.

Market Research and the RRAN Concept

Max Uptime's concept of Rapid Response as Needed came from some relatively informal market research conducted by the authors. Over the past two years we engaged IT management in conversation whenever possible and asked what they did and didn't like about the service arrangements they currently had and service offerings in general. A recurring comment was that rapid response was too expensive given the fact that it was only really needed occasionally. They also couldn't see why it should be priced as high as it is. They basically felt it was a rip-off, but that there wasn't anything they could do about it.

Following up on the idea, we posed as a market research firm and sent a brief questionnaire to 250 IT directors asking their opinion on the pricing of quick response service. We received 31 responses that essentially confirmed that they shared the opinions of those with whom we had talked.

That research led us to believe that significant inroads could be made into the market by offering a cleverly packaged quick response product. We would take some risk in that we would not receive as much money for providing a rapid response capability as other firms usually do, but our limited geographic coverage would enable us to respond quickly with minimal added cost.

The RRAN concept is designed to be a door opener that will help to give us our initial entrée into the market. It is almost certain to generate sales. However, in the long run, as the firm acquires more customers, it may become costly to the point of unprofitability. If that occurs, it can be slowly phased out without loss of market position.

Comment

Here's a good example of a creative use of the market research idea to build the reader's interest and your own credibility. This research isn't very scientific, and the results may be badly biased toward what the researchers wanted to hear. Nevertheless, the fact that our entrepreneurs went to this much trouble and have shown this much professional creativity leads the reader to believe that they will indeed be aggressive promoters of their own business once it's started. In other words, you get the idea that even if RRAN isn't as successful as they hope, Joe and Charlie will still make the business go.

Approach to Customers

Max Uptime will approach the market by making direct, personal contact with the IT directors of all the targeted companies in the area. A professional letter outlining our offerings will be sent to each of these decision-makers and followed up with a phone call the next week asking for an opportunity to make a presentation. A copy of the proposed letter is included as Appendix C. We expect this approach to generate a large number of face-to-face presentations, because IT departments are typically under considerable pressure to reduce cost.

The marketing effort will have to be fairly intense in the beginning but will diminish as business picks up. Having the best sales skills, Charles Conners will serve as the primary marketer. At least initially, that's all he'll do, while Joseph Updyke handles the service.

COMPETITIVE ANALYSIS AND MARKET SHARE

The Competition

Service providers in the BigCity area fall into three categories: manufacturers, national service companies, and small local independents. There are six major manufacturers:

AA	DD
BB	EE
CC	FF

There are two large national service firms, XXX and XXY, and four local operators:

> Maintenance, Inc.,
> Johnson and Bellows, Inc.,
> Service Masters, and
> High Tech Service, Inc.

Estimate of Relevant Market Size and Growth Rate

Size. The BigCity Chamber of Commerce lists 638 firms in the area in the target size range of from $3 to $30 million in revenues. We'll assume the average size of these firms is $10 million. In general, American companies spend 5% of revenues on IT and computer services and 20% of the IT budget generally goes into maintenance. This yields a target market size of:

$$638 \times \$10 \text{ million} \times 5\% \times 20\% = \$63.8 \text{ million}$$

Growth. The computer network industry is in a general recession at the current time. In the BigCity area, firms are struggling with reducing expenses rather than expanding operations. For planning purposes, it is both conservative and realistic to assume zero growth of the target market over the next few years.

Current Market Shares

Precise market share data is almost impossible to come by because of the restriction defining our target market in terms of company size and the fact that we're dealing with a single metropolitan area. However, we have been able to develop some informed estimates based on our own knowledge of the business and interviews with several other people. These estimates divide the market up as follows:

Manufacturers	50%
Large Service Providers	40%
Independents	10%

Clearly Max Uptime's most intense competition will come from the other local independents. Their approximate size in terms of revenues and staff as well as their market share and time in business is indicated below:

Firm	Technicians	Revenues	Market Share	Established
Maint Inc.	30	$3.0M	4.7%	1990
J & B Inc.	17	1.6M	2.5%	1986
Serv Mst	10	.9M	1.4%	1995
High Tech	7	.7M	1.1%	1998
Totals	64	$6.2M	9.8%	

Max Uptime's Projected Market Share

Max Uptime plans to grow to annual revenues of $1.1 million in the four-year time frame. Using the current market size, that translates to a 1.7% (1.1 / 63.8) market share. If the independent participants were to remain in their current positions, that would place us just ahead of Service Masters in the number three position.

The currently operating independents have managed to capture only 10% of the total service market although they've been in business on the average over ten years. It's important to understand that the reason for this seemingly poor performance isn't the reluctance of customers to use smaller firms. Rather, we believe it is because the four firms now in business have not aggressively presented themselves to the general market. Each business started with one or two accounts gained from the personal contacts of the founders and have grown largely through word of mouth. Max Uptime, on the other hand, plans an active solicitation campaign from the start, which will continue indefinitely.

Additionally, the current players have offered nothing innovative in terms of services or contracts. Their product is packaged identically with the manufacturers, but at a lower price. Max Uptime's strategy is based on managing the customer's perception of response time. This is a feature that we believe will prove highly attractive based on our research.

The Source of Share and the Response of Competitors

Since the local market is assumed not to be growing, Max Uptime's share will have to come from competing firms. We believe that about 70% of our business will come from people currently using manufacturers' service. This success will be a result of a three-pronged attack: (1) aggressive pricing, (2) intense marketing and solicitation, and (3) the appeal of the RRAN concept.

We expect no response from the manufacturers as a result of our inroads. Their loss will be small in terms of their size locally and imperceptible on the national level from which any retaliatory policy change would have to come.

About 20% of the business should come from the national service providers. It will generally be harder to take business from the nationals because they offer about a 20% discount off manufacturers' pricing. That makes our 30% discount less attractive to a customer using their service. Again, we don't expect any retaliatory action from these large companies due to our presence.

Only about 10% of revenues are expected to be taken from the local independents. This will have to be based on the RRAN concept, as our overall pricing won't be much different from theirs. In addition, it will be difficult to overcome the long-term relationship and loyalty built up between these firms and their customers.

It is quite likely that the local competitors will copy the RRAN idea once it shows itself to be a success. They will, however, be skeptical about it for some time. We estimate that it will be two years at the earliest before anyone else tries it. By that time, we'll be established. It's unlikely that the others will change their styles and emulate our marketing approach. We therefore don't believe that their late adoption of RRAN will change the market much.

IV
OPERATIONS

Comment

High-tech service is not an enterprise with which readers are likely to be familiar. Therefore, the plan has to provide a basic education in what's important to the business. You can't expect backers to invest in businesses they don't feel they understand, and you're their primary source of information.

This need to educate can be a business planning opportunity. It gives a planner an opportunity to explain what's important to his or her business and then illustrate how well those bases are covered. In a well-written plan, as readers discover the intricacies of the operation they become more and more impressed with the competence of the entrepreneurs and how well they understand their business.

BACKGROUND

The service business involves managing the provision of on-site technical maintenance and repair services for complicated electronic equipment. Service must be provided at customer sites because the equipment is generally not portable and is difficult to move. Further, the downtime involved in taking something back to the shop is unacceptable, so it must be fixed in place. Modern electronic equipment is designed to accommodate this requirement in that it is modular in nature. The operating components of most equipment are broken into circuit boards that can be removed and replaced in a simple operation once a fault is isolated.

Three kinds of service can be identified. The first is preventive maintenance, which is easy to schedule since it can be done at the provider's convenience within reasonable limits. The second is remedial maintenance of a noncritical nature. That is, a machine is malfunctioning in some way but is still doing most of its job. Service here should be prompt but needn't be immediate. The third is critical remedial maintenance—the machine is down. That kind of service is, of course, the biggest problem to customers and providers, because it needs to be performed very quickly depending on how critical the failed machine is to the customer's operation.

Simply stated, managing service operations involves getting qualified technicians on site with the right tools and spare parts in a reasonable amount of time. The problem is difficult because the need for and the urgency of remedial maintenance occurs on a random basis.

There are three major elements in the management of service operations:

> The availability and skill level of field technicians
> Spare parts
> Scheduling and dispatch

We'll talk about each in turn.

The Availability and Skill Level of Field Technicians

Managing the availability and skill level of field technicians involves recruiting and retaining quality people just as in any business. In this business, however, it also involves estimating staffing requirements given the amount of equipment under contract. It also involves being sure people are appropriately trained.

Staffing. Determining staffing requirements involves estimating the number of calls that will have to be accomplished each month. This involves projecting three things:

> The number of machines under contract
> The frequency of failure of those machines
> The distance between installations

The number of machines under contract is simply the firm's sales estimate. However, a sale in the maintenance business is a contract that extends into the future with the expectation of renewal indefinitely. Hence, sales and the number of machines under contract involves accumulating the sales of successive time periods. The idea is illustrated in the buildup of the financial projections.

The average frequency of failure is a statistic that is known for each type of machine installed. The technical term is the Mean Time Between Failures (MTBF). This figure is readily available for all equipment under consideration.

Travel is a major time consumer. The more dispersed the customer installations are, the more time is lost between calls. Firms that limit operations to densely populated areas where people can get from one call to the next in a few minutes have a significant cost advantage.

Training. The skill level of technicians is dependent on their training. In general, an individual has to have gone through a training course on every type of machine he or she is qualified to work on.

Training can be a considerable expense to larger companies because of its direct cost and the time lost when a technician has to leave the field to attend training. Large companies also hire new, entry-level techs who must be trained on virtually everything. Manufacturers also have to train people on new products as they emerge.

Small firms can have a significant cost advantage here if they hire only experienced technicians who have already been trained on the older equipment serviced by the smaller firms. It's also important to keep the turnover rate low to retain those trained people.

Spare Parts

The largest capital investment in the service business is a spare parts inventory. A service company must have a full complement of spares for everything it works on.

The number of spares required for a particular type of equipment depends on the number of units under contract. However, the investment per unit under contract goes down dramatically as the number of units increases. For example, if we have one unit of XYZ under contract, we need a complete complement of spares. However, if we add a second unit we don't need any more spares, because one batch is enough to maintain up to five units on line. Further, when we add a sixth unit of XYZ, we don't need an entire new batch of spares because all the components aren't equally prone to failure.

A higher number of spares are stocked for certain high-failure-rate components. These are generally carried by technicians as they travel, so there is some increase in spares as the number of techs increases.

Geography also plays an important role in sparing. If service is spread between two cities, a basic inventory is required in each. If the same level of business is consolidated into one city, the spare parts level can be greatly reduced.

Spares can be purchased directly from the manufacturer, but that tends to be expensive. An active used equipment market exists both in spares and whole units on older equipment. This is a cost-effective way to acquire spares, as these parts sell for a fraction of the cost of new ones. It is also frequently economical to purchase entire used units for use as spare parts.

Sparing requirements for all the equipment types we contemplate servicing are known. The total inventory requirement is easily projected as a function of the number of units under contract.

When inventories become substantial in size, a full-time inventory clerk/manager will be required. We don't expect to need this at Max Uptime until there are about five or six hired technicians on board. Until then, inventory management will be an additional duty of the field manager.

Scheduling and Dispatch

Efficient dispatch is central to effective response time and customer satisfaction. When customers experience equipment failures, they phone a central service number. The phone is answered by a dispatcher who logs the call and "opens" a service order. The dispatcher assigns calls to particular technicians based on his or her knowledge of where the techs are and what they're doing. Once a tech is designated to a call, his or her pager is activated. Techs are expected to respond to their pagers within thirty minutes by calling in to the dispatcher. At that time, the dispatcher gives the tech the assignment, and he or she gets to the trouble as quickly as he or she can. When the technician finishes the job, he or she calls in to the dispatcher and "clears" the call.

On a normal day, techs are scheduled to do routine preventive maintenance. That routine function is regularly interrupted by calls for remedial maintenance.

The difficulties involved in scheduling increase geometrically as the number of techs and equipment under contract increase. Large maintenance organizations have sophisticated dispatch centers, which take calls nationwide over an 800 network. For small companies, the problem is much less complex and can generally be handled by a single person who may have other duties as well.

At Max Uptime, dispatch will initially be handled by a clerical person, who will also double as a secretary and receptionist. An additional person will be required when there are approximately five field technicians.

MAX UPTIME'S OPERATIONS

Headquarters Office

The company will operate out of modest office and warehouse space in a central part of the city. The appearance of the facility is not important because customers rarely if ever visit the office. It serves as a home base for technicians, a stocking point for parts, a site for dispatch operations, and a place from which management can work. In addition, parts rework and repair is accomplished there as time is available.

Individual technicians may not visit the home office for days on end, as they are dispatched entirely by phone. Location is, however, important because parts must often be picked up by traveling techs or sent to customer sites. A central location therefore reduces travel time and expense.

Max Uptime has an option on a 3,000 square feet space in the back of the Paxton Industrial Park near the center of BigCity. The rent has been negotiated at $1,000 per month or $4 per foot per year. Some 2,000 sq. ft. will be used for parts storage and repair and to provide desk space for techs. The remainder will provide offices for the two founders and a secretary, who will also function as dispatcher in the beginning. At the end of the second year, another person will be added to help with the parts and dispatch activities.

Equipment

The business will require a minimal level of office furniture and equipment for parts repair. All items will be acquired secondhand. The most expensive items are two oscilloscopes at $2,000 each. Field techs are expected to have their own personal tools. The entire furniture and equipment list is expected to run under $12,000; the items are detailed in Appendix D. This figure will be capitalized and depreciated over five years, yielding a $200 per month depreciation expense.

Executive Compensation

The two founders will each draw salaries of $42,000 from the business once it is reasonably established. However, they are both willing to live on half of that during the first year to conserve cash flow.

Founders' Activities and Responsibilities

Marketing. Charlie Conners will handle all the marketing activities. This will be his primary responsibility. He will solicit and sell new customers as well as maintain an active communication with old customers to ensure their continued satisfaction. Continuing contact is especially important when the customer has recently experienced serious or prolonged equipment failure.

Travel and entertainment expenses are expected to be approximately $500 per month in the sales function.

Maintenance Operations. Joe Updyke will manage all service operations, including parts. In the beginning, he will function as a field technician himself. As more technicians are hired, Joe will gradually shift his role to manager.

He will incur travel expenses of approximately $300 per month in managing service operations.

RRAN Backup. An important facet of the founders' roles in the proposed business is that in the beginning both Joe and Charlie will make themselves available to respond to emergency requests for rapid response service. This resource will give the firm the flexibility to implement the RRAN concept in the early days when there aren't many hired technicians on board to draw from.

Dispatch

Dispatch for a service organization with fewer than five techs is not difficult. The function can be handled by a clerical person whose job keeps him or her near the phone. Initially, it isn't likely to take more than an hour a day. However, as the business grows, dispatch will become more time-consuming and require greater attention. It is anticipated that an additional person will be needed by the end of the second year.

The cost of dispatch includes providing at least two separate phone lines to receive incoming calls from technicians. In addition, each must be provided with a pager. Field personnel are expected to have their own cell phones. The company will reimburse reasonable air-time charges for calls to dispatch and customers.

Inventory Control and Management

Similar to dispatch, inventory control is relatively easy in a small organization but becomes demanding when the operation gets bigger. Initially, the service manager will handle ordering and stocking inventory, while the clerical person will be responsible for control and distribution to technicians. A simple manual system will suffice in the beginning to be replaced later on by a system on a personal computer.

Financial Services

Neither of the founders has any expertise in accounting for a small business. Max Uptime will therefore use the services of Jacobsen Bookkeeping for its financial record keeping and First National Bank's Payroll Services department for its payroll. It is estimated that these services will cost $200 per month initially and increase to $400 as the firm grows.

Training

Training expenses are expected to be minimal during the firm's first years. Max Uptime will hire only experienced techs who have already been formally trained on the equipment to be maintained. Brush-up and minor updating will be accomplished through technical manuals and self-study during slack periods.

Overhead Expenses

The costs associated with the items just discussed are considered overhead expenses and are summarized on a monthly basis over the first four years of operation as follows:

Monthly Overhead Expenses

	Year			
	1	2	3	4
Rent	$1,000	$1,000	$1,000	$1,000
Utilities/Insurance	300	300	300	300
Phones				
Office	100	100	100	100
Dispatch (w/pagers)	200	300	400	400
Officers' Expenses				
Sales (Conners)	500	500	500	500
Management (Updyke)	300	300	300	300
Officers' Salaries	3,500	7,000	7,000	7,000
Clerical Salaries	1,500	1,500	3,000	3,000
Bookkeeping & Bank Charges	200	300	300	400
Depreciation	200	200	200	200
	$7,800	$11,500	$13,100	$13,200

Break-Even Analysis

The following calculation estimates the level of revenue required to break even in each of the first two years of operation. The difference between the two years is due to the differing overhead expense levels in those years.

The direct cost of maintenance operations involves the salaries of technicians, travel expenses, the cost of parts, and a few miscellaneous items such as consumable supplies. These items fairly consistently run 60% to 62% of revenues if an organization makes efficient use of its manpower. That means the contribution margin is approximately 39%.

Overhead expenses have been projected in the last section, and an amount should be added to those figures to cover interest expense. Based on Max Uptime's financial projections presented in Section VI, a figure of $800 per month will be used to represent an average interest charge. Monthly overheads are then as follows:

	Year 1	Year 2
Monthly Expenses	$ 7,800	$ 11,500
Interest	800	800
Total Monthly	$ 8,600	$ 12,300
	× 12	× 12
Annual Expense Level	$103,200	$147,600

Dividing these figures by .39 then yields the annual revenue volume required to break even:

First year	$103,200 / .39 = $264,615
Second year	$147,600 / .39 = $378,461

These figures may seem large to the uninitiated, but one must keep in mind that maintenance is a cumulative business. That is, a unit that is sold today tends to remain under maintenance for several years. Each sale adds to a cumulatively building base of equipment under contract. Hence, relatively modest monthly sales build into a substantial repetitive revenue stream in short order. The financial projections anticipate reaching a break-even volume toward the end of the first year of operation.

Billable Hours and Pricing

Hired field technicians are paid for 40 hours per week, 52 weeks a year, a total of 2,080 hours. However, all these are not available for service and travel. The total must be reduced as follows:

Total paid hours		2,080
Less:		
Vacation, 2.5 weeks	100	
Sick time, 5 days	40	
Paid holidays, 10 days	80	
Paper work, 3 hrs/wk	140	
Training, minimal	25	385
		1,695
Efficiency factor		× .85
Net Available Hours		1,440

Next, we'll calculate a billing rate for time and material work. This is service that is not done under contract but on an as-needed basis on customer demand. We'll assume parts are priced independently to yield a reasonable profit, but that the labor billing must carry the firm's overhead. We'll price as of the third year of operations, when there are expected to be approximately six techs on board. Travel costs are about $3,500 per tech per year.

Total available hours	1,440 × 6 =	8,640 hrs
Costs:		
Tech compensation	$30,000 × 6 =	$180,000
Travel	$3,500 × 6 =	21,000
Overhead per plan ($13,100 per mo)		157,200
Interest expense (est)		10,000
Total		$368,200
Cost per hour	$368,200 / 8640 =	$42.62
Gross up for 15% pre-tax profit:	$42.62 / .85 =	$50.14

Using a rounded figure of $50 per hour compares very favorably to the $75 per hour charged by the major firms. Max Uptime is strategically positioned approximately 30% under the leaders in price.

Although some uncontracted (time and material) business is anticipated, this plan is built up without assuming any. This adds an element of conservatism to the forecast.

Business Organizational Form

Max Uptime will be organized as a Limited Liability Company (LLC). Incorporation will be handled by John Sandworth, a local attorney known to the founders. Legal costs are expected to be minimal.

V
MANAGEMENT AND STAFFING

The company will be managed entirely by its founders. Initially, Charles Conners will be responsible for all marketing functions and Joseph Updyke will handle operations. In the early years, Joe will be working as a field technician himself, and Charlie will be available for such duty as necessary in emergencies.

Headquarters Employees

There will be one headquarters employee to start, a general clerical person who will handle secretarial and administrative duties as well as dispatch and inventory control. As the firm grows, another such person will be added to handle the increased workload, especially with respect to dispatch and inventory. It is expected that this person will be required by the beginning of the third year.

Field Technician Staff

Field technicians will be hired as necessary to service the growing base of equipment on contract. The staffing plan for technicians is developed as part of the financial projection. The number of techs expected to be on board at the end of each year is as follows:

	Year			
	1	2	3	4
Field Technician Staff	3	6	8	11

Backgrounds of the Founders

Both founders are longtime residents of the BigCity area, a general description of the background of each follows:

Joseph P. Updyke

Joseph Updyke was born in BigCity and has lived here most of his life. He currently resides in Littleton, a nearby suburb where he owns his own home. Joe is 34, married, and has three children.

He attended Littleton High School, graduating in 1988. During high school he developed an interest in electronics and took industrial arts courses in that area. He worked part-time during his junior and senior years repairing TV sets for Moore Appliances of Littleton.

Upon graduation from high school, Joe enlisted in the Navy. After basic training he was designated an Electronics Technician and attended the Navy's twenty-week ET school. During his four years in the service, he advanced to the rank of Second Class Petty Officer (E5), the furthest possible in that period of time. He spent two years at sea and two years at a communications installation in Norfolk, Virginia. In both assignments he worked entirely on the maintenance of sophisticated electronics and computer equipment. In the last year he supervised as many as eight technicians.

After leaving the Navy, Joe returned to the BigCity area and took a technical job with SmallTech, a fledgling electronics company just getting started at the time. He worked for SmallTech for two years until the company failed. He then joined BigTech, also in a technical role. Joe was a field technician for BigTech for four years and was then promoted to district manager. He has been in that job for seven years, and supervises fifteen people.

Joe is active in the Littleton Methodist Church and is a member of the Littleton School Board. He also coaches the local Little League on which his oldest son plays.

Joe Updyke is a broadly experienced electronics specialist as well as a seasoned supervisor of others in the field. He is also a solid, reliable family man who has demonstrated a commitment to his community.

He is interested in taking his special skills and background and using them to grow beyond the opportunities available in a large company. He approaches this task with enthusiasm and a commitment to succeed.

Charles F. Conners

Charles Conners has lived in the BigCity area for nine years. He currently owns his home in Brockton, a nearby suburb where he lives with his wife of eleven years and their two children. He is 32 years old.

Charlie was born and raised in New York City. He went to high school there, after which he attended Queens College, also in New York, studying history. He spent two years in college before financial problems forced him to suspend his higher education. After a year in the food service industry, Charlie enrolled in LaValle Tech, a one-year trade school in electronics. He subsequently graduated with honors.

After receiving his certificate as an electronics technician, Charlie joined Large, Inc., a manufacturer of small computers in Plainfield, New Jersey. He spent two years as a field technician with Large and was recruited by BigTech to move to BigCity. He's been with that firm ever since, a period of nine years.

During his time with BigTech, Charlie has risen to the grade of Senior Field Technician. That is the highest grade achievable for a technical specialist.

Charlie is a particularly gregarious and outgoing person. He genuinely enjoys personal contact in business and is good at it. In his senior technical capacity, he is often called upon by the sales force to assist in presentations and to iron out problems when customers are less than satisfied with products or services. He has become exceptionally effective in these difficult situations.

At the same time, he has become personally acquainted with a large number of IT directors in the area who have come to respect his knowledge and integrity in the field. He enjoys an excellent reputation among the technical professionals in the neighborhood.

For the last three years, Charlie has been pursuing a college degree in the evening at Brockton State College. He lacks only two courses to graduate with a Bachelor's Degree in Business Administration, concentrating in Marketing.

Charlie perceives Max Uptime as an opportunity to put his special set of skills and contacts to work. His combination of marketing and technical talents will position the company as an important contender in the high-tech service marketplace in the near future.

Supporting Documentation

Résumés and personal references of the principals are included in Appendix E.

VI
FINANCIAL PROJECTIONS

The financial projections of this section are built up beginning with assumptions about the company's ability to sell service contracts. Those sales lead to an installed base of equipment under contract that grows over the forecasted time frame. Revenue and cost estimates flow from that base of equipment along with some important balance sheet items. This section discusses the development of those figures in detail. Overhead expenses and the assumptions behind them were presented in the operations section. Revenue, cost, overhead, and balance sheet figures are combined in this section to produce Max Uptime's forecasted financial statements.

The Complexity of Forecasting Service

The forecasting techniques used in the service business tend to be relatively complex. The methodology is presented in detail below so that the interested reader can follow the business assumptions underlying the plan exactly. A reader interested only in an overview can skim this material and move directly to the financial statements themselves. We begin with a brief summary of the technique.

Comment

This is a tough part of the presentation. No matter how good a planner/writer you are, it's hard to present involved arithmetic calculations in an interesting or entertaining way. In the preceding paragraph we warn readers about what's coming, but also tell them that they can skip the detail if they want to trust us. This is an effective technique. Reviewers will frequently opt not to go through your detail if they know it's available. However, if not offered the choice, they might think you're hiding something and begin to feel uneasy about the whole plan. Some writers may be more comfortable putting the following detailed explanation of technique in an appendix. That's perfectly fine as long as it's available to the reader. The following overview section, however, should definitely be in the body of the plan.

AN OVERVIEW OF THE FORECASTING APPROACH

All business forecasting must begin with revenue that is based on sales activity. In the service business, revenue and sales are related on a cumulative basis. That is, a service contract sold today stretches into the future for at least a year. If performance is assumed to be satisfactory, indefinite renewal can also be expected. Therefore, the revenue dollars flowing into the business in any future time period depend not on the sales of contracts in that period, but on the cumulative sales to date as of that time, net of any cancellations that may have occurred.

Conceptually, a service business builds up a base (sometimes called the *installed base*) of equipment under contract over time. The forecast size of that base dictates the level of revenues that can be expected to flow into the organization in future time periods. The size of the base also determines the level of cost that will be incurred in its support. Therefore, the first step in financially planning a service business is developing a forecast of the installed base of equipment under contract. From that we develop predictions of both revenue and cost. Overhead expenses are handled separately, being less related to the base.

Revenue

Once a forecast of the base is developed, revenue follows directly. It is simply predicted as the number of units under contract multiplied by an average price per unit. Sophisticated planning over longer periods can include increasing or decreasing prices in future years due to inflation or changes in the competitive environment.

Cost

Forecasting the cost of service is not so simple. It also begins with the installed base, but involves a complex series of relationships among the cost-producing elements of the business. Basically, we must predict how much service any unit needs in terms of hours and the number of calls that will be made on it. From that we have to develop the number of people it will take to service the base and what it will cost to get them on site.

In general, a unit under contract needs regular preventive maintenance and repair when it fails partially or completely. Work on malfunctioning or failed equipment is called remedial service or remedial maintenance.

Preventive maintenance is done in accordance with schedules recommended by the equipment manufacturers and is readily predicted. Remedial needs can't be forecasted with certainty, but their frequency can be estimated through the mean time between failure (MTBF) statistic provided by manufacturers. This figure is an estimate of the number of operating hours that tends to elapse between equipment failures. MTBF's are excellent predictors when substantial numbers of units are involved.

For both remedial and preventive maintenance, it is possible to predict the average service time a call will take on any piece of equipment.

Therefore, since the exact preventive service requirements are known and the average remedial service requirements can be estimated from the MTBF, it is possible to statistically predict the average number of calls per month a typical unit will require, as well as the average elapsed service time per call.

This leads to an estimate of the service personnel required to maintain any particular unit. The company's total personnel requirement is then the sum of the individual requirements over all the units forecast to be under contract.

It's important to understand that this statistical approach allows one to predict total service requirements in terms of both hours and number of calls. Further, if the average travel time and cost per call is known, total travel time and cost can also be predicted.

Each field technician has a consistent number of hours available per month to apply to hands-on service and travel. That figure, along with the hours required by the installed base of equipment, leads directly to the number of field technicians that will be required to support the equipment in each planned time period. That figure leads to an estimate of the salary cost of operations.

Spares Inventory and the Cost of Parts

The spare parts inventory that has to be purchased and carried on the balance sheet is also related to the installed base under service. The more units there are, the more spares are needed. However, as the number of units installed in an area increases, spares usage can become more efficient and fewer dollars per unit has to be tied up in inventory.

The monthly cost of parts is forecast as a relatively constant percent of service revenues. Historically, this figure runs at about 30% for businesses like Max Uptime.

THE DETAILED FORECAST

This section presents the detailed assumptions about cost and revenues that lead to the projections of Max Uptime's financial future that conclude the section. It also outlines the calculations that constitute the forecasting method.

Comment

This section can do two things for Joe and Charlie. First, of course, it does what it purports to do: It tells the reader exactly how they put together their forecast and what assumptions they made. Perhaps more important, however, it shows the audience how astute and meticulous they are. Readers will be impressed with the level of thought and detail behind the projections and with the entrepreneurs' understanding of their business. Don't underestimate the importance of this last point. A detailed presentation like this will establish the planners as experts in the eyes of the audience. It can build tremendous credibility.

It's also important to note that this is not a technical discussion. It discusses business issues: hours, miles, and the associated costs. These are the things that financial backers are interested in.

Unfortunately, it's also true that this section can backfire on the planner if it isn't done well. If the presentation is confusing, incomplete or, worst of all, incorrect, credibility can be irretrievably lost.

Summarizing Equipment Characteristics by Size

The forecasting process is simplified by summarizing the various types of equipment Max Uptime plans to service into three categories: small, medium, and large. We begin by estimating the average monthly revenue, the mean time between failure (MTBF), the number of preventive calls per month, and the average working time per call for each size. These assumptions come from experience and product information supplied by the equipment manufacturers. The per unit averages are tabulated as follows:

	Revenue	MTBF (Hrs)	Preventive Calls/mo	Time/call (Hrs)
Small	$30	2,000	.1	.5
Medium	$120	500	.5	1.0
Large	$600	200	2.0	2.0

Mean time between failure is stated in terms of operating hours on the equipment. Notice how the maintenance activity increases with the size of the equipment.

Smaller pieces of equipment that are purely electronic, like personal computers, tend to operate for very long periods without service. Many need no preventive maintenance at all. However, electro-mechanical equipment of any size tends to fail frequently and requires preventive service. Printers are a good example of the latter.

Separating the equipment by size enables us to forecast each category separately. That ability is important because we expect to be more successful in selling service on small units initially when customers view us as a new and untried organization. Later, as Max Uptime's reputation grows, we will have more success with larger units.

The Installed Base Forecast

Forecasting the installed base begins by projecting the sale of maintenance contracts into the future by equipment category. In early periods the base within each category can be thought of as simply the accumulation of all contracts sold to date. Later, the possibility of some cancellations or nonre-newals must be recognized. These will occur for reasons other than dissatisfaction with our service. Customers will sometimes discontinue the use of certain equipment or upgrade to new equipment that we won't handle. To accommodate the occasional loss of a contract, the sales forecast is taken to represent net sales; that is, the net of new units less canceled or unrenewed units.

The rate of net new additions to the base will increase over the first six months as we penetrate the most likely customer candidates, especially those already personally known to us. After that, winning new accounts will become more difficult, and the rate of new business will be somewhat slower. By the third and fourth year we will also be seeing some of the cancellation effect discussed in the last paragraph. The net effect is that the highest rate of additions to the base will be seen in the second year. Thereafter, growth will continue, but slowly.

Forecasting the base is simply a matter of accumulating the net sales projections from period to period within each product category. For example:

<u>Small Units</u>

Period	<u>1</u>	<u>2</u>	<u>3</u>	<u>4</u>	<u>5</u>	<u>6</u>	
Net Units Sold	2	3	4	5	7	9	...
Units on Contract	2	5	9	14	21	30	...

The Revenue Forecast

Revenue is then the units on contract or base figure multiplied by an assumed average monthly price per unit:

Revenue (@$30)	$60	$150	$270	$420	$630	$900

Total revenue is simply the sum of this projection over all three equipment categories.

Forecasting the Cost of Revenue

Cost flows directly from the installed base through manpower and travel time and expense estimates. The calculation is somewhat involved so we'll take it a step at a time.

Developing Per Unit Time Requirements

We'll assume that the average piece of commercial equipment operates 12 hours a day, 25 days a month—that's 300 hours per month. Dividing that figure by the MTBF gives an estimate of the number of remedial calls per month the equipment generates. For example 300 / 2000 = .15 calls per month for small units. In other words, under this kind of use, each machine can be expected to fail once in 6.7 (1 / .15) months. The other results are as follows:

	MTBF	Remedial calls/mo
Small	2,000	.15
Medium	500	.60
Large	200	1.50

Next, we'll develop the total number of direct labor hours required per unit per month by adding the remedial and preventive calls and multiplying the total by the average number of hours required for each call. The per unit calculation is:

	Remedial calls/mo	+ Preventive calls/mo	= Total Calls/mo	× Hours/call	= Total Dir Hrs
Small	.15	.1	.25	.5	.125
Medium	.6	.5	1.10	1.0	1.10
Large	1.5	2.0	3.50	2.0	7.00

The last column represents the number of "hands-on" hours per month it will take to maintain one unit of equipment in each category. It does not, however, include travel time. That will be considered next.

Field technicians generally go from one customer's site directly to another. Therefore, the average travel time between calls depends on the average distance between customers. That distance depends on the density of customers under contract within the BigCity area. The more there are, the closer they are together. This means that travel times will be longer in the first year when the company has relatively few customers, but will shorten as the base of equipment on contract increases.

We'll assume that travel time between customer sites will decrease for the first three years, but will be more or less constant after that. The forecasted number of hours between sites is as follows.

	Year		
	1	2	3
Travel time per call	.5	.33	.25

Next, since we know the average number of calls by equipment type and the travel time by year, we can forecast the average number of travel hours that will be required per unit per month for each equipment type in each year.

	Calls/unit/mo	×	Travel Hrs/call by yr			=	Travel Hrs/unit/mo by yr		
			1	2	3		1	2	3
Small	.25						.125	.083	.063
Medium	1.10		.5	.33	.25		.550	.363	.275
Large	3.50						1.750	1.160	.875

(To get each row of the right-hand table, multiply the number of calls per unit per month in the equipment category by the time factor in that year. For example, the first row is .25 × .5 = .125, .25 × .33 = .083, and .25 × .25 = .063. Get the second row by doing the same thing, substituting 1.10 for .25, and so on.)

We're finally ready to derive a forecast of the total technician hours per unit per month that will be required to maintain equipment in each category, and then in each year. We'll do this by adding our earlier forecast of direct hours by equipment category to the travel hours by category and by year we've just developed.

	Direct Hrs/unit/mo	+	Travel Hrs/unit/mo by yr by category by yr			=	Total Tech Hours/unit/mo		
			1	2	3		1	2	3
Small	.125		.125	.083	.063		.250	.208	.188
Medium	1.10		.550	.363	.275		1.650	1.460	.138
Large	7.00		1.75	1.160	.875		8.750	8.160	7.880

The number of hours required to service a category of equipment in a given month within a future year is developed by multiplying the appropriate figure from the right-hand table by the units on contract for that period. For example, using the units on contract illustration in the Installed Base Forecast earlier in this section, we had the following base of equipment for small units in the first year:

Units on Contract   2   5   9   14   21   30   .   .   .   .

The total hours required to maintain these units would be obtained by multiplying by the entry for year 1 and small units from the table (.250). The result is as follows:

Total Technician Hours   .5   1.25   2.25   3.5   5.25   7.5

Adding this result over all three equipment types gives the number of person-hours that will be required to support the contracted product base in each future month.

Keep in mind that we're working with monthly forecasting parameters, which change as we move from one type of equipment to another and from year to year.

A further example is appropriate. Suppose in some month of the second year our units on contract forecast is as follows:

Small	567
Medium	312
Large	140

Then, we would multiply each of these figures by the second-year factors from the table to come up with the total hours required to service the base:

Small	567 × .208	=	117.9
Medium	312 × 1.46	=	455.5
Large	140 × 8.16	=	1,142.4
	Total		1,715.8

This total represents the number of hours that will be required to sustain the contracted base in that month.

The Required Staff of Field Technicians and Salary Cost

In the operations section of the plan, we developed the number of hours that each technician on board would be available for direct labor and travel. This is a relatively constant figure that isn't expected to change much as we move into the future. The annual figure given there was 1,440 hours, which is equivalent to 120 hours per month.

Dividing the monthly available hours per person into the person-hours requirement of the last section gives an estimate of the number of field technicians that will be required in that month. Continuing the example, the required headcount would be:

$$1715.8 / 120 = 14.3$$

Of course, fractional people aren't possible, so we must plan for 15 field technicians.

This figure is reduced by one in the first two years to reflect the fact that one of the founders will be doing technician work until the organization grows large enough to require his full-time service as a manager. It is then multiplied by the planned salary of individual field technicians to arrive at the cost of hired field technicians line on the income statement.

Local Travel Costs

It is customary in the industry to require field technicians to travel in their own cars. They're paid a monthly allowance for the use of their automobiles, plus a flat rate per mile. Max Uptime plans to pay each driver $200 per month plus 40 cents a mile. Given these assumptions, we can predict the cost of travel as the base of equipment under contract grows if we simply make another assumption about the number of miles between calls. As the base grows, the distance between sites will shrink as follows:

	Year		
	1	2	3
Miles per call	5	4	3

This along with the average number of calls per unit per month allows us to develop a travel cost per unit per month by equipment category and by year as follows:

	Calls/unit/mo	×	rate/mile	×	Miles/call by yr			=	Travel cost/unit/mo by yr		
					1	2	3		1	2	3
Small	.25								.5	.4	.3
Medium	1.1		.40		5	4	3		2.2	1.8	1.3
Large	3.5								7.0	5.6	4.2

The figures from the table on the right are multiplied by the forecast units on contract in each future time period and summed over the three equipment categories to arrive at the total mileage cost in any future month. That sum is then added to the fixed amount paid to each driver ($200) times the number of drivers on board to arrive at the travel cost line on the income statement.

Sparing Requirements and the Cost of Parts

The spare parts inventory required at any point in time depends on the number of units under contract at that time. However, coverage becomes more efficient as the equipment density in an area increases. Therefore, fewer parts per unit installed are needed as the business grows. We have assumed that the dollar cost of spares required to support each unit of equipment by category by year is as follows:

	Spares Inventory/unit by year		
	1	2	3
Small	$100	$80	$70
Medium	$300	$240	$210
Large	$500	$400	$350

The spares inventory required in any equipment category in any future month is obtained by multiplying the number of units on contract in that category in that month by the figure from the table for the appropriate year. This figure summed over all categories is the total spares inventory, which is input directly to the balance sheet forecast. However, management believes a minimum spares inventory of $20,000 will be necessary to get into business, so that figure is used when the calculation above results in a smaller figure.

The cost of parts consumed in the maintenance process is simply estimated at 30% of revenues throughout the forecast period.

Miscellaneous Cost

Miscellaneous cost is estimated at $150 per technician per month.

Interest Rate

The financial projections are based on a loan interest rate of 12% compounded monthly.

PRESENTATION OF THE FINANCIAL FORECAST

A four-year financial forecast for Max Uptime is presented in the following pages. The first year is detailed by month while the following three years are presented by quarter. The presentation shows the development of the installed base by equipment category as well as the required number of technician hours in each category in each time period. Total revenue is shown along with total personnel requirements leading to the planned staffing level.

Financial statements are shown in standard formats. These include income statements, balance sheets, and statements of cash flow for each forecasted year. A summary of key elements of the financial projections follows the detailed statements on page 271. A verbal evaluation is included on page 272.

Max Uptime, Inc.
Unit Sales and Base Forecast
First Year by Month

MONTHS

	1	2	3	4	5	6	7	8	9	10	11	12	TOTAL
Small Units													
Units Sold	2	5	7	10	10	10	10	10	10	10	10	10	104
Units on Contract	2	7	14	24	34	44	54	64	74	84	94	104	104
Average Price $30.00													
Revenue	$60	$210	$420	$720	$1,020	$1,320	$1,620	$1,920	$2,220	$2,520	$2,820	$3,120	$17,970
Total Tech Hrs/Unit/Month 0.25 Tech HOURS	0.5	1.75	3.5	6	8.5	11	13.5	16	18.5	21	23.5	26	149.75
Medium Units													
Units Sold	1	2	3	3	3	3	3	4	4	4	4	4	38
Units on Contract	1	3	6	9	12	15	18	22	26	30	34	38	38
Average Price $120.00													
Revenue	$120	$360	$720	$1,080	$1,440	$1,800	$2,160	$2,640	$3,120	$3,600	$4,080	$4,560	$25,680
Total Tech Hrs/Unit/Month 1.65 Tech HOURS	1.65	4.95	9.9	14.85	19.8	24.75	29.7	36.3	42.9	49.5	56.1	62.7	353.1
Large Units													
Units Sold	0	0	1	1	2	2	2	2	2	2	2	2	18
Units on Contract	0	0	1	2	4	6	8	10	12	14	16	18	18
Average Price $600.00													
Revenue	$0	$0	$600	$1,200	$2,400	$3,600	$4,800	$6,000	$7,200	$8,400	$9,600	$10,800	$54,600
Total Tech Hrs/Unit/Month 8.75 Tech HOURS	0	0	8.75	17.5	35	52.5	70	87.5	105	122.5	140	157.5	796.25
Total Revenue	$180	$570	$1,740	$3,000	$4,860	$6,720	$8,580	$10,560	$12,540	$14,520	$16,500	$18,480	$98,250
Total Tech Hrs/Month	2.15	6.7	22.15	38.35	63.3	88.25	113.2	139.8	166.4	193	219.6	246.2	1,299.1
Direct Hrs Per Tech													
FT Manpower	0.02	0.06	0.18	0.32	0.53	0.74	0.94	1.17	1.39	1.61	1.83	2.05	
Number Techs Required	1	1	1	1	1	1	1	2	2	2	2	3	

Sparing Requirements Per Unit Installed by Equipment Type

Small	Medium	Large
$100	$300	$500

Spares Inventory	1	2	3	4	5	6	7	8	9	10	11	12	TOTAL
Small	$200	$700	$1,400	$2,400	$3,400	$4,400	$5,400	$6,400	$7,400	$8,400	$9,400	$10,400	
Medium	$300	$900	$1,800	$2,700	$3,600	$4,500	$5,400	$6,600	$7,800	$9,000	$10,200	$11,400	
Large	$0	$0	$500	$1,000	$2,000	$3,000	$4,000	$5,000	$6,000	$7,000	$8,000	$9,000	
Total	$500	$1,600	$3,700	$6,100	$9,000	$11,900	$14,800	$18,000	$21,200	$24,400	$27,600	$30,800	

Travel Costs
Cost/Month/Unit Total Travel Cost—Mileage

		1	2	3	4	5	6	7	8	9	10	11	12	TOTAL
Small	$0.50	Small	$1.00	$3.50	$7.00	$12.00	$17.00	$22.00	$27.00	$32.00	$37.00	$42.00	$47.00	$52.00	$299.50
Medium	$2.20	Medium	$2.20	$6.60	$13.20	$19.80	$26.40	$33.00	$39.60	$48.40	$57.20	$66.00	$74.80	$83.60	$470.80
Large	$7.00	Large	$0.00	$0.00	$7.00	$14.00	$28.00	$42.00	$56.00	$70.00	$84.00	$98.00	$112.00	$126.00	$637.00
		Total	$3.20	$10.10	$27.20	$45.80	$71.40	$97.00	$122.60	$150.40	$178.20	$206.00	$233.80	$261.60	$1,407.30

	1	2	3	4	5	6	7	8	9	10	11	12	TOTAL
Fixed $200.00 Paid Each Tech	$200.00	$200.00	$200.00	$200.00	$200.00	$200.00	$200.00	$400.00	$400.00	$400.00	$400.00	$600.00	$3,600.00
Total Travel Costs	$203.20	$210.10	$227.20	$245.80	$271.40	$297.00	$322.60	$550.40	$578.20	$606.00	$633.80	$861.60	$5,007.30

Max Uptime, Inc.
Income Statement
First Year by Month

MONTHS

		1	2	3	4	5	6	7	8	9	10	11	12	TOTAL
Revenue		$180	$570	$1,740	$3,000	$4,860	$6,720	$8,580	$10,560	$12,540	$14,520	$16,500	$18,480	$98,250
Cost														
Hired Techs at Average of	$3,000.00 Per Mo	$0	$0	$0	$0	$0	$0	$0	$3,000	$3,000	$3,000	$3,000	$6,000	$18,000
Travel		$203	$210	$227	$246	$271	$297	$323	$550	$578	$606	$634	$862	$5,007
Parts at	0.3 of Revenue	$54	$171	$522	$900	$1,458	$2,016	$2,574	$3,168	$3,762	$4,356	$4,950	$5,544	$29,475
Misc/Tech	$150.00	$150	$150	$150	$150	$150	$150	$150	$300	$300	$300	$300	$450	$2,700
Total Cost		$407	$531	$899	$1,296	$1,879	$2,463	$3,047	$7,018	$7,640	$8,262	$8,884	$12,856	$55,182
Gross Margin		($227)	$39	$841	$1,704	$2,981	$4,257	$5,533	$3,542	$4,900	$6,258	$7,616	$5,624	$43,068
Expenses														
Rent		$1,000	$1,000	$1,000	$1,000	$1,000	$1,000	$1,000	$1,000	$1,000	$1,000	$1,000	$1,000	$12,000
Officers Salaries		$3,500	$3,500	$3,500	$3,500	$3,500	$3,500	$3,500	$3,500	$3,500	$3,500	$3,500	$3,500	$42,000
Management Expenses		$300	$300	$300	$300	$300	$300	$300	$300	$300	$300	$300	$300	$3,600
Sales Expenses		$500	$500	$500	$500	$500	$500	$500	$500	$500	$500	$500	$500	$6,000
Util/Insur		$300	$300	$300	$300	$300	$300	$300	$300	$300	$300	$300	$300	$3,600
Clerical Salaries		$1,500	$1,500	$1,500	$1,500	$1,500	$1,500	$1,500	$1,500	$1,500	$1,500	$1,500	$1,500	$18,000
Bookkeeping & Bank Charges		$200	$200	$200	$200	$200	$200	$200	$200	$200	$200	$200	$200	$2,400
Depreciation		$200	$200	$200	$200	$200	$200	$200	$200	$200	$200	$200	$200	$2,400
Phone (Office)		$100	$100	$100	$100	$100	$100	$100	$100	$100	$100	$100	$100	$1,200
Phone (Dispatch)		$200	$200	$200	$200	$200	$200	$200	$200	$200	$200	$200	$200	$2,400
Misc		$300	$300	$300	$300	$300	$300	$300	$300	$300	$300	$300	$300	$3,600
Total		$8,100	$8,100	$8,100	$8,100	$8,100	$8,100	$8,100	$8,100	$8,100	$8,100	$8,100	$8,100	$97,200
EBIT		($8,327)	($8,061)	($7,259)	($6,396)	($5,119)	($3,843)	($2,567)	($4,558)	($3,200)	($1,842)	($484)	($2,476)	($54,132)
Interest		$175	$260	$346	$430	$510	$580	$640	$710	$790	$880	$950	$1,030	$7,301
EBT		($8,502)	($8,321)	($7,605)	($6,826)	($5,629)	($4,423)	($3,207)	($5,268)	($3,990)	($2,722)	($1,434)	($3,506)	($61,433)
Tax		$0	$0	$0	$0	$0	$0	$0	$0	$0	$0	$0	$0	$0
EAT		($8,502)	($8,321)	($7,605)	($6,826)	($5,629)	($4,423)	($3,207)	($5,268)	($3,990)	($2,722)	($1,434)	($3,506)	($61,433)
Dividend														$0

Max Uptime, Inc.
Balance Sheet
First Year by Month

MONTHS

	Opening	1	2	3	4	5	6	7	8	9	10	11	12
Assets													
Cash	$5,000	$5,000	$5,000	$5,000	$5,000	$5,000	$5,000	$5,000	$5,000	$5,000	$5,000	$5,000	$5,000
Accounts Receivable		$180	$660	$2,070	$4,013	$6,795	$9,900	$13,155	$16,530	$19,965	$23,430	$26,895	$30,360
Inventory	$20,000	$20,000	$20,000	$20,000	$20,000	$20,000	$20,000	$20,000	$20,000	$21,200	$24,400	$27,600	$30,800
Current Assets	$25,000	$25,180	$25,660	$27,070	$29,013	$31,795	$34,900	$38,155	$41,530	$46,165	$52,830	$59,495	$66,160
Deposits	$1,500	$1,500	$1,500	$1,500	$1,500	$1,500	$1,500	$1,500	$1,500	$1,500	$1,500	$1,500	$1,500
Fixed Assets													
Gross	$12,000	$12,000	$12,000	$12,000	$12,000	$12,000	$12,000	$12,000	$12,000	$12,000	$12,000	$12,000	$12,000
Accumulated Depreciation	$0	($200)	($400)	($600)	($800)	($1,000)	($1,200)	($1,400)	($1,600)	($1,800)	($2,000)	($2,200)	($2,400)
Net	$12,000	$11,800	$11,600	$11,400	$11,200	$11,000	$10,800	$10,600	$10,400	$10,200	$10,000	$9,800	$9,600
Total Assets	$38,500	$38,480	$38,760	$39,970	$41,713	$44,295	$47,200	$50,255	$53,430	$57,865	$64,330	$70,795	$77,260
Liabilities													
Accounts Payable	$0	$54	$171	$522	$900	$1,458	$2,016	$2,574	$3,168	$3,762	$4,356	$4,950	$5,544
Current Liabilities	$0	$54	$171	$522	$900	$1,458	$2,016	$2,574	$3,168	$3,762	$4,356	$4,950	$5,544
Debt	$13,500	$21,928	$30,412	$38,877	$47,067	$54,721	$61,491	$67,194	$75,044	$82,875	$91,468	$98,773	$108,149
Equity	$25,000	$16,498	$8,177	$571	($6,254)	($11,884)	($16,307)	($19,513)	($24,782)	($28,772)	($31,494)	($32,928)	($36,433)
Total Liabilities & Equity	$38,500	$38,480	$38,760	$39,970	$41,713	$44,295	$47,200	$50,255	$53,430	$57,865	$64,330	$70,795	$77,260

Max Uptime, Inc.
Cash Flow Statement
First Year by Month

MONTHS

	1	2	3	4	5	6	7	8	9	10	11	12	TOTAL
Cash from Operating Activities													
EAT	($8,502)	($8,321)	($7,605)	($6,826)	($5,629)	($4,423)	($3,207)	($5,268)	($3,990)	($2,722)	($1,434)	($3,506)	($61,433)
Depreciation	$200	$200	$200	$200	$200	$200	$200	$200	$200	$200	$200	$200	$2,400
Decr/(Incr) in A/R	($180)	($480)	($1,410)	($1,943)	($2,783)	($3,105)	($3,255)	($3,375)	($3,435)	($3,465)	($3,465)	($3,465)	($30,360)
Decr/(Incr) in Inv	$0	$0	$0	$0	$0	$0	$0	$0	($1,200)	($3,200)	($3,200)	($3,200)	($10,800)
Incr/(Decr) in A/P	$54	$117	$351	$378	$558	$558	$558	$594	$594	$594	$594	$594	$5,544
Cash from Operations	($8,428)	($8,484)	($8,464)	($8,190)	($7,654)	($6,770)	($5,704)	($7,849)	($7,831)	($8,593)	($7,305)	($9,377)	($94,649)
Cash from Investing Activities													$0
Decr/(Incr) in Fixed Assets	$0	$0	$0	$0	$0	$0	$0	$0	$0	$0	$0	$0	$0
Cash from Financing Activities													$0
Incr/(Decr) in Debt	$8,428	$8,484	$8,464	$8,190	$7,654	$6,770	$5,704	$7,849	$7,831	$8,593	$7,305	$9,377	$94,649
Dividends	$0	$0	$0	$0	$0	$0	$0	$0	$0	$0	$0	$0	$0
Cash from Fin	$8,428	$8,484	$8,464	$8,190	$7,654	$6,770	$5,704	$7,849	$7,831	$8,593	$7,305	$9,377	$94,649
Net Cash Flow	$0	$0	($0)	$0	$0	$0	($0)	$0	($0)	$0	$0	($0)	$0
Beginning Cash Balance	$5,000	$5,000	$5,000	$5,000	$5,000	$5,000	$5,000	$5,000	$5,000	$5,000	$5,000	$5,000	
Net Cash Flow	$0	$0	($0)	$0	$0	$0	($0)	$0	($0)	$0	$0	($0)	
Ending Cash Balance	$5,000	$5,000	$5,000	$5,000	$5,000	$5,000	$5,000	$5,000	$5,000	$5,000	$5,000	$5,000	

Max Uptime, Inc.
Unit Sales and Base Forecast
Second Year by Quarter

		QUARTERS				
		1	2	3	4	TOTAL
Small Units						
Units Sold		35	35	35	35	140
Units on Contract		139	174	209	244	766
Average Price	50					
Revenue		$12,510	$15,660	$18,810	$21,960	$68,940
Total Tech Hrs/Unit/Mo	0.208	86.736	108.576	130.416	152.256	477.984
Medium Units						
Units Sold		12	12	12	12	48
Units on Contract		50	62	74	86	272
Average Price	50					
Revenue		$18,000	$22,320	$26,640	$30,960	$97,920
Total Tech Hrs/Unit/Mo	1.463	219.45	272.118	324.786	377.454	1,193.808
Large Units						
Units Sold		9	9	9	9	36
Units on Contract		27	36	45	54	162
Average Price	50					
Revenue		$48,600	$64,800	$81,000	$97,200	$291,600
Total Tech Hrs/Unit/Mo	8.155	660.555	880.74	1,100.925	1,321.11	3,963.33
Revenue		$79,110	$102,780	$126,450	$150,120	$458,460
Total Tech Hrs/Qtr		966.741	1,261.434	1,556.127	1,850.82	5,635.122
Technicians		2.69	3.50	4.32	5.14	
Number Techs Required		3	4	5	6	

Sparing Requirements Per Unit Installed by Equipment Type

Small	Medium	Large				
$80	$240	$400				

Spares Inventory						
Small			$11,120	$13,920	$16,720	$19,520
Medium			$12,000	$14,880	$17,760	$20,640
Large			$10,800	$14,400	$18,000	$21,600
Total			$33,920	$43,200	$52,480	$61,760

Travel Costs						
Cost/Mo/Unit						
Small	$0.40	$166.80	$208.80	$250.80	$292.80	$919.20
Medium	$1.76	$264.00	$327.36	$390.72	$454.08	$1,436.16
Large	$5.60	$453.60	$604.80	$756.00	$907.20	$2,721.60
Total		$884.40	$1,140.96	$1,397.52	$1,654.08	$5,076.96
Fixed		$1,800.00	$2,400.00	$3,000.00	$3,600.00	$10,800.00
Total Travel Costs		$2,684.40	$3,540.96	$4,397.52	$5,254.08	$15,876.96

Max Uptime, Inc.
Income Statement
Second Year by Quarter

			QUARTERS		
	1	2	3	4	TOTAL
Revenue	$79,110	$102,780	$126,450	$150,120	$458,460
Cost					
Hired Techs	$18,000	$27,000	$36,000	$45,000	$126,000
Travel	$2,684	$3,541	$4,398	$5,254	$15,877
Parts	$23,733	$30,834	$37,935	$45,036	$137,538
Misc/Tech $150	$1,350	$1,800	$2,250	$2,700	$8,100
Total Cost	$45,767	$63,175	$80,583	$97,990	$287,514
Gross Margin	$33,343	$39,605	$45,867	$52,130	$170,945
Expenses					
Rent	$3,000	$3,000	$3,000	$3,000	$12,000
Salaries	$21,000	$21,000	$21,000	$21,000	$84,000
Mgt Expenses	$900	$900	$900	$900	$3,600
Sales Expenses	$1,500	$1,500	$1,500	$1,500	$6,000
Util/Insur	$900	$900	$900	$900	$3,600
Clerical Salaries	$4,500	$4,500	$4,500	$4,500	$18,000
Bookkeeping & Bank Charges	$900	$900	$900	$900	$3,600
Depreciation	$600	$600	$600	$600	$2,400
Phone (Office)	$300	$300	$300	$300	$1,200
Phone (Dispatch)	$600	$600	$600	$600	$2,400
Misc	$900	$900	$900	$900	$3,600
Total	$35,100	$35,100	$35,100	$35,100	$140,400
EBIT	($1,757)	$4,505	$10,767	$17,030	$30,545
Interest	$3,400	$3,780	$4,160	$4,360	$15,700
EBT	($5,157)	$725	$6,607	$12,670	$14,845
Tax	$0	$0			$0
EAT	($5,157)	$725	$6,607	$12,670	$14,845
Dividends					$0

Max Uptime, Inc.
Balance Sheet
Second Year by Quarter

	QUARTERS			
	1	2	3	4
Assets				
Cash	$7,500	$7,500	$7,500	$7,500
Accounts Receivable	$32,963	$42,825	$52,688	$62,550
Inventory	$33,920	$43,200	$52,480	$61,760
Current Assets	$74,383	$93,525	$112,668	$131,810
Deposits	$1,500	$1,500	$1,500	$1,500
Fixed Assets				
Gross	$12,000	$12,000	$12,000	$12,000
Accumulated				
Depreciation	($3,000)	($3,600)	($4,200)	($4,800)
Net	$9,000	$8,400	$7,800	$7,200
Total Assets	$84,883	$103,425	$121,968	$140,510
Liabilities				
Accts Payable	$7,911	$10,278	$12,645	$15,012
Current Liabs	$7,911	$10,278	$12,645	$15,012
Debt	$118,562	$134,013	$143,581	$147,086
Equity	($41,591)	($40,866)	($34,258)	($21,588)
Total Liabilities &				
Equity	$84,883	$103,425	$121,968	$140,510

Max Uptime, Inc.
Cash Flow Statement
Second Year by Quarter

| | QUARTERS | | | | |
	1	2	3	4	TOTAL
Cash from Operating Activities					
EAT	($5,157)	$725	$6,607	$12,670	$14,845
Depreciation	$600	$600	$600	$600	$2,400
Decr/(Incr) in A/R	($2,603)	($9,863)	($9,863)	($9,863)	($32,190)
Decr/(Incr) in Inventory	($3,120)	($9,280)	($9,280)	($9,280)	($30,960)
Incr/(Decr) in A/P	$2,367	$2,367	$2,367	$2,367	$9,468
Cash from Operations	($7,913)	($15,450)	($9,568)	($3,506)	($36,437)
Cash from Investing Activities					
Decr/(Incr) in Fixed Assets	$0	$0	$0	$0	$0
Cash from Financing Activities					
Incr/(Decr) in Debt	$10,413	$15,450	$9,568	$3,506	$38,937
Dividends	$0	$0	$0	$0	$0
Cash from Financing	$10,413	$15,450	$9,568	$3,506	$38,937
Net Cash Flow	$2,500	($0)	$0	($0)	$2,500
Beginning Cash Balance	$5,000	$7,500	$7,500	$7,500	$27,500
Net Cash Flow	$2,500	($0)	$0	($0)	$2,500
Ending Cash Balance	$7,500	$7,500	$7,500	$7,500	$30,000

Max Uptime, Inc.
Unit Sales and Base Forecast
Third Year by Quarter

		QUARTERS				
		1	2	3	4	TOTAL
Small Units						
Units Sold		30	30	25	25	110
Units on Contract		274	304	329	354	
Average Price	50					
Revenue		$24,660	$27,360	$29,610	$31,860	$113,490
Total Tech Hrs/Unit/Mo	0.188	154.536	171.456	185.556	199.656	711.204
Medium Units						
Units Sold		11	10	10	8	39
Units on Contract		97	107	117	125	
Average Price	50					
Revenue		$34,920	$38,520	$42,120	$45,000	$160,560
Total Tech Hrs/Unit/Mo	1.375	400.125	441.375	482.625	515.625	1,839.75
Large Units						
Units Sold		9	8	8	8	33
Units on Contract		63	71	79	87	
Average Price	50					
Revenue		$113,400	$127,800	$142,200	$156,600	$540,000
Total Tech Hrs/Unit/Mo	7.875	1,488.375	1,677.375	1,866.375	2,055.375	7,087.5
Revenue		$172,980	$193,680	$213,930	$233,460	$814,050
Total Tech Hrs/Qtr		2,043.036	2,290.206	2,534.556	2,770.656	9,638.454
FT Manpower		5.68	6.36	7.04	7.70	
Number Techs Required		6	7	8	8	

Sparing Requirements Per Unit Installed by Equipment Type

Small	Medium	Large					
$70	$210	$350					
Spares Inventory							
Small				$19,180	$21,280	$23,030	$24,780
Medium				$20,370	$22,470	$24,570	$26,250
Large				$22,050	$24,850	$27,650	$30,450
Total				$61,600	$68,600	$75,250	$81,480

Travel Costs						
Cost/Mo/Unit						
Small	$0.30	$246.60	$273.60	$296.10	$318.60	$1,134.90
Medium	$1.32	$384.12	$423.72	$463.32	$495.00	$1,766.16
Large	$4.20	$793.80	$894.60	$995.40	$1,096.20	$3,780.00
Total		$1,424.52	$1,591.92	$1,754.82	$1,909.80	$6,681.06
Fixed		$3,600.00	$4,200.00	$4,800.00	$4,800.00	$17,400.00
Total Travel Costs		$5,024.52	$5,791.92	$6,554.82	$6,709.80	$24,081.06

Max Uptime, Inc.
Income Statement
Third Year by Quarter

| | QUARTERS | | | | |
	1	2	3	4	TOTAL
Revenue	$172,980	$193,680	$213,930	$233,460	$814,050
Cost					
Hired Techs	$45,000	$54,000	$63,000	$63,000	$225,000
Travel	$5,025	$5,792	$6,555	$6,710	$24,081
Parts	$51,894	$58,104	$64,179	$70,038	$244,215
Misc/Tech $150	$2,700	$3,150	$3,600	$3,600	$13,050
Total Cost	$104,619	$121,046	$137,334	$143,348	$506,346
Gross Margin	$68,361	$72,634	$76,596	$90,112	$307,704
Expenses					
Rent	$3,000	$3,000	$3,000	$3,000	$12,000
Salaries	$21,000	$21,000	$21,000	$21,000	$84,000
Mgt Expenses	$900	$900	$900	$900	$3,600
Sales Expenses	$1,500	$1,500	$1,500	$1,500	$6,000
Util/Insur	$900	$900	$900	$900	$3,600
Clerical Salaries	$9,000	$9,000	$9,000	$9,000	$36,000
Bookkeeping & Bank Charges	$900	$900	$900	$900	$3,600
Depreciation	$600	$600	$600	$600	$2,400
Phone (Office)	$300	$300	$300	$300	$1,200
Phone (Dispatch)	$600	$600	$600	$600	$2,400
Misc	$900	$900	$900	$900	$3,600
Total	$39,600	$39,600	$39,600	$39,600	$158,400
EBIT	$28,761	$33,034	$36,996	$50,512	$149,304
Interest	$4,180	$3,730	$3,340	$2,820	$14,070
EBT	$24,581	$29,304	$33,656	$47,692	$135,234
Tax	$0	$1,973	$9,424	$13,354	$24,751
EAT	$24,581	$27,331	$24,232	$34,338	$110,483
Dividends			$0	$0	$0

Max Uptime, Inc.
Balance Sheet
Third Year by Quarter

| | QUARTERS | | | |
	1	2	3	4
Assets				
Cash	$10,000	$10,000	$10,000	$10,000
Accounts Receivable	$72,075	$80,700	$89,138	$97,275
Inventory	$61,600	$68,600	$75,250	$81,480
Current Assets	$143,675	$159,300	$174,388	$188,755
Deposits	$1,500	$1,500	$1,500	$1,500
Fixed Assets				
Gross	$12,000	$12,000	$12,000	$12,000
Accumulated Depreciation	($5,400)	($6,000)	($6,600)	($7,200)
Net	$6,600	$6,000	$5,400	$4,800
Total Assets	$151,775	$166,800	$181,288	$195,055
Liabilities				
Accounts Payable	$17,298	$19,368	$21,393	$23,346
Current Liabilities	$17,298	$19,368	$21,393	$23,346
Debt	$131,484	$117,108	$105,338	$82,814
Equity	$2,993	$30,324	$54,557	$88,895
Total Liabilities & Equity	$151,775	$166,800	$181,288	$195,055

Max Uptime, Inc.
Cash Flow Statement
Third Year by Quarter

| | QUARTERS | | | | |
	1	2	3	4	TOTAL
Cash from Operating Activities					
EAT	$24,581	$27,331	$24,232	$34,338	$110,483
Depreciation	$600	$600	$600	$600	$2,400
Decr/(Incr) in A/R	($9,525)	($8,625)	($8,438)	($8,138)	($34,725)
Decr/(Incr) in Inventory	$160	($7,000)	($6,650)	($6,230)	($19,720)
Incr/(Decr) in A/P	$2,286	$2,070	$2,025	$1,953	$8,334
Cash from Operations	$18,102	$14,376	$11,770	$22,524	$66,772
Cash from Investing Activities					
Decr/(Incr) in Fixed Assets	$0	$0	$0	$0	$0
Cash from Financing Activities					
Incr/(Decr) in Debt	($15,602)	($14,376)	($11,770)	($22,524)	($64,272)
Dividends	$0	$0	$0	$0	$0
Cash from Financing	($15,602)	($14,376)	($11,770)	($22,524)	($64,272)
Net Cash Flow	$2,500	($0)	$0	($0)	$2,500
Beginning Cash Balance	$7,500	$10,000	$10,000	$10,000	
Net Cash Flow	$2,500	($0)	$0	($0)	
Ending Cash Balance	$10,000	$10,000	$10,000	$10,000	

Max Uptime, Inc.
Unit Sales and Base Forecast
Fourth Year by Quarter

| | | QUARTERS | | | | |
		1	2	3	4	TOTAL
Small Units						
Units Sold		20	20	20	20	80
Units on Contract		374	394	414	434	
Average Price	50					
Revenue		$33,660	$35,460	$37,260	$39,060	$145,440
Total Tech Hrs/Unit/Mo	0.188	210.936	222.216	233.496	244.776	911.424
Medium Units						
Units Sold		8	8	8	8	32
Units on Contract		133	141	149	157	
Average Price	50					
Revenue		$47,880	$50,760	$53,640	$56,520	$208,800
Total Tech Hrs/Unit/Mo	1.375	548.625	581.625	614.625	647.625	2,392.5
Large Units						
Units Sold		8	8	8	8	32
Units on Contract		95	103	111	119	
Average Price	50					
Revenue		$171,000	$185,400	$199,800	$214,200	$770,400
Total Tech Hrs/Unit/Mo	7.875	2,244.375	2,433.375	2,622.375	2,811.375	10,111.5
Revenue		$252,540	$271,620	$290,700	$309,780	$1,124,640
Total Tech Hrs/Qtr		3,003.936	3,237.216	3,470.496	3,703.776	13,415.424
FT Manpower		8.34	8.99	9.64	10.29	
Number Techs Required		9	9	10	11	

Sparing Requirements Per Unit Installed by Equipment Type

Small	Medium	Large
$70	$210	$350

Spares Inventory

		1	2	3	4	
Small		$26,180	$27,580	$28,980	$30,380	
Medium		$27,930	$29,610	$31,290	$32,970	
Large		$33,250	$36,050	$38,850	$41,650	
Total		$87,360	$93,240	$99,120	$105,000	

Travel Costs
Cost/Mo/Unit

		1	2	3	4	
Small	$0.30	$336.60	$354.60	$372.60	$390.60	$1,454.40
Medium	$1.32	$526.68	$558.36	$590.04	$621.72	$2,296.80
Large	$4.20	$1,197.00	$1,297.80	$1,398.60	$1,499.40	$5,392.80
Total		$2,060.28	$2,210.76	$2,361.24	$2,511.72	$9,144.00
Fixed		$5,400.00	$5,400.00	$6,000.00	$6,600.00	$23,400.00
Total Travel Costs		$7,460.28	$7,610.76	$8,361.24	$9,111.72	$32,544.00

Max Uptime, Inc.
Income Statement
Fourth Year by Quarter

	QUARTERS				
	1	2	3	4	TOTAL
Revenue	$252,540	$271,620	$290,780	$309,780	$1,124,640
Cost					
Hired Techs	$72,000	$72,000	$81,000	$90,000	$315,000
Travel	$7,460	$7,611	$8,361	$9,112	$32,544
Parts	$75,762	$81,486	$87,210	$92,934	$337,392
Misc/Tech $150.00	$4,050	$4,050	$4,500	$4,950	$17,550
Total Cost	$159,272	$165,147	$181,071	$196,996	$702,486
Gross Margin	$93,268	$106,473	$109,629	$112,784	$422,154
Expenses					
Rent	$3,000	$3,000	$3,000	$3,000	$12,000
Salaries	$21,000	$21,000	$21,000	$21,000	$84,000
Mgt Expenses	$900	$900	$900	$900	$3,600
Sales Expenses	$1,500	$1,500	$1,500	$1,500	$6,000
Util/Insur	$900	$900	$900	$900	$3,600
Clerical Salaries	$9,000	$9,000	$9,000	$9,000	$36,000
Bookkeeping & Bank Charges	$1,200	$1,200	$1,200	$1,200	$4,800
Depreciation	$600	$600	$600	$600	$2,400
Phone (Office)	$300	$300	$300	$300	$1,200
Phone (Dispatch)	$600	$600	$600	$600	$2,400
Misc	$900	$900	$900	$900	$3,600
Total	$39,900	$39,900	$39,900	$39,900	$159,600
EBIT	$53,368	$66,573	$69,729	$72,884	$262,554
Interest	$2,100	$1,180	$300	$0	$3,580
EBT	$51,268	$65,393	$69,429	$72,884	$258,974
Tax	$14,355	$18,310	$19,440	$20,408	$72,513
EAT	$36,913	$47,083	$49,989	$52,477	$186,461
Dividends			$17,205	$41,154	$58,359

Max Uptime, Inc.
Balance Sheet
Fourth Year by Quarter

| | QUARTERS | | | |
	1	2	3	4
Assets				
Cash	$10,000	$10,000	$10,000	$10,000
Accounts Receivable	$105,225	$113,175	$121,125	$129,075
Inventory	$87,360	$93,240	$99,120	$105,000
Current Assets	$202,585	$216,415	$230,245	$244,075
Deposits	$1,500	$1,500	$1,500	$1,500
Fixed Assets				
Gross	$12,000	$12,00	$12,00	$12,00
Accumulated Depreciation	($7,800)	($8,400)	($9,000)	($9,600)
Net	$4,200	$3,600	$3,000	$2,400
Total Assets	$208,285	$221,515	$234,745	$247,975
Liabilities				
Accounts Payable	$25,254	$27,162	$29,070	$30,978
Current Liabilities	$25,254	$27,162	$29,070	$30,978
Debt	$57,223	$21,462	$0	($0)
Equity	$125,808	$172,891	$205,675	$216,997
Total Liabilities & Equity	$208,285	$221,515	$234,745	$247,975

Max Uptime, Inc.
Cash Flow Statement
Fourth Year by Quarter

	QUARTERS				
	1	2	3	4	TOTAL
Cash from Operating Activities					
EAT	$36,913	$47,083	$49,989	$52,477	$186,461
Depreciation	$600	$600	$600	$600	$2,400
Decr/(Incr) in A/R	($7,950)	($7,950)	($7,950)	($7,950)	($31,800)
Decr/(Incr) in Inventory	($5,880)	($5,880)	($5,880)	($5,880)	($23,520)
Incr/(Decr) in A/P	$1,908	$1,908	$1,908	$1,908	$7,632
Cash from Operations	$25,591	$35,761	$38,667	$41,155	$141,173
Cash from Investing Activities					
Decr/(Incr) in Fixed Assets	$0	$0	$0	$0	$0
Cash from Financing Activities					
Incr/(Decr) in Debt	($25,591)	($35,761)	($21,462)	($1)	($82,814)
Dividends	$0	$0	($17,205)	($41,154)	($58,359)
Cash from Financing	($25,591)	($35,761)	($38,667)	($41,155)	($141,173)
Net Cash Flow	($0)	($0)	($0)	($0)	($0)
Beginning Cash Balance	$10,000	$10,000	$10,000	$10,000	
Net Cash Flow	($0)	($0)	($0)	($0)	
Ending Cash Balance	$10,000	$10,000	$10,000	$10,000	

A SUMMARY OF THE FORECASTED FINANCIAL RESULTS

The following summarizes the installed base, the technical staffing plan, and key financial information by year:

	Years			
	1	2	3	4
Units on Contract				
Small	104	244	354	434
Medium	38	86	125	157
Large	18	54	87	119
Number of Hired				
Field Technicians	3	6	8	11
Revenue detail		($000)		
Small	18.0	68.9	113.5	145.4
Medium	25.7	97.9	160.6	208.8
Large	54.6	291.6	540.0	770.4

Summary Income Statements
($000)

	Years			
	1	2	3	4
Revenue	98.3	458.5	814.1	1,124.6
Cost	55.2	287.5	506.3	702.5
Gross Margin	43.1	170.9	307.7	422.1
Expense	97.2	140.4	158.1	159.6
Interest	7.3	15.7	14.1	3.6
EBT	(61.4)	14.8	135.2	259.0
EAT	(61.4)	14.8	110.5	186.5
Dividends				58.4

Selected Balance Sheet Items
($000)

	Selected Ratios			
Total Asset Turnover	1.3	3.3	4.2	4.5
ROS	–	3.2%	13.6%	16.6%
ROA	–	10.6%	56.6%	75.2%
ROE	–	–	124.3%	85.9%

	End of Years				
	0	1	2	3	4
Inventory	20.0	30.8	61.8	81.5	105.0
Accounts Receivable	-0-	30.4	62.6	97.3	129.1
Total Assets	38.5	77.3	140.5	195.1	248.0
Debt	13.5	108.1	147.1	82.8	-0-
Equity	25.0	(36.4)	(21.6)	88.9	217.0

Evaluation and Summary

Revenue is expected to grow to $1.1 million in the four-year period forecasted. The debt will be drawn as needed to support growth in working capital. It will peak at approximately $150,000 near the end of the second year. After that time, internally generated cash will rapidly pay down the amount outstanding, fully repaying the obligation in the second quarter of the fourth year. No earnings will be drawn out of the company until the debt is repaid.

Max Uptime will operate at a loss in the first year, but will turn profitable in the second quarter of the second year. After that the momentum of the growth in the installed base will carry the firm into solid profitability. The fourth year will see a healthy return on sales of over 16% and returns on assets and equity of 75% and 86%, respectively. These last may seem unrealistically high to those unfamiliar with the service business, but are achievable because of the low investment in plant and equipment necessary in this field. It should be noted in this regard that the balance sheet consists almost entirely of receivables and inventory.

Comment

In most plans it's a good idea to talk about contingency planning, that is, what you will do if things don't go as well as planned. That usually means if revenues are a lot slower in coming in than expected. Unfortunately, if that happens to Max Uptime there isn't much they can do about it. The founders can continue to work for half pay past the first year, but few other expenses can be significantly reduced. They simply have to plow ahead and drive toward their break-even point.

Therefore, since they don't really have a contingency plan, it's better not to say anything in the document. However, be prepared to answer questions about the possibility of problems, because they're sure to be asked.

APPENDICES

A. Target customer list

B. List of equipment maintained

C. Letter to IT directors

D. Equipment list

E. Résumés and personal references

(The appendices are not included as their illustrative value is minimal.)

GLOSSARY

Absorption
The accounting process in which overhead cost is included in the cost of manufactured product. A concept within *cost accounting* and *standard cost*.

Acceleration Clause
A clause in a loan agreement that makes the entire debt due and payable immediately if the borrower defaults, usually by missing one or more payments.

Accelerator
A provision in a sales compensation (commission) plan that increases the percentage commission paid on sales above the salesperson's quota.

Accounting Period
The time period for which the books of account are closed and financial statements are produced. Generally months, quarters, or years. Virtually all companies have a basic annual period. Larger firms also tend to recognize quarterly or monthly periods.

Accounts Payable
Amounts owed for products and services purchased on credit in the normal course of business.

Accounts Receivable
Amounts to be received from customers as a result of credit sales.

Accrual
An accounting entry or a balance sheet account reflecting an unbilled liability—that is, a debt known to be owed by the firm on which the paperwork has yet to be received.

Acquiring Bank
A bank through which an e-commerce merchant receives credit card payments.

Allowance for Doubtful Accounts
Also known as *bad debt reserve*. An amount offsetting the recorded value of accounts receivable to allow for the fact that in the normal course of business some receivables will never be collected.

Asset Management Ratios
Financial ratios designed to highlight how effectively a company utilizes assets such as receivables, inventory, and equipment.

Average Collection Period (ACP)
Also known as *days sales outstanding* (DSO). The time it takes to collect the average dollar of credit sales. Average receivables balance divided by revenue times 360.

Balance Sheet
A financial statement showing all of the firm's assets, liabilities, and equities at a single point in time.

Bandwidth
A measure of the data transfer capacity of a web host's connection between the Internet and an e-commerce web site.

Billable Hours
In a personal service business, the time a service provider actually spends performing services for customers.

Board of Directors
The group who appoint senior management and control the operations of a corporation. The directors are elected by stockholders.

Bond
A financial device through which a company borrows money from many lenders at the same time. Buying a company's bond is actually lending it money.

Books
Also known as *books of account*. The financial records of a business. May be in computer form rather than in actual books. *Financial books* use accounting practices designed to reflect actual

operations and are for display to most interested parties. *Tax books* use accounting practices allowed or required by the tax code and may be somewhat different from financial books. There is nothing wrong or illegal with having both tax and financial books.

Break-Even Analysis
A technique to estimate the sales level required for a business to just break even in terms of profit and loss, that is, to earn zero profit.

Brick-and-Mortar Business
In the jargon of e-commerce, a traditional, off-line or non–e-commerce business.

Budget
A short-term, detailed plan for running a business on a day-to-day basis. Largely a financial projection.

Business Broker
An individual or company that arranges the sale of businesses for a commission.

Business Format Franchise
See Franchise.

Business Model
A concise statement of how a business markets, produces, and distributes what it sells and the resulting financial relationships between revenue, cost, and profit.

Business Plan
A written portrayal of the future of a business venture including descriptive text and numerical projections.

Buy-Sell Agreement
An agreement among business owners concerning the departure or death of an owner. It contains a method for establishing the price remaining owners must pay to those who leave for their shares of the firm. Buy-sell agreements can also limit an owner's ability to sell his or her interest to outside parties.

Bylaws
A set of rules by which a corporation is run. Bylaws are generally agreed upon by the stockholders at the time of incorporation or shortly thereafter. In small companies, the most important issues addressed are the management

responsibilities of individual stockholders, each person's compensation, how departing stockholders will be paid for their shares of the business, and which decisions require approval by supermajorities of stockholders.

Capital
Money provided to support the large, long-lived assets of a business. Also the assets themselves. More loosely, the money to get started in business. In accounting, the sum of the values of long-term debt and equity.

Capital Assets
Also known as *capital equipment*. Long-lived assets used in running a business.

Capitalized Earnings
A technique to establish the current lump-sum worth of a stream of earnings projected indefinitely into the future. The periodic earnings figure divided by the relevant interest rate in decimal form. That is, if the interest rate is 10%, $50 a year indefinitely is worth:
$50 / .10 = $500.

Card-not-present (transaction)
A credit card purchase in which the seller cannot physically examine the buyer's credit card. Virtually all e-commerce transactions are card-not-present, which creates security problems.

Cash Flow Statement
A financial statement showing where a business has gotten its cash and what it has done with it during an accounting period. More formally called the Statement of Changes in Financial Position. Also called the *Statement of Sources and Uses* or *Sources and Applications of Cash*.

Chat Room
A web site at which a number of Internet users can simultaneously enter questions or comments that are viewed by everyone "in" the room. In the context of e-commerce, a customer service representative (CSR) often leads the "discussion" answering questions from anyone. The answers are then available to everyone in the room.

Clean-up Clause
A clause in short-term credit agreements requiring the borrower to be out of debt for some

period each year. Ensures that short-term credit is used for short-term purposes.

Close

Also known as *closing the books* or the *accounting close*. Entering all of a period's transactions into the books of account, and summarizing, balancing, and producing financial statements for the period just ended.

Closely Held Corporation

Closely held corporations have three characteristics: (1) a small number of shareholders, (2) no market for their stock, and (3) shareholders controlling a majority of the stock participate in management.

Collateral

Assets pledged to secure a loan which, if the borrower fails to pay, belong to the lender to the extent necessary to pay off the loan.

Commercial Realtor

A real estate broker or salesperson who specializes in business or commercial property.

Commission Plan

Also known as *compensation* plan or *comp* plan. The rules by which commissions are paid to salespeople. Includes rates and quotas.

Common Size Income Statement

An income statement with each line item stated as a percentage of revenue rather than as a number of dollars.

Competitive Advantage

In the context of strategic management, something that gives a firm an edge over its competition. Based on a strength or distinctive competence. A distinctive competence that is used effectively produces a competitive advantage.

Competitive Analysis

The systematic study and evaluation of a business's competitors. Generally a part of the marketing section of a business plan.

Contingency Plan

A plan of action to minimize the effect of unexpectedly adverse conditions. A worst-case scenario.

Contribution

The revenue from a sale less the variable cost of the product sold. Also the contribution margin when expressed as a percentage of the revenue.

Corporate Tax (Rates)

Tax (rates) paid by incorporated businesses on pre-tax earnings.

Corporation (C-Type Corporation)

A fictitious legal entity that runs a business on behalf of its stockholder owners. Characterized by limited liability for the stockholders. Traditional, C-type corporations are subject to corporate taxation on business profits, which can lead to double taxation when profits are paid to stockholders as dividends.

Cost

Money spent by a business on materials or activities that are closely related to production of its product or service.

Cost Accounting (System)

The accounting techniques and methods employed in the factory. The term is usually applicable to manufacturing operations. *See* Standard Cost.

Covenant

An agreement associated with borrowing money. Lenders generally attempt to limit the risk-taking latitude of firms borrowing money while their loans are outstanding. Covenants preclude certain activities and require others in an effort to ensure conservative business behavior by the borrower. They may also preclude the business owners from withdrawing assets. Also called *indenture*.

Current Assets and Liabilities

Assets that are expected, in the normal course of business, to be converted to cash within one year, and liabilities that are expected to require cash within one year.

Current Ratio

Current assets divided by current liabilities. A measure of the firm's liquidity, or its ability to meet its short-term financial obligations.

Customer Service Representative (CSR)

An employee who assists customers with product or administrative problems.

dba

Doing business as. A term describing a proprietorship operating under a name other than that of the proprietor. E.g., John Smith dba Smith Fine Art Studio.

Debt

Borrowed money, long or short term. Long-term debt plus equity constitutes the firm's capital.

Debt Management Ratios

Ratios designed to highlight how effectively a firm makes use of borrowed money. The major focus of debt management ratios is whether the firm has too much debt.

Debt-to-Equity Ratio

The proportionate relationship between debt and equity in a firm's capital. For example if a company is financed with $75,000 of borrowed money and $25,000 of the owner's own money (equity), its capital (of $100,000) is three-to-one debt to equity.

Debt Service

The payment required due to the existence of debt. Includes interest and any required repayment of principal.

Depreciation

An accounting device to spread the cost of a long-lived asset over the period in which it is expected to give service. *Straight-line depreciation* spreads the cost evenly. *Accelerated depreciation* puts more cost in the early periods of an asset's life and less in the later periods. *Accumulated depreciation* is an offset to the original cost of an asset on a company's books to reflect depreciation previously taken. The Net Book Value of an asset is its original cost less accumulated depreciation to date.

Development

The process of making a viable product out of a laboratory prototype. Also enhancing processes and functions within a business.

Differentiation

A technique of making a product or service stand out among others by adding features that add value to certain customers. *A differentiation*

strategy is an overall approach to a business based on differentiation.

Distinctive Competence

In the context of strategic management, a strength in something that matters in the firm's competitive environment.

Domain Name

The name of an e-commerce business, which is also its address on the Internet. Domain names are of the form www.examplename.com.

Dotcom

An Internet-based, e-commerce business.

Double Taxation of Earnings

A major disadvantage of the corporate form of business organization. Earnings are subject to a corporate income tax. The after-tax profit can be paid to stockholders as dividends, which are then subject to a personal income tax. Thus, the earnings are taxed twice. Avoidable for small businesses through formation as an S-type corporation or an LLC.

Earnings Before Interest and Taxes (EBIT)

A measure of the profitability of operations without regard to the method by which the company is financed (by debt or by equity).

E-Commerce

Business activity which is primarily conducted over the Internet. E-commerce enterprises are generally referred to as dotcoms.

E-Mail

Correspondence sent electronically over the Internet.

Encryption Software

Computer programs that encode information before it's transmitted over the Internet and decode it when received. Senders and receivers must have compatible software and keys to the encoding algorithm.

Equipment List

Also known as *capital equipment list*. The list of major pieces that a business anticipates purchasing in the time frame covered by the plan. An important part of the business plan.

Equity
The owner's interest in a business.

Executive Summary
A brief summary of a business document presented at its beginning.

Expense
Money spent by a business on a regular basis that is not closely related to production (e.g., the salaries of marketing people and accountants).

Financial Statement
A numerical presentation drawn from the books of account at the end of an accounting period that indicates the financial performance of the business during that period. Generally, the income statement, the balance sheet, and the cash flow statement.

Firewall
A computer between the Internet and a network that prevents hostile or intrusive incoming data from accessing the system.

Fixed Assets
Long-lived assets used in a business. Not necessarily fixed in place (e.g., a truck).

Fixed Costs
Costs that do not change when the levels of production or sales change (e.g., rent).

Fixtures
Items attached to real estate. Trade fixtures are items specifically used in a business.

Focus or Focus Strategy
See Niche Market and Niche Strategy.

Forecast
A short-term financial projection of where the momentum of a business will carry it. Sometimes used to refer to any financial projection.

Form of Business Organization
One of several statutory arrangements under which a business can be owned and operated. The predominant forms are sole proprietorship, partnership, and corporation although there are variations within the latter two categories.

Franchise
A business relationship in which the owner of a successful enterprise (the franchisor) licenses another (the franchisee) to copy his or her products and/or methods in return for a fee. The franchisor is expected to provide continuing advice and support in return for a continuing royalty. A business format franchise provides a turnkey package to the franchisee.

Fringe Benefits
Benefits provided for employees in addition to wages. Largely medical and life insurance. The value of fringe benefits is generally not taxable income to employees.

Funds
Cash. (The technical accounting definitions are slightly different, but for practical purposes funds and cash are interchangeable words.)

General Partner(ship)
A partner who participates in operating the partnership business and is exposed to unlimited liability. All of the partners in a general partnership. In a limited partnership, there must be at least one general partner while the others, usually passive investors, enjoy limited liability.

Gross Margin
Revenues less costs.

Hacker
One who electronically breaks into computer systems, usually to steal or vandalize.

Income Statement
A financial statement showing revenues less costs and expenses. Provides an indication of the firm's earnings during a period.

Inventory
Items held by a business for resale.

Inventory Reserve
An amount offsetting the stated amount of inventory to recognize that some material may be unusable for a variety of reasons.

Inventory Turnover
Cost of goods sold divided by average inventory. A measure of the effectiveness with which inventory is managed.

Joint and Several Liability
When two or more people are jointly and severally liable for a claim, the claimant can recover

entirely against any one of them regardless of degree of fault.

Keyword

A descriptive term used to find relevant web sites on the Internet. An Internet browser searches sites for keywords.

Leverage

The extent to which a firm is financed with borrowed money. A firm with a great deal of debt relative to its equity is said to be heavily leveraged.

Liability

An amount owed by a business to any outsider. Generally any financial obligation.

Limited Liability

A concept associated with the corporate form of doing business. Stockholders, the owners of the business, are financially at risk only to the extent of their investment in the business. Alternatively stated, a claimant can sue the business only for its assets and not for the personal assets of the owners. In the context of small businesses, the idea is often circumvented. That is, the financial separation of a business from its owners who operate it is not always easy.

Limited Liability Company (LLC)

A business form that is essentially a corporation, but is characterized by pass through taxation. LLCs are similar to S-type corporations but are free of several rules that restrict the operation of S-types. (*See* Corporation, S-Type Corporation).

Limited Partnership

A partnership in which some of the partners, usually passive investors who don't participate in the business, have limited liability. In a limited partnership, there must be at least one general partner who runs the business and has unlimited liability.

Link

A point-and-click connection on a web site to another web site.

Liquidity

With respect to an asset, the relative ease with which it can be turned into cash without substantial loss. A liquid asset is easily converted to cash. With respect to a business, its ability to pay its bills in the short run as a result of adequate or inadequate cash flow (PERT).

Liquidity Ratios

Financial ratios designed to highlight a firm's ability to pay its bills in the short run.

Location Analysis

The systematic acquisition and evaluation of information relevant to selecting a site for a business.

Login

The process of entering a secure web site, usually requiring a password.

Majority Interest

An owner or group of owners who either own or belong to a group whose members together own an interest large enough to control the firm.

Marketing Plan

A company's overall approach to marketing its products and services. Generally included in the marketing section of a business plan. Distinguished from a sales plan, which is a more detailed forecast of exactly what will be sold in the near future.

Mean Time Between Failure (MTBF)

The average operating period between physical failures for certain equipment. Common terminology in high-tech fields.

Milestone

An identifiable event in a plan to accomplish some end. Usually a point in time at which some subset of goals have been completed. *See* Program Evaluation and Review Technique.

Minority Interest

An owner or group of owners whose interest is too small to control the firm.

Mission

A brief statement of why an enterprise is in business and what it plans to become.

Net Book Value (NBV)

See Depreciation.

Net Income

Revenues less all costs and expenses including interest and taxes. Also known as *earnings* or *profit after tax* (EAT or PAT), the proverbial bottom line.

Niche Market
A relatively small, distinct market segment. The customers in a niche generally have some need that is being overlooked or poorly served by the major competitors serving the market.

Niche Strategy
A business strategy based on serving customers in an identifiable niche market. Also called a *Focus Strategy*.

Notes Payable
A balance sheet account reflecting short-term indebtedness supported by notes. *See* Promissory Note.

Operating Agreement
A document that stipulates the internal rules under which a business organized as a Limited Liability Company (LLC) is run.

Operating Plan
A fairly detailed business planning document usually encompassing about a year. Often an *annual plan*. Used to actually run the business, as opposed to a strategic plan, which is a more visionary exercise.

Organization Chart
A graphic depiction of the reporting relationships and managerial responsibilities within an organization.

Overhead
Expense and cost items not generally related in amount to production or sales. Also called *Fixed Costs*.

Partnership
An unincorporated form of business organization in which two or more individuals combine to operate an enterprise. In a *general partnership*, all partners participate in running the business and are liable for its debts. In a *limited partnership*, the limited partners invest only money and do not participate in running the business, which is managed by at least one general partner. The liability of limited partners is limited to their investment.

Partnership Agreement
An agreement between partners that spells out their duties, authority, and entitlements to income and ownership of a business organized as a partnership.

Pass Through Taxation
A form of business taxation in which a firm's earnings are "passed through" untaxed to its owners becoming personal income to them (i.e., there is no corporate income tax).

Password
A secret code used to identify individuals who are authorized to enter a secure place or receive secure information. In e-commerce, needed to enter a secure web site.

Payment Gateway
The connection between an e-commerce business and the credit card network that authorizes payment.

Personal Identification Number (PIN)
A secret number assigned to individuals, usually customers, to verify their identities in electronic transactions.

Personal Tax (rate)
Tax (rate) paid by people or households on their income.

Piercing the Corporate Veil
Stripping the owner(s) of a corporation of limited liability in a court of law by showing that they treated the business as an extension of themselves rather than as a separate legal entity.

Pre-incorporation Agreement
A written agreement between the founding stockholders of a corporation that, among other things, spells out their responsibilities, compensations, roles in management, and their rights to payment if they depart. Executed before incorporation with content generally transferred to corporate bylaws afterward.

Price Earnings Ratio (P/E Ratio)
The price of a firm's stock divided by its most recent earnings per share. A fundamental of valuation in stock markets.

Private Key

An e-business's key to encryption software for messages and data sent by its customers.

Profitability Ratios

Financial ratios designed to highlight how well a firm earns money. Three ratios state profitability relative to sales, assets, and owners equity.

Pro Forma

"As if" or "projected," in accounting terms. Used with projected financial statements. Pro forma financial statements are projections cast as if the assumptions of the business plan happened.

Program Evaluation and Review Technique (PERT)

A graphic technique for planning large-scale projects. Establishes milestones and shows the order in which they must be accomplished.

Promissory Note

Also known as *note*. An instrument reflecting indebtedness, usually short term.

Proprietorship

A form of business organization in which the entrepreneur is personally the business, is exposed to unlimited liability, and recognizes the business's profit as personal income for tax purposes.

Proxy Server

Prevents outsiders from identifying individual computers within a system thereby increasing the security of the network from hackers.

Public Key

A customer's key to encryption software for messages and data sent to an e-business.

Quick Ratio

Also known as the *acid test*. Current assets less inventories divided by current liabilities. A measure of a firm's liquidity.

Ratio Analysis

A technique for evaluating the financial health of a business by forming ratios from groups of numbers drawn from the financial statements. A firm's ratios are compared to those of other firms, to its own ratios in prior periods, and to planned ratios in order to assess its financial condition.

Research

The process of looking for a new product, service, or technology. In a business environment the search is usually focused and there is generally reason to believe the objective can be found.

Research and Development (R & D)

Often the engineering department in a company

Response Time

In certain service businesses, the time elapsed from the customer's placement of an order for remedial service until the arrival of the service technician on site.

Retained Earnings

Part of *equity*. The sum of prior profits not paid out to shareholders as dividends.

Return on Assets (ROA)

Net income (profit after tax) divided by total assets. A measure of profitability and asset utilization.

Return on Equity (ROE)

Net income divided by equity. A measure of profitability combined with asset utilization and the effective use of borrowed money.

Return on Investment (ROI)

Net income divided by the money invested in a business, sometimes debt plus equity, but most commonly just equity making the term equivalent to ROE. Frequently used with investments in projects that are not whole businesses. Also used in investments in securities.

Return on Sales (ROS)

Net income divided by sales revenue. A measure of profitability without regard to asset utilization.

Revenue

The money derived from selling a firm's products or services. Also called *sales* or *sales revenue*.

Right of First Refusal

The right to purchase something before it's offered to another. Corporate bylaws often give existing stockholders the right of first refusal on the purchase of new stock before it's offered to outsiders.

Sales Plan

A detailed projection of units and prices to be sold in the near future. Distinguished from a *marketing plan*, which is a broader, more strategic statement of approach to marketing and selling.

Screening Router

A router directs electronic packets of information around computer networks. A screening router scans the information, blocking potentially hostile packets, thereby making it more difficult to attack the system.

Search Engines

Web sites that provide links to other sites based on keyword descriptions.

Secure, security

Protected from theft or damage. In e-commerce the term generally refers to data stored at or transmitted to or from an e-commerce enterprise. It also refers to making the e-business's own computer system safe from invasion by anyone attempting to damage it or steal information.

Secure Sockets Layer (SSL)

The leading encryption program for sending secure information over the Internet.

Server

Computer hardware at a web host's physical site on which e-commerce web sites are maintained and made available to the Internet.

Service Business

A business that *primarily* sells personal services, although some products may also be sold to customers. For example, an auto repair shop sells parts and labor but is primarily in business to provide the labor.

Small Business Administration (SBA)

A government agency set up to provide free assistance to small businesses. Under certain conditions, it will guarantee loans to small businesses.

Sole Proprietorship

A form of business organization in which an entrepreneur simply goes into business. The business and the owner are legally indistinguishable.

Sponsored Link

A paid appearance by an e-commerce web site on the result of a search conducted by a search engine. Basically advertising on the search engine.

Spreadsheet

A wide columnar worksheet for making numerical and financial calculations. In personal computer jargon, a program that presents the user with such a display into which numbers are input and calculations programmed. The computer then carries out the indicated calculations on the input numbers.

Squeeze Out

A tactic in which a majority interest in a corporation or a partnership forces an unwanted minority interest out of the business, usually without fair compensation for his or her share of the enterprise.

Staffing Plan

The projected personnel requirements by job type for an organization. The staffing plan leads to a hiring plan or schedule.

Standard Cost

The planned production cost of a complex manufactured project including elements of labor, material, and overhead.

Standard Cost System

A cost accounting system that develops planned standard costs and captures actual factory costs segregated in the same way to facilitate comparisons between plan and actual.

Statement of Changes in Financial Position

See Cash Flow Statement.

Stock Option

The right to buy a stock at a specified price over a designated period regardless of its market price.

Strategic Plan

A long-range planning document addressing very broad, fundamental issues. Usually executed as a separate document only by larger companies.

Strategy

The overall plan for running a business.

S-Type Corporation

A corporate form providing pass-through taxation. Largely eclipsed by the LLC.

Strength

In the jargon of strategic management, something a company does well.

Supermajority

Some percentage substantially more than half such as 75% or 80%. Corporate bylaws often require that supermajorities of stockholders approve certain major decisions such as merging with other companies.

Target Audience

The people your business plan is being written for. Generally potential financial backers.

Term

The length of time a debt is to be outstanding.

Terms of Sale

The conditions under which one firm is willing to sell to another. Usually involves credit terms. "Two-ten, net thirty" is typical meaning a 2% discount is offered if the buyer pays in ten days; otherwise the entire amount is due in thirty days. Customers often violate the terms of sale slightly to conserve cash, say by paying in forty or fifty days. This practice is called *stretching payables* or *leaning on the trade.*

Times Interest Earned

Earnings before interest and taxes (EBIT) divided by interest. Measures the firm's ability to service its debt and indicates a firm's ability to handle more debt. Also known as a *coverage ratio.*

Tort

A legal term meaning a wrong or injury that generally results in a liability to the injured party. In a commercial context, an injury caused by a business. For example, the manufacturer of a defective product that injures a consumer may be liable for his or her lost income, medical expenses and for a court determined amount to compensate for pain and suffering.

Trade Credit

The practice of companies selling to one another on credit in the normal course of business.

Uniform Partnership Act (UPA)

A law governing partnerships adopted in some form by all states except Louisiana. The UPA provides a set of default rules that come into effect when there is no partnership agreement. If people work together without an agreement as to business form, the law assumes they're a partnership subject to the UPA.

User Interface

The features of a web site's design that affect how customers navigate the site, find what they want, and place orders.

Variable Cost

A cost that changes proportionately with the level of production and sales (materials and production labor, for example).

Variance

The difference between a planned or budgeted amount and the corresponding actual dollar figure.

Venture Capitalist

A backer who puts equity money into usually high-risk new businesses, seeking large returns on the investments. The money invested is known as venture capital.

Web Browser

A computer program through which a user accesses the Internet.

Web Host

A company that maintains computer hardware that connects web sites to the Internet for a fee. E-commerce web sites are resident on their host's servers, and administered from places of business.

Web Site

A "location" on the Internet that consists of a series of images called web pages that appear on users' computer screens when they access the site. An e-commerce web site generally provides information about product and availability and takes orders.

Working Capital

The money required to run a business on a day-to-day basis. In accounting the difference between current assets and current liabilities. Sometimes called net *working capital.*

Write-off

The removal of an asset from the books of account, usually upon recognition that it is worthless. Often results in a reduction in profit.

REFERENCES

Abele, Derek F., *Defining the Business: The Starting Point of Strategic Planning* (Englewood Cliffs, NJ: Prentice Hall, 1980) p. 169.

Lasher, William R., *Practical Financial Management* (Mason, OH: Thomson–SouthWestern, 2005).

Porter, Michael E., *Competitive Strategies: Technologies for Analyzing Industries and Competitors*, (New York: Free Press, 1980).

Rayport, Jeffrey and Bernard J. Jaworski, *Introduction to E-Commerce*, (New York, New York: McGraw Hill Higher Education, 2002).

INDEX